Spatial Agency

Other Ways Of Doing Architecture

First published 2011
by Routledge
2 Park Square, Milton Park, Abingdon, Oxon, OX14 4RN

Simultaneously published in the USA and Canada
by Routledge
711 Third Avenue, New York, NY 10017

Routledge is an imprint of the Taylor & Francis Group, an informa business

Text pages designed by Ben Weaver and typeset by Adam Cheltsov in
F Grotesk by Radim Pesko, and Galaxie Polaris Condensed by Chester Jenkins
Printed and bound in India by Replika Press, Pvt. Ltd, Sonepat, Haryana

British Library Cataloguing in Publication Data
A catalogue record for this book is available from the British Library

Library of Congress Cataloging-in-Publication Data
A catalog record has been requested for this book

ISBN13: 978-0-415-57192-0 (hbk)
ISBN13: 978-0-415-57193-7 (pbk)

Spatial Agency

Other Ways Of Doing Architecture

Nishat Awan

Tatjana Schneider

Jeremy Till

ROUTLEDGE

London and New York

$20K House IV construction, Newbern, AL (2009). Courtesy Rural Studio (p.193)

Asiye eTafuleni. 'Working in Warwick: Including Street Traders in Urban Plans'. Photo: Dennis Gilbert (p.103)

An issue of Making Policy Public, CUP 2009. Photo: Prudence Katze (p.115)

Passage 56 community garden. Ph: atelier d'architecture autogérée (p.105)

Bauhäusle. Ph: Peter Blundell Jones (p.107)

PS². City supplements walking tour. Courtesy Ruth Morrow (p.95)

St Joseph ReBuild Center. Courtesy Detroit Collaborative Design Center (p.127)

Arcosanti. Silt-cast construction on the roof of West Housing. Ph: Ivan Pintar (p.132)

Day-care centre dream-tree. Courtesy Baupiloten (p.109)

Drejerbanken cohousing. Ph: William Sherlaw (p.122)

Booklet accompanying the roundtable discussion:
Year Out as first encounter with architectural practice.
Front members room, 1st Dec 2006, 2pm

Exploring Practice Year Out Accounts

Alternative Practices &

public works. 'Exploring Practice' programme (p.190)

Research Initiatives Cluster
Architectural Association

Haus-Rucker-Co. Oase No.7. Ph: Hein Engelskirchen (p.155)

New Alchemy Institute. Cape Cod Ark. Courtesy John Todd (p.176)

Raumlabor, Cape Fear. Courtesy Raumlabor (p.191)

Football House, California. Courtesy Jersey Devil (p.159)

Urban voids, Philadelphia. Strategy for the self-reparation of the urban tissue. Image: Ecosistema Urbano

Woodland art trail. Ph: muf (p.175)

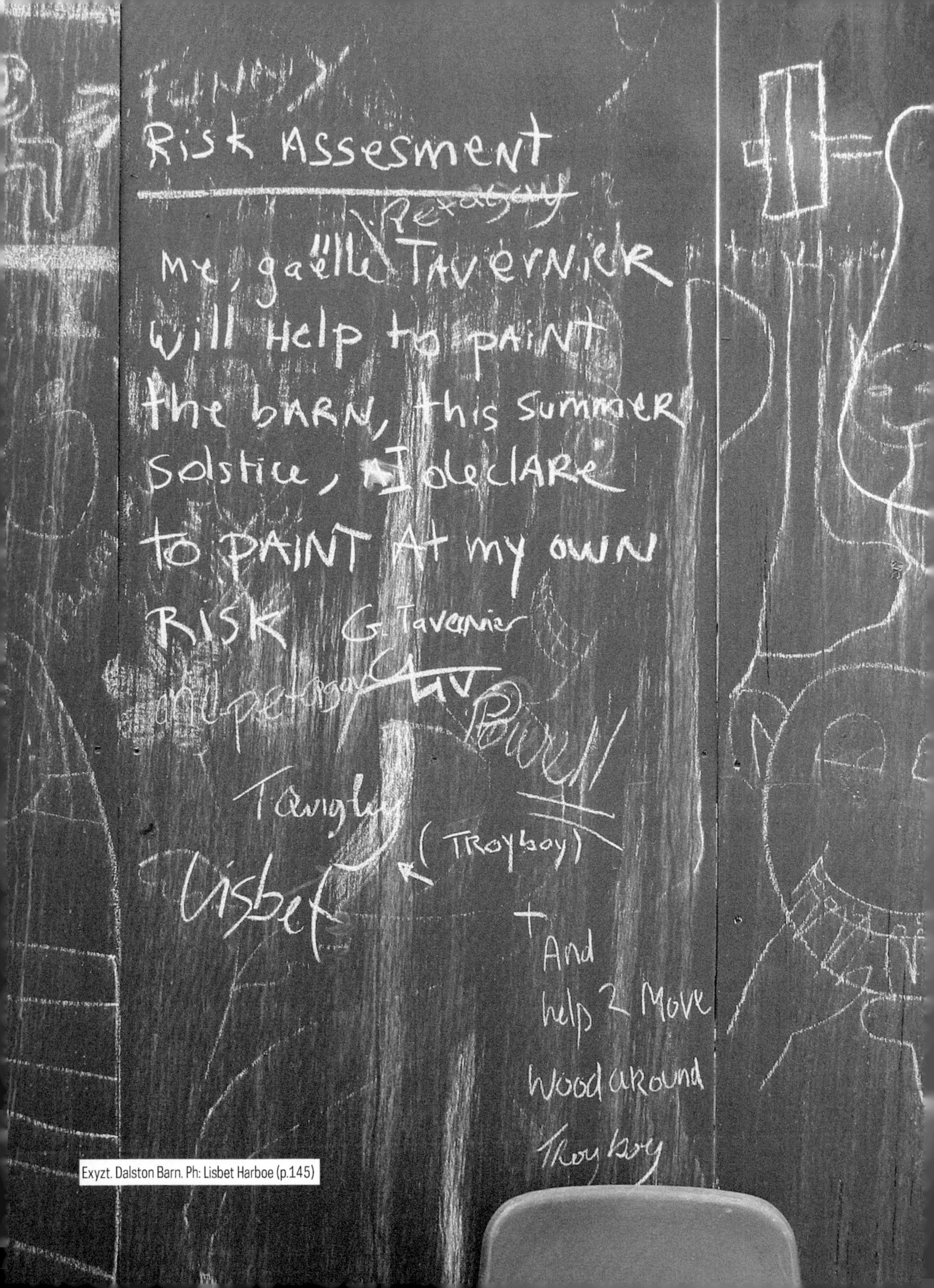

Risk Assesment

Me, gaëlle TAVERNIER
will help to paint
the barn, this summer
solstice, I declare
to PAINT At my own
RISK   G. Tavernier
and Petagay

Tavigly
Lisbet   (TRoyboy)

And
help 2 Move
Wood around
Troy boy

Exyzt. Dalston Barn. Ph: Lisbet Harboe (p.145)

LIC Township, Ahmedabad. Ph: Vāstu-Shilpā Consultants (p.205)

Post-apocalyptic settlement on the CCA front lawn as part of the Year 3000 day-camp, 2008. Courtesy CCA (p.113)

CONTENTS

INTRODUCTION

A few years ago the French sociologist Bruno Latour self-criticised *Actor-Network-Theory*, his seminal contribution to social theory. "There are four things that do not work with Actor-Network-Theory," he notes, only half-jokingly, "the word actor, the word, network, the word theory and the hyphen."[1] In a similar spirit we became uncomfortable with the working title of this book, *Alternative Architectural Practice*. These three words became increasingly limiting in a project that we wanted to be expansive and empowering. This introduction will therefore trace the journey from *Alternative Architectural Practice* to *Spatial Agency*, starting with an explanation as to why the first three words "do not work".

Alternative

As soon as one says the word "alternative" it begs the question: "alternative to what?" In order to establish an alternative it is first necessary to define the norm against which it is set, and with this three issues immediately arise. First, the interpretation of the norm will differ according to who is doing the defining. As the authors of the *Dictionary of Alternatives* note, "one person's alternative is another person's orthodoxy."[2] There is no agreed understanding of what constitutes the inviolate centre of architectural culture, and so the definition of the alternative becomes difficult to pin down. Second, the alternative is necessarily reactive to the norm, and thus may remain in thrall to it. In some cases in this book the critique of the norm is explicit, and the resulting alternatives establish another way of constructing practice – for example, the feminist move away from the patriarchal underpinnings of so much architecture practice. But often, as in any binary structure, the alternative becomes bound by exactly

the terms of reference that it would wish to escape. The alternative is always caught in the shadow of the thing that it posits itself against. The result is that the alternative is inevitably defined by the norm, whilst the norm remains largely undisturbed by the irritant it overshadows. Third, the dialectical operation of the alternative suggests that, in the will to criticise the norm, one should abandon all the structures and rituals of the norm. The alternative marks itself through casting off the attributes of the centre, and in this there is a danger that the baby will be thrown out with the bathwater, as opposed to the possibility of assuming a hybrid stance that might keep those characteristics of the centre that are still worthwhile or appropriate, but doing so in a manner that reframes them in new guises or with revised motivations. In our context this means avoiding the temptation to ditch the traditional architectural skills of design and spatial intelligence (because they might in some way be tainted with the brush of normality), but instead seeing how they might be exploited in different ways and contexts. This is not to dismiss the value of alternative approaches and the power of the term as such but for the purpose of this project alternative became a hindrance to the underlying critical inquiry. Instead, we wanted our project to be able to engage with projects and practices not through their overt alterity but through the possibilities that they offered.

These three issues with the "alternative" revealed themselves at a symposium that we organised as part of the research project on which this book is based. Nearly all the speakers at the conference, which was called *Alternate Currents*, started their talks with a definition of what their work was alternative to. Although there was a general sense that mainstream architectural practice is not engaged enough with political and social contexts, no clear consensus as to how to create alternatives was formed. The positing of these multiple alternatives was at the same time affirming as it was frustrating. Affirming because of the hope that doing things in other ways was both possible and empowering, frustrating because the centre was often left so untroubled or unchanged by these alternative actions. Rather than defining common ground and shared tools, the defining of each individual position as "alternative" also led to the need of each of the presenters to demarcate and defend their own position with some force; each person became alternative to the others.[3]

Yet, there clearly are strong normalising tendencies of mainstream architectural production; we can see them all around us: the conforming city of office and apartment blocks, the city of sameness, indifference and of non-engagement, but also of conflict. We didn't want to hide behind something that could be seen as marginal because of its associated implication of being ineffectual, so the large number of examples collected in this book are intended to present a powerful counter, an otherness, to this centre. The book does not see these actions as marginal, because as soon as one accepts the dialectic of margin/centre then one inevitably submits to the terms of reference of the centre. If the centre has been found wanting – as was so spectacularly exposed in the 2008–2009 economic collapse – then what right has it to define, and so control, what constitutes the "margins"? In many ways the tenets of the centre are unravelling by themselves in front of our very eyes, most poignantly in the form of the global environmental crisis and the accompanying social divisions, and so what we present are not merely reactions to established "mainstream" practices but empowering examples

from the past and present from around the globe that provide pointers as to how one might operate not only in uncertain times but as a matter of principle. Some of the work in the book is motivated by a critique of certain aspects of normative structures; critique, however, is always used as a means to positive action, not as an end in itself. In this much, the term alternative didn't work for us, because the work presented here should not be read as alternative and therefore potentially marginal, but on its own terms and merits, presenting a new paradigm as to how to operate – a paradigm that has thus far been largely written out of the standard histories of architecture.

Architectural

The second term that we found limiting was "architectural". The standard definition of an architect is someone who designs buildings, and the vast majority of architects do indeed spend most of their time designing and detailing buildings. There is, of course, nothing wrong with this per se, but the concentration on the building as the primary locus of architectural production brings with it certain limitations. First, is the association of architecture with the building as object. Architectural culture – expressed through reviews, awards and publications – tends to prioritise aspects associated with the static properties of objects: the visual, the technical, and the atemporal. Hence the dominance of aesthetics, style, form and technique in the usual discussion of architecture, and with this the suppression of the more volatile aspects of buildings: the processes of their production, their occupation, their temporality, and their relations to society and nature. The definition of architecture in terms of object-buildings thus excludes just those aspects of world that cause architects discomfort, because these often unpredictable and contingent aspects are those over which they have limited power, whereas the static aspects are those over which architects sill retain nominal control, in terms of being able to manipulate form and technique. What is found in the work in this book is that a loss of control is seen not as a threat to professional credibility, but as an inevitable condition that must be worked with in a positive light. Buildings and spaces are treated as part of a dynamic context of networks. The standard tools of aesthetics and making are insufficient to negotiate these networks on their own, and so the examples collated here use other priorities and ways of working as part of their toolkit.

The second limit we found in the association of architecture with buildings is that the equation *architecture=building* magnifies the commodification of architecture. Buildings are all too easily appropriated into the commodity exchange of the marketplace: "progressive", "innovative", "efficient", "iconic" or "landmark" buildings are seen to have higher exchange value within this system, and it is thus that the signifiers of progress, innovation, efficiency and income generation have become the hallmarks of successful architects in times of fiscal growth. In the economic excesses of the 2000s, the rampant displays of so-called progress and innovation went unchecked as architects tried to outbid themselves with tricks of excessive form and technique. Aligning architecture so closely to the control and values of the marketplace not only shuts down other ways of thinking and operating, but also begs the question as what to do when the foundations of the market are undermined by its own excessive actions? Or rather, if buildings have been reduced to commodities, what happens to architecture when the commodity exchange of architecture is staunched? The answer was all too apparent in the early days of the 2009 recession, with architects and other built environment professionals topping the lists of unemployment growth, taking with them an even bigger number of construction workers.

New ways of working and behaving are demanded if we are to avoid being impotent passengers on the rollercoaster of boom and bust cycles. Clues as to these other ways are given by the examples in the book, most of which prioritise values outside the normal terms of reference of the economic market, namely those of social, environmental and ethical justice. As we shall see, these are issues that are best addressed within the dynamic context of social space, rather than within the static context of architecture as building, hence our move from the limits of the term "architectural" to the more open possibilities of the "spatial". But, again, this does not mean abandoning the skills and ways of thinking that go into the production of buildings; instead we argue that they can be deployed and developed in other settings as well.

The third limit of the word "architectural" is that it suggests that only architects are involved in the creative production of the built environment. Architecture as a profession is based on the need for architecture (as practice and product) to be the protected domain of the architect. The standard histories of architecture focus almost exclusively on the guiding hand of the individual architect, and in this exclude the multiple voices and actions of others. Architects, as is argued in the book *Informal City*, "fail to see, let alone analyse or capitalize upon, the informal aspects of urban life because they lack a professional vocabulary for describing them. Their vision is shaped and, therefore, also limited by their theories, which [...] fail to confront critically real-world issues. The present-day city calls for a profound reorientation in the manner in which we study it: we believe in working at the intersections of the individual and the collective, the real and the virtual in a multiplicity of parallel engagements."[4] As can be seen from many of the examples in the book, it is clear to our spatial agents that spatial production belongs to a much wider group of actors – from artists to users, from politicians to builders – with a diverse range of skills and intents. To acknowledge this breadth, we moved away from the limits of the word "architecture", with its implications that it is the sole domain of the architect, and moved to the wider possibilities of space.

~~Practice~~

The third term that we found limiting was "practice", mainly because of its connotations of habit and unreflective action. Although much solace is given to architects by Donald Schön's famous identification of architecture with a certain type of reflective practice,[5] the reality of much architectural practice is circumscribed by much more instrumental demands, in which action is determined in reaction to the short-term priorities of clients and the market. Practice also brings with it connotations of repetition – "practice makes perfect" – as if architectural practice is a matter of refining particular stylistic or technical tropes over time, and applying them to any given context without real concern for the particular. Famous architects are usually those who have developed, through practice, a defining character to their work. The architectural results can be seen from the global reach of international modernism to the way that contemporary icons impose standard formal solutions with little regard for local conditions, because it is these solutions that constitute the architect's signature. If such practice is guided by theory, it is theory of the traditional type, based on the model of the natural sciences, which attempts to develop universal and systematic methods removed from the vagaries of the particular.[6]

One response to this tying of traditional theory to normative practice is to introduce the word "critical" to theory. Critical is here not seen as a merely negative function but one which starts with a critical evaluation of existing conditions in order to make them better. "We do not anticipate the world dogmatically," says Marx, "but rather wish to find the new world through criticism of the old."[7] Traditional architectural practice may be associated with predetermined action, or of anticipating the world dogmatically, through its habit of playing out established themes. Against this a critical practice or rather, to use the accepted word, "praxis", starts with an open-ended evaluation of the particular external conditions, out of which action arises with no predetermined outcome but with the intention to be transformative. It is this attention to external dynamics and structures that differentiates critical praxis from the internalised concerns of so much so-called "critical architecture", a term which has come under increasing scrutiny in recent architectural discourse.[8] Critical architecture and its accompanying theories, particularly in the guise developed in the US East Coast academies,[9] revolves around a retying of architecture's internal knots, in which critical attention is focused solely on architecture's own concerns and obsessions. What results is a spiralling effect of critique, which effectively asserts architecture's presumed autonomy. Praxis, in the sense of action propelled by a critical understanding of external conditions, moves away from the normative concerns and structures of traditional practice, and also away from the endless deferral and retreat of "critical" theory and practice. It is such praxis that one can sense running through the projects in the book.

Spatial Agency

While it may appear churlish to open a book with an unravelling of some standard terms, it is at least consistent with this notion of praxis and led us to the phrase *Spatial Agency*.

Spatial does not so much replace architectural as a term, but radically expands it. It is now generally understood that space describes something more than the idea of empty stuff found between physical objects, or of the white expanses left between the black lines of architects' drawings. As the residue of the construction of those lines, space is abstracted and emptied of its social content, so better and easier to subject to control. The key text in challenging the hold of abstract space was Henri Lefebvre's 1974 book *The Production of Space*, first translated in to English in 1991. Of the many memorable phrases in the book, one summarises the argument most succinctly: "(social) space is a (social) product."[10] At a stroke, Lefebvre wrests the production of space from the clutches of specialists, most notably architects and planners, and places it in a much broader social context.

A very different spatial understanding arises out of Lefebvre's redefinition. First is that production is a shared enterprise. Of course, professionals are involved in the process, but social space explicitly acknowledges the contribution of others, and with this dismisses the notion of expert authorship that the professions still cling to. Second, social space is dynamic space; its production continues over time and is not fixed to a single moment of completion. This dynamic inevitably shifts the focus of spatial attention away from the static objects of display that constitute the foreground of so much architectural production, and moves it onto the continuous cycle of spatial production, and to all the people and processes that go into it. The dynamic, and hence temporal, nature of space means that spatial production must be understood as part of an evolving sequence, with no fixed start or finish, and that multiple actors contribute at various stages. Third, social space is intractably political space, in so much as people live out their lives in this space, and so one has to be continuously alert to the effects of that space on those lives. It is too easy in the abstraction of space that takes place in drawings and models, to see it as some kind of neutral ether which, as Lefebvre notes, "the architect has before him (like) a slice of space cut from larger wholes… (and) takes this portion of space as a 'given' and works on it according to his tastes, technical skills, ideas and preferences."[11] But this apparent neutrality and abstraction is simply not the case: social space, as inherently political, is charged with the dynamics of power/empowerment, interaction/isolation, control/freedom, and so on. What can be seen in the examples in the book is an awareness of these dynamics, with responses that eschew any pretence that architectural, and hence spatial, production can be treated as a neutral action. They remind us that every line on an architectural drawing should be sensed as the anticipation of a future social relationship, and not merely as a harbinger of aesthetics or as an instruction to a contractor. They also point to the possibility of achieving transformation in manners beyond the drawing of lines.

Lefebvre's analysis of space, written as it was in 1974, now has to be supplemented by other factors that have multiplied since, most clearly the issues of globalisation, climate change, and the rise of the virtual – all of which have clear implications for spatial production. We live, as Zygmunt Bauman argues so compellingly, in liquid times,[12] which means that all the producers of space are enmeshed in the intertwining and restless arms of social networks, global networks, ecological networks and virtual networks. Such engagement with wider spatial forces is both frightening and necessary. Frightening because they present a challenge to the safety-blanket of self-reflexive language that architecture has wrapped itself in since the Renaissance: exposed to the multiple, and often conflicting, forces of these networks, architecture's pretence to any autonomy is shattered. Necessary because unless one at least recognizes these networks and architecture's place within them, then the likely fate that awaits architects is to be shunted in to a cul-de-sac away from the networks, there to be reduced to polishers of static form and technical manipulators of stuff in the name of efficiency and progress. These are activities that consolidate, and pander to, the demands of the capitalist production of space, with shining form just another bauble in the endless production of commodities, and efficiency part

of a wider programme of spatial control in which lives are measured and ruled by the dictates of the market. Zoned cities, smaller dwellings, the privatisation of the public realm and contractor-led provision of public buildings are just a few of the consequences.

Although we are critical of the values that have led to this reduction, and the apparent inability of the architectural profession to escape the trap it has set itself, our intention is not one of abandoning architectural intelligence. Quite the opposite. The book is meant as an inspiration as to how that intelligence can be exercised in a much broader spatial field, one that acknowledges the social, global, ecological and virtual networks. As will be seen, the reasons (why), context (where) and means (how) of that engagement are also greatly expanded beyond the traditional role of the architect. But far from killing off any role for architects, the intent is to posit a much richer set of activities that give new scope, and hope, for architectural activity; hence the subtitle of the book, *Other Ways of Doing Architecture*. Equally, if the introduction of the term "spatial" challenges the protective nature of the term "architectural", and in so doing dissolves the protection of the title that the profession has so dearly clung to since Victorian times, then we do not see this as a negative consequence. Protection of a small patch of territory – that of designing buildings – has allowed others to claim the larger networks. Now is the time to step over the self-defined boundaries of the profession and share in that expansive spatial field, or more particularly to act as spatial agents.

Spatial **Agency**

Agency as a term has only relatively recently been introduced into architectural discourse,[13] but has a long history in social and political theory. Agency is traditionally held in a dialectic pairing with structure. Agency is described as the ability of the individual to act independently of the constraining structures of society; structure is seen as the way that society is organized. Discussion in classic social theory then centres on which of the two has primacy over the other. Do the accumulated actions of individuals constitute the overarching societal structures, or are the latter so overwhelming as to allow no scope for individual action and freedom? Such dialectic of agency and structure is played out in architectural practice. On the one hand, as agent, there is hope that the creative actions of individuals will effect change. On the other hand, as an operation within a social structure, architecture can be described an act determined by economic and social forces, and the architect reduced to a technical facilitator with decisions effectively made by others. This dialectic of agency and structure constructs the stereotypical images of the architect as either the individual genius who singlehandedly takes on the world or else the lackey of commercial forces – a tension that Ayn Rand parodied in her 1943 novel and subsequent film *The Fountainhead*, with the genius architect Howard Roark contrasted with his saviour cum nemesis, the commercial architect, Peter Keating. In reality the productions of a tiny minority of elite architects perpetuate the myth of the power of individual agency, and the glamour of their products masks the way that the vast majority of architectural production is in the thrall of economic and political forces. The individual agents may exist, but in such a minority that they are an ineffectual foil to the production of dross that emits from the overriding economic structure.

In terms of spatial agency, neither side of the agency/structure dialectic is appropriate. The primacy of the freedom of the individual to act suggests a lack of engagement with both the limits and opportunities of wider spatial and societal structures, and sanctions the retreat into an autonomous world of form-making and crafting, undisturbed by external factors. On the other hand, the primacy of structure would lead us to believe that individual action in the spatial field is always at best constrained by, at worst completely determined by, the overarching societal structures. This leads to despair as to the efficacy of any action, and with it the abrogation of wider responsibilities: why bother to attempt to effect change if that attempt is inevitably overcome by others? The answer is played out all too commonly in the withdrawal of architecture from a critical engagement with societal structures.

To avoid on the one hand the ineffectual solipsism of individual agents or on the other hand despair in the face of overarching structures, one has to get away from the idea of agency and structure as a dualism, as two opposing conditions. Instead, as Anthony Giddens has argued, agency and structure should be understood as a duality, two linked but separately identifiable conditions. "Human agency and structure," he writes, "are logically implicated with one another."[14] This duality of agency accords with other recent investigations of the relation of action to society, and in particular those coming from Actor Network Theory (ANT), in which any societal event or object is only understood as embedded in a set of associations between human and non-human.[15] For architecture, this means that buildings are not seen as determinants of society (the primacy of the individual) nor as determined by society (the primacy of structure) but rather as in society.

It is Giddens' take on agency that we follow in this book. He argues that agents are neither completely free as individuals, nor are they completely entrapped by structure. Spatial agents are neither impotent nor all powerful: they are negotiators of existing conditions in order to partially reform them. Spatial agency implies that action to engage transformatively with structure is possible, but will only be effective if one is alert to the constraints and opportunities that the structure presents. "Action depends on the capability of the individual to 'make a difference' to a pre-existing state of affairs or course of events," writes Giddens, "... agency means being able to intervene in the world, or to refrain from such intervention, with the effect of influencing a specific process or state of affairs."[16] The idea that withdrawing from a situation might be as appropriate an action as intervening is an interesting one in an architectural context. The normal modus operandi for an architect is to add something physical to the world; this alternative suggests that, in the spirit of Cedric Price, the addition of a building is not necessarily the best solution to a spatial problem and that there are other ways of making a spatial difference.[17]

This conception of spatial agency brings with it a number of other features. First is the notion of intent. Agents act with intent but that intent is necessarily shaped and reshaped by the context within which the agent in working. An agent's action is guided by an initial transformative intent, but because of the dynamics of the structural context, that intent has to be responsive and flexible. This is very different from the determinist view of the world in which things play out according to preordained patterns, either because of the will of agents to act as individuals come what may, or because of the power of the structure to control all individual actions. Against such fixity, Giddens states clearly that "agency presumes the capability of acting otherwise."[18] To act "otherwise" is counterintuitive to the professional mindset, which is based on the assumption that stable knowledge will inevitably lead to a certain solution. Professions rely on this assertion of stable knowledge in order to give themselves authority over others, and so to accept acting otherwise is to recognise the limits of one's authority, and to relinquish the sole hold of fixed and certain knowledge. If agents are indeed to allow themselves to act otherwise, then the knowledge that they bring to the table must be negotiable, flexible and, above all, shared with others. Agents act not alone but as part of a mutual enterprise, hence Giddens' term "mutual knowledge" as a defining feature of the agent's makeup. Mutual knowledge is not determined by professional norms and expectations, but rather is founded in exchange, in negotiation, out of hunch, out of intuition. Mutual knowledge means abandoning the hierarchies embedded in most professional relationships ("I know more than you do,") and instead welcoming contributions from everyone in the spirit of a shared enterprise. Many of the people in the book are not professionals in the protective sense of the word, or indeed care about this alleged status, but instead engage with the world as expert citizens, working with others, the citizen experts, on equal terms.

In contrast to what Giddens calls "discursive consciousness", in which matters are explicit and explainable, mutual knowledge is "practical in character." But the discursive and the practical are by no means mutually exclusive: "the line between discursive and practical consciousness is fluctuating and permeable,"[19] he argues, suggesting that each draws on the other in the act of agency. The discursive realm, allows the development of knowledge away from the immediate demands of the everyday; mutual knowledge is about the practical deployment of knowledge within the everyday. Each needs the other. Without the realism of mutual knowledge, discursive consciousness floats free into spheres of impossible purity. Without the discursive, mutual knowledge will lose any sense of distance and vision as it is ground down by the particular demands of each condition. These transactions between the discursive and the practical present a challenge to professional norms, both academic and architectural, which have traditionally tended towards the higher ground of the discursive. If one cannot explicate, then one cannot claim authority; hence the domination of the discursive over the practical, of discourse over doing, and with this the marginalisation of discourse as it increasingly needs to feed off itself, discourse on discourse, in an ever-spiralling effect of internalisation.

Our call for a move beyond discourse for the sake of discourse does not throw away discursive consciousness but sees it working with and on behalf of practical transformative action.

In foregrounding the necessity of working with others, agency inevitably exposes the professional to issues of power, and in particular of how power might be used, and how it might be abused, by professionals acting as spatial agents. Agency is intractably tied to power – an early definition of agent in the *Oxford English Dictionary* is: "one who exerts power or produces an effect".[20] The words used here are telling: power exerted is the power of one person over another, which is hardly consistent with the notion of shared responsibility. A better definition in relation to spatial agency is that the agent is one who effects change through the *empowerment* of others, allowing them to engage in their spatial environments in ways previously unknown or unavailable to them, opening up new freedoms and potentials as a result of reconfigured social space.

It is through the notion of empowerment that the word agency can be taken at face value, in terms of acting as an agent with and on behalf of others; not in the sense of simply reacting to the often short-term market-led demands of clients and developers, but in the sense being responsive to the longer-term desires and needs of the multitude of others who build, live in, work in, occupy, and experience architecture and social space. In this way agency fits the previous identification of the temporality and contingency of spatial production, because in being alert to the coming wants and needs of others, one has to project visions and solutions onto an uncertain future.

The combination of visions and solutions introduces a complexity to the idea of spatial agency that one does not get in traditional theories of agency. In the latter, agents intervene directly in the world through their actions. In spatial agency, their agency is effected both through actions and visions, but also through the resulting spatial solutions. It resides in both the human and the non-human, and spatial agents have to be responsible for all aspects of their actions, from their initial relationship with others to enabling the production of physical relations and social structures, because all are means of playing out their intent. Spatial agency is here as much about modes of behaviour as it is about modes of making. In Bruno Latour's term, critical attention is shifted from architecture as a matter of fact to architecture as a matter of concern.[21] As matters of fact, buildings can be subjected to rules and methods, and they can be treated as things on their own terms. As matters of concern, they enter into socially embedded networks, in which the consequences of architecture are of much more significance than the objects of architecture.

Choosing Spatial Agency

This book contains 136 examples of spatial agency. As with any such collection, the natural reaction of the reader is first to see what has been included, and then question what has been left out. Clearly, space restricted the number of entries, and equally clearly there are omissions, some because we failed to spot them, some because they failed to meet our criteria for inclusion.[22] But the real point of lists is not to agree with them, but to argue about inclusions and exclusions, and in this wrangle form one's own sense of the subject. This is what we did between the three of us, and we now offer up our list for further debate and refinement. The selection as it stands is inevitably partial, in both senses of the word: it is both incomplete and also a reflection of our own tendencies. In order to get some consistency in our choices, we used three criteria against which to measure potential entries: spatial judgement, mutual knowledge and critical awareness.

Spatial judgement refers to the ability to exercise spatial decisions. In this it exceeds, but does not exclude, spatial intelligence, which has been understood as an innate human capability and a defining feature of the architectural and other creative professions.[23] Where spatial intelligence tends to concentrate on the ability to work in three dimensions, and thus to focus on the formal aspects of spatial production, our understanding of spatial judgement prioritises the social aspects of space, and the way that the formal affects them. It follows that, in selecting examples on the basis of spatial judgement, we were looking more at the way that they initiate empowering social relationships than at formal sophistication, the latter of which has been for so long the paradigm of architectural excellence.

Mutual knowledge refers to Giddens' term, discussed above; it indicates the willingness of spatial agents to both share their knowledge in an open manner, and also to respect the knowledge of others.

Mutual knowledge implies openness as to what may contribute to spatial production, so that the instinct of the amateur is accepted as having equal potential as the established methods of the supposed "expert". Mutual knowledge expands the means by which knowledge may be displayed and developed. Thus stories (which can be shared) are as productive as drawings (which often exclude the non-expert), and actions are privileged as much as things.

Finally, critical awareness refers to the need for spatial agents to act in a critical manner – "critical" here designating not a negative stance but an evaluative one that is aware of the opportunities and challenges, freedoms and restrictions, of the given context. Critical awareness also relates to the need to be self-critical, and so avoid imposing the same solutions onto different places, just playing out the old tropes in an unthinking manner.

To make the cut, examples had to meet at least two of these criteria, and preferably achieve well against all three. Just being spectacular in one area was not enough, which tended to exclude virtuoso architects (who may excel in an aspect of spatial judgement, but fail on the other criteria) and the individual critic (whose work remains isolated from others and from spatial production). Looking through the final list, a certain flavour becomes evident. An early twitter about the *Spatial Agency* website called it "terribly worthy", which we suspect was not meant as a compliment.[24] But if worthiness can be removed from its pious associations and returned to its Middle English origins of worth, then perhaps it is not such a bad acknowledgement that spatial agency is something that adds social value to the world. The examples of individuals, groups and projects collated in this book all show a desire to critically interrogate the status quo, and change it for the better. They show architecture's capacity for transformative action and, even more importantly, how the role of the architect can be extended to take into account the consequences of architecture as much as the objects of architecture.

This research project was set off by a frustration with the conservative tendencies of so much architectural practice. It would have been easy enough to be relentlessly damning about the limited preoccupations of the profession, but as we progressed through the research, this negative turn was replaced by a much more buoyant approach, inspired by the examples in the book, which leave us in admiration for their mixture of canniness, bravery and optimism. It is possible to appreciate the work on its own terms and in its own setting, but the ambition is that the various approaches can be applied in a much wider range of contexts. Because much of the work included here has never made it into the pages of orthodox architectural histories, the temptation may be to damn it with faint praise as interesting but marginal. But this would be to deny the inherent strength of the work to effect change at a wider level. Just because a project has been developed in the Global South among slum dwellers does not mean that its lessons and ethics cannot be adapted to a northern city. These are ways of thinking and behaving that are relevant, and applicable, in a multitude of design contexts, from the commercial office block to the infrastructure of a favela. Taken together, the examples are testimony to the possibility of how, by looking at the world in the different way, one is able to find other ways of doing architecture.

The following chapters outline how the wider lessons of spatial agency may be employed to enact such change. *The Motivations of Spatial Agency* sets out the various reasons that spatial agents have set out on their chosen path. *The Sites of Spatial Agency* shows the means and locations of spatial agency. *The Operation of Spatial Agency* explains how spatial agency has been, and might be, enacted. The final part of the book is a lexicon of enacted examples of spatial agency.

1 Bruno Latour, 'On recalling ANT', in *Actor Network Theory and after* (Oxford: Blackwell, 1999), pp. 15–25.

2 Martin Parker, Valerie Fournier and Patrick Reedy, *The Dictionary of Alternatives: Utopianism and Organization* (London: Zed Books Ltd, 2007), xi.

3 For a summary of the issues raised by the symposium see Eeva Berglund, 'Exploring the Social and Political. Are Architects Still Relevant to Architecture?', *Architectural Research Quarterly*, 12 (2008), 105–11. For the papers presented at the symposium see the same issue of *ARQ* and 'Alternate Currents', *Field: A Free Journal for Architecture*, ed. by Jeremy Till and Tatjana Schneider, 2 (2008) <http://www.field-journal.org>.

4 Alfredo Brillembourg, Kristin Feireiss and Hubert Klumpner, *Informal City – Caracas case* (Munich: Prestel, 2005), 19.

5 Donald A. Schön, *The reflective practitioner: how professionals think in action* (New York: Basic Books, 1983).

6 As Max Horkheimer notes in his seminal paper *Traditional and Critical Theory*. Traditional theory is "a universal systematic science, not limited to any particular subject matter but embracing all possible objects. This is published in Max Horkheimer, *Critical theory: selected essays* (New York: Continuum, 1982), 188–243. Typical of such normative theories in architecture is the contemporary obsession with theories of form, such as parametrics, in which abstract and universalised principles are used to direct practice, oblivious of the constraints or opportunities of particular contexts.

7 Karl Marx, 'Letter to Arnold Ruge, September 1843', accessed from <http://www.marxists.org/archive/marx/works/1843/letters/43_09.htm>.

8 For a recent collection of essays on the subject see: *Critical Architecture*, ed. by Jane Rendell and others (London: Routledge, 2007).

9 For a good summary of the issues see: George Baird, 'Criticality and its discontents', *Harvard Design Magazine*, 21 (2004), 1–6.

10 Henri Lefebvre, *The Production of Space* (Oxford: Blackwell, 1991), 26.

11 Lefebvre, 360.

12 Zygmunt Bauman, *Liquid Modernity* (Cambridge: Polity Press, 1997).

13 Two recent publications that have focussed on the issue of agency in architecture are: Kenny Cupers and Isabelle Doucet, eds., 'Agency in Architecture: Reframing Criticality in Theory and Practice', *Footprint*, no. 4 (2009), and Florian Kossak and others, *Agency: Working With Uncertain Architectures* (London: Routledge, 2009).

14 Anthony Giddens, *Social Theory and Modern Sociology* (Cambridge: Polity, 1987), 220.

15 Bruno Latour, *Reassembling the Social: an introduction to Actor-Network-Theory* (Oxford: Oxford University Press, 2005).

16 Anthony Giddens, *The Constitution of Society: Outline of the Theory of Structuration* (Berkeley: University of California Press, 1984), 14.

17 See introduction to: Cedric Price, *Cedric Price: Works II* (London: Architectural Association, 1984).

18 Giddens (1987), 216.

19 Giddens (1984), 4.

20 Giddens, 9. See also the section 'Agency and Power', pp.14ff.

21 Bruno Latour, 'Why has critique run out of steam? From matters of fact to matters of concern', *Critical Inquiry*, 30 (2004), 225–248.

22 An expanded range of entries can be found on the accompanying website, www.spatialagency.net, which also offers the opportunity to point out omissions.

23 Leon Van Schaik, *Spatial Intelligence: new futures for architecture* (London: Wiley, 2008).

24 Kieran Long, kieranlong, 2010 <http://twitter.com/kieranlong>. "Jeremy Till's new database is terrible (sic.) worthy and wordy, but is a great and much-needed resource."

1

THE MOTIVATIONS OF SPATIAL AGENCY

If you ask a potential architecture student why they want to study architecture, the most common response is along the lines: "I want to design buildings and make the world a better place." Implicit in this answer is the assumption that there is a causal link between designing a building and making the world a better place, and it is this link that architects cling to through the thick and thin of practice. Where a poet might condense grief in to a few lines, a photographer depict suffering or a novelist expound at length on sadness, it would be strange to see an architect who deliberately set out to inflict misery on its occupants, or who designed a project that purposely made the world a worse place. Architects start out instinctually optimistic, and even if this hope is tempered and frustrated over time by the barriers that have to be overcome, the initial motivation of betterment still remains. Although immediate goals such as getting the building completed on time, satisfying the client or just plain survival might occupy the daily attention of the architect, they are normally overseen by higher aspirations, however vaguely defined.

The question then arises as to exactly what constitutes "better", and what means are used to achieve it? The answer may be suggested in the second most common response to why students want to study architecture, namely "because it is a combination of art and science". Architectural hope is here invested in the muse of artistic genius combined with the authority of scientific reason, and the accompanying focus on aesthetics and technique, which become the primary measures of architectural achievement. As we have seen, spatial agency does not so much dispense with these measures, but supplements them with many others, and so expands the definition of what might constitute "better". Rather than connecting

architectural optimism solely with the look and making of stuff – most clearly in the timeworn affiliation of happiness with beauty – spatial agency holds to the idea of betterment but associates it with a more fluid set of processes and social conditions.

Our apparent scepticism of the efficacy of beauty as a medium for the greater good does not imply the corollary of the promotion of ugliness. Instead it comes from a belief that beauty has been used too often as an excuse to retreat from some of the more contested areas of contemporary life, as if a timeless sense of beauty will lift us from our daily grind. It may be that the connection between beauty and betterment is so taken for granted that the motivation to make the world a better place is surreptitiously replaced with the more simple, and more controllable, motivation of making beautiful stuff, in the belief that architects can do good by doing what they do best, namely designing delightful things.

To argue that there is not a direct, causal, link between beauty and happiness, or at a wider level between aesthetics and ethics, is not to argue for the dismissal of the role of aesthetics and tectonics, but to more realistically understand the role they play in the context of the much wider set of social conditions to which architecture contributes. This effectively relieves the pressure on the design of the perfected object beautiful, and of its reception as the be-all and end-all of architectural culture. By all means craft the building, compose the elevation, worry over the detail, but at the same time see these as just some tasks in service to another. Beauty may be one approach to achieving betterment, but it is not a sufficient one. When Zygmunt Bauman writes that "beauty, alongside happiness, has been one of the most exciting promises and guiding ideals of the restless modern spirit,"[1] what he is pinpointing is the hope that beauty holds out but may never deliver. The excitement is there in discussions of new formal and technical possibilities, which tend to dominate architectural discourse, but they represent a false hope because they are conceived of away from the world in which the results are eventually located, and so the beauty, and its associated hope, is scarred by other actions. In contrast, the motivations of spatial agency arise not from without but from within the contested areas of spatial production, and have more explicit aims than the fuzzy hope to make the world a better place. Because the motivations for spatial agency are more grounded and more focused, it is also likely that the resulting actions and results will be more resilient in the face of worldly contingencies.

In what follows, we identify five issues that have motivated the examples of spatial agency in the book: politics, the profession, pedagogy, humanitarian crises and ecology. It is not as if these issues are in any way mutually exclusive, but for the sake of clarity they will be taken one at a time.

Politics

To say that architecture is political is to state a truism; to say that architects tend to avoid politics is to assert a generality. Architecture is immanently political because it is part of spatial production, and this is political in the way that it clearly influences social relations. The extent and form of this influence is open to debate, as will be seen in the varying approaches to the political taken by spatial agents, but what is common to them all is an acknowledgement that the production of space is inherently political and that to participate in its production entails not only the taking into account of momentary social responsibilities but also the appreci-ation of long-term consequences. Architecture or, more precisely, space affects and effects social relations in the most profound ways, from the very personal (in a phenomenological engagement with stuff, space, light, materials) to the very political (in the way that the dynamics of power are played out in space). Adopting the feminist maxim ("the personal is political"[2]) buildings conjoin personal space and political space. In recognition of the role that architecture plays in part of (and it really is only part of) the production of that social space, designers have to face up to the responsibility of affecting the social dynamics of others in ways beyond the delivery of beauty. The key political responsibility of the architect lies not in the refinement of the building as static visual commodity, but as a contributor to the creation of empowering spatial, and hence social, relationships in the name of others.

This acknowledgement differs from the attitude of many contemporary architects, whose very silence on the political status of their work is indicative of a certain unease, in which the projection of a personal belief (of the politics of left or right) onto the public is seen to challenge the objective view that professionals are meant to bring to the table. The shift in the professions from their original role as keepers of a particular branch of socially important knowledge into expert agents for an increasingly technocratic society has been accompanied with a suppression of a sense of social duty, and with it a waning of political intent.[3] The result is either an uncomfortable silence or else the transfer of politics from the dynamics of society to the statics of the object.[4] When challenged about the lack of social relevance in their work, progressive formalists will respond, "but there is a politics of aesthetics," which is true, but these politics are usually conducted on their own self-referential terms.

The eschewal of politics may also arise out of the apparent failure of the more overtly political mission of the golden age of modernism in the 1930s and 1950s, when architecture was employed as both instrument and representation of social reform. It was a doctrinaire alliance, with the ordering tendencies of modernist architecture eliding with those of modernity, and the progressive aesthetics of modernist architecture signalling a societal break from the burdens and injustices of tradition. Charles Jencks' announcement of the death of modernism in the opening pages of his book The Language of post-modern Architecture, with the description of the demolition of the Pruitt-Igoe estate in St Louis, brilliantly conjoined social demise with architectural failure.[5] He draws on the myth that design was primarily responsible for the societal collapse on the estate (overlooking the contributing institutional, racial and economic factors[6]), and so at a stroke demonises architecture's association with social issues and then breaks any attachment in his replace-ment of modernism by postmodernism. The latter, now apparently rid of political bonds, was free to explore new stylistic avenues – the "language" of the book's title. But just to push aside politics does not mean that they go away. Quite the opposite. As Mary McLeod notes in her seminal article, *Architecture and Politics in the Reagan Era*, the retreat of postmodern architects into discussions of style was accompanied by a capitulation to the political forces of Reaganism. "Architecture's value no longer lay in its redemptive social value," she argues, "but rather in its communicative power as a cultural object", and this power has significant value in the economics of that and this era.[7]

The recent turn identified by certain theorists towards a pragmatic laissez-faire does not avoid this trap, but is maybe more honest in its recognition of architecture's complicity with prevailing political and economic forces.[8] Thus in a recent interview, Rem Koolhaas notes that "our position is that, once unleashed, whether you want it or not, (globalization) is what is 'normal', so you have to inscribe yourself within it rather than try to work against it or to stop it. Not uncritically, but..."[9] There is a sense of realism in the so-called "projective" architecture of the 2000s that moves architecture out of the cul-de-sac of "critical" architecture, where architectural theory resided in the 1980s and 1990s, and moves it into the fast lane of late capitalism. But such is the speed of the traffic that architects are left with little choice but go with the flow, sometimes enjoying the new formal possibilities that the speed throws up, sometimes finding the gaps in the traffic that allow them to explore new social potentials. In the former category one might place the work of pragmatic formalists such as Foreign Office Architects,[10] in the latter the earlier cultural work of OMA such as the Kunsthal in Rotterdam or the Seattle Public Library. However, what is missing in all this new pragmatism, whether of the "stars" or the "mainstream" (who have been pragmatic all along), is a sense of political or ethical intent. Roemer van Toorn is clear about the dangers of the laissez-faire in this respect: "instead of taking responsibility for the design, instead of having the courage to steer flows in a certain direction, the ethical and political consequences arising from the design decisions are left to market realism, and the architect retreats into the givens of his discipline. In that way... projective practices... are formalistic."[11]

Many of the examples of spatial agency specifically do not accept a laissez-faire attitude: they might be pragmatic, but never are formalistic for the sake of form; they start out with a clear transformative intent and *do* try to produce work that has both a political and ethical content, challenging the perceived and real limitations of each new project. In this, the pragmatics of spatial agency are different from the pragmatism of architecture. Where the latter resigns itself to the wider forces – "why resist what cannot be resisted?" – and so effectively withdraws from the political, the former engages but in a manner that avoids modernism's alliance with epic social reform, be it of the left or of the right – and not only because most projects are much more modest in scale. If modernisms politics were naïve in their resort to notions of social determinism or grand spatial utopias which were meant to deliver social utopias, then the politics of spatial agency need to be more knowing and nuanced, adapting to their circumstances. Here the politics of spatial agency fit well with Roberto Mangabeira Ungers call for realistic trajectories of context change,[12] in which he identifies that even in the seemingly most intractable situations, there are opportunities for destabilisation and transformation. "Even the most entrenched formative context," he writes, "can be dissolved by escalating practical and imaginative conflict."[13] The conjunction here of practicality and imagination is important, because it brings two operations that are sometimes kept apart, and so asks spatial agents to be at the same time realist and visionary. This leaves the door open for architectural intelligence, founded as it is on the intersection the creative and the real, to operate in a wider field. Spatial agency often starts with an understanding of the political implications of a given context, and uses that understanding as a means to creatively transform space for the better, or more particularly to transform the lives of the people within that space for the better through close attention to how space affects social and phenomenal relationships. The clearest examples of the application of this attention are those architect-politicians who have chosen to move from working with architectural space to influence social change, to using politics to effect spatial change (which in turn influences social transformation). There is a small but influential group of politicians who come from architectural backgrounds, and it is maybe no coincidence that the cities or regions that they are associated with are also at the forefront of the urban debate. The Brazilian, Jamie Lerner, Mayor of Curitiba and Governor of Paraná, is the best known of the architect-mayors, but there are others such as Ilmar Reepalu, the mayor of the Swedish city of Malmo, under whose tenure the city has become an exemplar of sustainable urban renewal.[15]

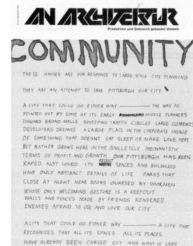

[Fig.2.1] These magazine covers are from the magazine An Architektur which critically analyses the production and use of the built environment through graphic works, interviews, annotated key texts and edited issues. The group comments in an interview with Marie Bruun Yde and Signe Sophie Bøggild of the blogsite openhagen "We have to articulate that planning and design is by no means only a question of form, but always implies – often unacknowledged by the architects – political decisions. Architecture is always in a political field and that this is exactly the realm where we want it to be."

The precise motivation of the political agency differs from example to example, but there are some broad groupings. The first are those whose motivation is primarily driven by a clear political position. That these positions as represented in the book are generally of the left is not just down to our own political sensibilities; it is also because there are precious few examples of spatial agency that are *explicitly* motivated by the politics of the right (some recent Centri Sociali in Italy are the only ones included in the lexicon, showing the potential of self-organising systems to be appropriated by left and right alike), though, as many others have argued, it is possible to identify pragmatic/projective/postcritical/ mainstream practice as implicitly or tacitly aligning itself with the centre or right ground of politics. It may be too that our selection criteria are self-fulfilling in their orientation to the left, with in particular the demand for mutual knowledge ruling out any libertarians who still take Ayn Rand seriously.[16]

Probably the most explicit examples of politically motivated spatial agency come from the neo-Marxists. The German group An Architektur, [Fig.2.1] the US writer Mike Davis, the Scottish cooperative G.L.A.S. (p.132) and the German/American academic Peter Marcuse each in their own way start out from a critique of the effects of capitalism and the neo-liberal economy on spatial production. It is possible to dismiss these approaches as hopelessly ideological, but that would be to miss the emancipatory intent that lies behind their unveiling of the spatial consequences of the controlling power systems.

It is impossible, for example, not to feel first appalled and then moved to some form of action after reading Mike Davis' *Planet of Slums*,[17] his devastating account of how the rapid urbanisation of the world has left vast swathes of people living in sub-standard conditions.

Exactly what that action might be can be seen in another grouping of spatial agents, those whose stance is clearly antithetical to the political status quo, but who play out their politics primarily through spatial interventions or actions rather than through critique, whether the Italian architect Giancarlo de Carlo's approach that arose out of his anti-fascist past and alignment with the Italian anarchist movement, the Brazilian group Morar de Outras Maneiras' (MOM) [Fig.2.2] Marxist background which informs their design of interfaces for favela dwellers in order to allow them a degree of autonomy, or Noero Wolff Architects, whose Jo Noero must be the only architect to have made an acceptance speech for a major architectural award that included the words "hegemony", "justice" and "imperialist".[18] The action of others, such as the feminist praxis of Matrix in the UK or the resistance of District Six in South Africa, is more specifically motivated by the politics of gender or race, in each case working against dominant power structures. The real inspiration of these forms of spatial agency is that they give us hope that there are other ways of operating politically and transformatively in a spatial context.

That such clearly articulated political positions are not common in architectural circles is both worrying and understandable: worrying because without such alternatives being posited, the status quo will simply gather strength; understandable because of the power of the dominant forces. It takes a brave professional to stand up to a corporate client and profess a feminist/Marxist/anarchist position, which is why some explicitly politically motivated agents, such as Estudio Teddy Cruz and atelier d'architecture autogérée, have chosen to self-initiate projects rather than wait for a potentially disapproving client to come to them.

A second, much larger, grouping of spatial agents are still politically motivated but operate in the wider name of social justice. The starting point here is one that relates social inequalities to spatial conditions, and then tries to alleviate these injustices through some form of action or intervention. The end game is often similar to the final intent of the more overtly political stances, but social justice as a concept allows for a more mediated encounter with political forces. For example, groups such as Abahlali baseMjondolo and Shack/Slum Dwellers International, both in South Africa, have identified the achievement of land tenure, and accompanying economic stability, as the single most important key for the urban poor to achieve some form of political strength and the beginnings of social justice. This way of working with tactics that are related to space but are not solely physical applies also outside of the Global South. For example, the Spanish activist Santiago Cirugeda, [Fig.2.3] who through creative engagement with the regulatory framework opens up possibilities for others to appropriate space.

These examples may cause some discomfort to a strictly architectural audience, because they achieve their effect not primarily through the visible, but through a reinscription of the invisible processes that make the visible possible. In this context Michelle Provoost of the Dutch architectural historian collective Crimson presents

[Fig.2.2] Teaching space at Aglomerado da Serra, Belo Horizonte, Brazil. The work of the Brazilian group Morar de Outras Maneiras draws on and works with the informal production of space in the Brazilian favelas. This teaching space in the favela Aglomerado da Serra in Belo Horizonte was built using materials already owned by a small local institution, but had not been considered by them as useable. MOM acted as advisors and helped to design the structure, but their main input came through the design of a mediating process, which was meant to "remove social constraints, freeing the exchange of ideas and technical information. It is intended to strengthen people's experience, opinion and judgment, or in short, to enhance their autonomy." Ph: MOM, 2006

[Fig.2.3] Santiago Cirugeda's Strategies for Subversive Urban Occupation. The Spanish architect Santiago Cirugeda and his practice Recetas Urbanas challenge what it might mean to be and practice as an architect, by questioning and subverting regulations, laws and conventions. He challenges the notion that the architect is the author, and thereby the solely recognised designer, and produces urban prescriptions that can be used and utilised by anyone who may want to try them out, stating: "A cheap architecture is more important than a fashion architecture, architecture should be available for everybody." Image: Santiago Cirugeda/Recetas Urbanas

an interesting hypothesis: "could it be that architectural significance and relevance are inversely proportional to the visibility of the architecture or the conspicuousness of the architectural image?"[19] The short answer is "yes and no and yes". Yes, in so much as the reverse is often true, with the most striking, most visible, architecture also the most indicative of the power of the market, and so emblematic of the accompanying loss of significance of the role of the architect. No, because "not all flashy buildings are empty shells." But yes in so much as there are many examples of how the architect can operate modestly and invisibly, but to great effect, through an intelligent and imaginative engagement with the economic, social and political contexts of spatial production, and that it is here that the architect regains a prominent role, and with it a social significance. Provoost is wonderfully clear in articulating a position, and illustrating it with built examples, in which the architect transcends the Vitruvian offer of knowledge, expertise and evocation; instead she finds innovation and inspiration in projects that "allow architects to penetrate to the heart of architectural production, because they experiment with new methods of organization, commissioning and financing and ignore 'business as usual'". This is a position that avoids the laissez faire of the pragmatist and is prepared to engage productively with wider forces, with their reward expressed in the less obviously visible world of political dynamics rather than the extremely visible world of formal dynamics.

The politics of spatial agency accord with Chantal Mouffe's theory of "agonistic politics", which sees space as a "battleground where different hegemonic projects are confronted, without any possibility of final reconciliation".[20] Such a space is defined by a multiplicity of agencies in continual confrontation and negotiation, in a process that may involve students of architecture, architects, artists, urban planners, policy makers and ordinary citizens – all of whom recognise the political implications of their actions.

Professionalism

The second motivation for spatial agency is linked to the first. We have seen how politically motivated agency often leads to action that challenges preconceived notions of what it is to be an architect. In some cases, as covered in this section, it is such a challenge to received professional definitions and methods that is the primary motivation of a person or group's agency.

Professions, and still more the bodies that represent them, have a split personality in relation to the tenets of spatial agency. On the one hand there is the founding mission of all professions to serve society thought the development and deployment of a branch of knowledge. This sense of contributing to the public good, however vaguely framed, is consistent with the empowering thrust of spatial agency. However, the means of achieving this mission, as overseen by professional codes and values, generally contradict the premise of agency. The main problem is the self-protectionist nature of all professions. Although the founding charters of the professional bodies are full of noble public intent, the reality of their institutional structures fast move in to compromise this aspiration. All professional bodies, and the architectural ones are no different, are torn between public service and private protection, awkwardly criss-crossing the line between learned body and subscription club. But in the end, architects are defined by the knowledge and rituals that the bodies preserve. A closed loop is set up whereby the profession designates knowledge which architects must possess – a process that is started in education whereby the professional institutions such as the RIBA assess how students are taught according to the set content – which in turn prescribes what architects do,

design buildings, and the buildings in turn become the constituents of the professional knowledge. Spatial agency ruptures this professional closure, first in its inclusion of others, amateurs, in the processes and secondly in its rejection of the building as the sole source and representation of expertise.

The groups that most clearly articulated this rupture were the Architects' Revolutionary Council (ARC) and the associated New Architecture Movement (NAM). These UK organisations of the 1970s confronted the profession head-on and were explicitly oppositional of the RIBA and all it stood for, calling not only for a democratically controlled council but also for a revision of the educational system that they regarded as the starting point for the creation of self-referential professional bodies. Although short-lived, their legacy of a mixture of political ire, anti-institutional polemic and wit (has there ever been a better architectural slogan than ARC's: "If crime doesn't pay… where do architects get all their money?") lives on in the blogosphere.[21] ARC and NAM were particularly critical of the elitist nature of the profession, both in terms of the hierarchical structure of architectural practice and in terms of whom it served. The latter point was more specifically addressed by a number of groups from the 1960s onwards, who were highly critical of the way that the profession did not serve large parts of the population, in particular the urban and rural poor as well as other marginalised sections of society. The main motivation of movements such as the Community Design Centers in the USA and Community Technical Aid Centres in the UK was to bring professional services to people and communities who would otherwise not have access to them. Working with disenfranchised communities continues today with the practice of various groups including Atelier-3/Rural Architecture Studio in Taiwan, and the Design Corps in the USA. All of these groups shift professional attention from simply providing expertise (though they do this too) into broader fields of advocacy and facilitation on behalf of others, without suppressing the role that professional knowledge plays when it comes to setting up, detailing, financing, and running a project.

It is exactly such an extension of the role of the professional that motivates another group of spatial agents. Pioneering in this respect is the work of the 1960s Brazilian radicals Arquitectura Nova, including Sérgio Ferro, who are too little known in the Anglophone world, but influential in Latin America. Ferro started

[Fig.2.4] The dwellings in Iquique designed by Elemental demonstrate just how relevant design is in conditions of scarcity, both at a micro and a macro scale. Rather than detached houses, a comb-like variation on row housing was developed to make the most of financial resources as well as outdoor space. Instead of providing a finished house, the inhabitants were given a basic raw unit that they could then complete, and some external slack space that could be used for building extensions. Elemental understood and made use of the strong self-build tradition of the people who were to move into these houses, and translated this into a built structure that allowed them to claim it as their own. Alejandro Aravena, one of the co-founders of the practice, says "Communication has been a relevant factor for us. We speak in the same level with the families, the users of our housing projects, without paternalism, without false expectations and at the same time, transmitting trust and telling them that we have a professional knowledge which would help them in their problems." The housing at Iquique before and after the self-built additions. Ph: Taduez Jalocha (before), Cristobal Palma (after)

with a direct critique of the profession's obsession with design, and in particular the architectural drawing which for him represented a domain of remote and abstracted expertise that inevitably alienated architecture from its processes of production. Arquitectura Nova therefore turned their attention to the construction of buildings, and all the people involved in the processes, because they believed that "it was through identification with building, not design, that a radical architecture could be achieved." [22] The spirit of this approach lives on in the form of the *mutirão*, collective building efforts that inform the self-built production of some Latin American social housing. The role of the professional here ranges from one of technical facilitator and experimenter, to one

of designing systems of production and means of communication that enable the self-builders to operate in as efficient and democratic a manner as possible. [23] A similar intent of applying design intelligence to a broad set of scenarios can also be seen in examples as diverse as 00:/ in the UK and Elemental [Fig.2.4] in Chile, both of whom are acutely aware of the need to understand and intervene in the micro-economics and social networks at stake in the design and production of any environment.

What is clear is that this expanded field also demands the professional to engage with a new set of tools, some of which may be outside the traditional comfort zone of the design-forming tools of drawing and modelling. In their list of tools for spatial agency, 00:/

include: *interviews, visioning workshop, mind mapping, residency, consultation, scenario testing, collaboration, co-design, business development, stats analysis, design guide, technical investigation, policy writing, prototyping*. Others might add their own tools (say *brief writing, game playing, web 2.0, storytelling, open source software*, and so on and on), by which time we are in a danger of having a cacophony of methods that threatens the very viability of professional stability. From the Renaissance onwards architecture has been identified with *disegno*, with design as manifested through drawing, therefore it might be seen that the expansion of the repertory so radically beyond *disegno* means the dispersal of the profession. However, this expansion is not a negative turn, because the dispersal is one that allows architecture to open up to others, and include them in its processes. If architectural drawing, with its codes, abstractions and mystique of artistry, tends, as Sérgio Ferro argued, to seclude architecture from spatial dynamics, then these other tools enable it to engage with them. Some of the most inventive examples of spatial agency focus on the design of these tools, seeing them as the prime means to unlock the potential of a given situation. Thus the creative energy of Chora and public works [Fig.2.5] is invested as much in the vehicles to reach to the solution as it is in the solution itself. There is a quote, variously attributed to Mark Twain or Abraham Maslow, which perfectly summarises professional attitudes: "To a man with a hammer, everything looks like a nail." The hammer is both a strength because it forges the zone of professional expertise, but it is also a weakness because the world is not just nails, hence the expansion of the range of available tools. The French phrase for the professional mindset, *déformation professionnelle* puns on the idea of professional formation (*formation professionnelle*) captures the dangers of seeing the world through too limited a lens. Spatial agency, as seen in this section, translates *déformation professionnelle* more literally, and more positively, as a deformation that is a reformation of professional values and methods.

Pedagogy

The next motivation for spatial agency comes from those who believe that in order to achieve this professional reformation, one has to start further down the line with professional education. Architectural

[Fig.2.5] "Where does a shop start?" and "One Day Shop in Loughborough". The project list of public works contains a long list of tools for engagement and actions: thus a mobile porch is timetabled with activities and the international village shop is "an open and experimental platform for the development and exchange of local produce across a network of rural and urban spaces" that can take on any form and environment imaginable – as shown so delightfully in the set of pictures above, a public mobile mapping station whose aim it was to index "a variety of [Folkestone's] different informal and formal cultural spaces, interests and networks." Ph: public works

[Fig.2.6] The Montreal Biosphère by Fuller built in 1967. Richard Buckminster Fuller (1895–1983) was an architect and designer whose design philosophy of 'more for less' was applied across a range of projects, from the design of a car, housing, boats, games, to perhaps his most famous design the geodesic dome. One of the first to recognise the finite nature of natural resources, Fuller was convinced that design and technology could offer solutions to the problems of the management of resources, especially with regard to transportation and building. His geodesic domes (pictured) inspired a whole host of architects and designers, most famously perhaps they were used and adapted at the hippie commune in Colorado, Drop City. Their application being important for demonstrating that Fuller's ideas could also be applied in a low-tech manner. A prolific designer and thinker, his systems thinking and emphasis on access to and invention of tools for living were concepts that proved to be a major inspiration for Stewart Brand, the co-founder of the Whole Earth Catalog. Ph: Ryan Mallard

education is notably under-theorised as an underlying discipline, though is clearly intensely theorised as a set of surface actions. It has remained largely unbothered by reformist educational movements such as critical pedagogy,[24] with the result that its central structures and methods have altered little since they were founded in the École des Beaux Arts in the early C19. Thus the continuation of the master tutor and willing servant students, the privileging of the visual, the inculcation of absurd modes of behaviour (sleep deprivation, aggressive defensiveness, internal competition), the raising of individuals on to pedestals, all these and more self-perpetuate in schools of architecture around the world, a strange form of interbreeding with tutors passing the architectural gene to students who in turn become tutors who perform the same rituals. The stasis of the underlying system is left undisturbed because we are distracted by the speed of change on the surface. Because things look different from year to year, from school to school, from unit to unit, the frantic display of architectural education suggests progress is being made, whereas in fact the core is left unchallenged.

There have been very few attempts to propose wholesale revisions to the structures and methods of architectural education. Most celebrated was the Bauhaus, but that quickly reverted to type (albeit modernist-looking type rather than classical-looking type) under the directorship of Mies van der Rohe. Perhaps most radical of all was the short-lived experiment at the Bartlett, University College London, under

the directorship of Richard Llewelyn Davies when drawing boards were pushed to one side and replaced with the empirical methods of the sciences, and the longer lasting Black Mountain College in the US, which from 1933 to 1956 ran an "education in democracy" which placed creativity at the core, and included Buckminster Fuller [Fig.2.6] as one of the tutors.[25] In Germany HfG Ulm (School of Design, Ulm) had a specifically political intent and replaced subject/profession based departments with thematic groups. Others have attempted to change the values from within academia, in particular through introducing an ethical dimension to architectural education, which makes students aware at an early stage of their wider social responsibilities. Best known of these initiatives is the Rural Studio, where students are immersed in the complexities of one of the poorest counties in the US. As the late, and great, Samuel Mockbee, founder of the Rural Studio, notes the primary aim of the education there is not a general worthiness, but has a longer term ambition for the students "to be more sensitive to the power and promise of what they do, to be more concerned with the good effects of architecture rather than with 'good intentions'".[26]

Elsewhere Baupiloten [Fig.2.7] in Germany, the Live Projects programme at the University of Sheffield, and the Yale Building Project have each in their own way devised programmes that take the students beyond the self-defining milieu of the school studio, and thus introduced the dynamics of spatial agency.

[Fig.2.7] Workshop with children of the Familienservice school; children exploring a model; engaging the inhabitants of student halls in the refurbishment of their buildings. The Baupiloten course at the Technical University Berlin is an explicit attempt to reform the faculty's teaching programme. It brings the practicing architect Susanne Hofmann and a group of students in their 4th and 5th years of architectural education together with real life clients who are mostly pupils, parents and teaching staff. For the students, participating in this course gives them opportunity to work on these relatively small design projects from the first meeting and sketch through to the building or intervention. And, for the end users, the Baupiloten course presents a chance to be directly engaged in the design process. Courtesy Baupiloten / Susanne Hofmann

[Fig.2.8] The Baban Seth Community Classroom in Navi Mumbai. James Soane writes in his article about Maurice Mitchell's new book *Learning from Delhi*, that "Mitchell argues that the relevance of the studio is to implicate the architect within a social and often political framework where he/she must act with integrity and learning." Mitchell and his students at the London Metropolitan University act on these principles. The book gives an overview of this practice, which is run under the research programme Architecture of Rapid Change and Scarce Resources, and includes projects such as the Baban Seth Community Classroom in Navi Mumbai (pictured). Ph: Bo Tang

[Fig.2.9] Construction of drains by residents of a slum neighbourhood. The Orangi Pilot Project (OPP) in Karachi, Pakistan, is "a living training ground for extending the model of community managed sanitation to other settlements, other cities and other parts of Asia." It is evidence that communities, against opposition from engineers and often also NGOs, can build and maintain their own water supply and sewage system with assistance from the OPP. The organisation of the technical infrastructure, as seen in the picture, is not only a way of organising the settlements or improving their lives but is also "consolidating their right to stay." Ph: OPP Research and Training Institute

Most recently the inspiring work of Maurice Mitchell's [Fig.2.8] students at London Metropolitan University has shown how new forms of education explicitly lead to alternative forms of practice, in this case the idea of the architect as detective, uncovering the spatial potential of sites in Delhi.[27]

The principles of spatial agency have probably been engaged with most profoundly in educational settings outside of the academy, with examples such as Asiye eTafuleni in South Africa and Arif Hasan [Fig.2.9] in Pakistan. In India, Ankur have been instrumental in taking the tenets of radical pedagogy to the streets. Their *cybermohalla* project, in collaboration with Sarai, creates local technology hubs (mohalla meaning neighbourhood in Hindi and Urdu) "as a means for talking about one's 'place' in the city, and in cyberspace."[28] In all these cases, the decision has been made to invest agency in empowering others through various educational programmes focused on equipping people with the tools and awareness to allow them to take on spatial issues themselves. In the spirit of the notion of mutual knowledge, these pedagogical approaches are not ones of a prescriptive imposition of knowledge, but of a drawing out of the vernacular intelligence that the communities already possess. It is such an approach that often motivates the next grouping.

Humanitarian Crises

In relation to other professions, architects came late to setting up agencies to help in times of humanitarian crisis. French doctors founded *Médecins Sans Frontières* (MSF) in 1971 and French engineers followed with *Ingénieurs Sans Frontières* in 1982, which in turn lead to the growth of the international federation of *Engineers Without Borders* in the 1990s. In contrast the international federation *Architectes Sans Frontières* (ASF)[29] was not formally constituted until 2007, though some of the national groups were set up earlier, and there were individual pioneers such as Fred Cuny. (p.99) It would be wrong to attribute this tardiness to a lack of social conscience in the part of the architectural community. More likely it is indicative of the complexities of architectural production. A broken bone or broken bridge can be dealt with as immediate fixes (though clearly MSF and EWB also have longer term strategies), whereas the provision of shelter is a much more long drawn out process.

Over the years much architectural ingenuity has been devoted to the design of emergency shelters, most famously Shigeru Ban's (p.99) cardboard buildings after the 1995 Kobe earthquake, and Nader Khalili's [Fig.2.10] SuperAdobe constructions. However, the continuing evidence, whether in the US after Hurricane Katrina or in Pakistan after the disastrous 2010 floods, is that these and other efforts have not penetrated the wider field, with the dropping of tents still the standard solution despite their climatic and social limitations. As Ian Davis notes: "There must be few subjects in the spectrum of man's buildings where so much effort has been expended, so much money spent, and yet where paradoxically so little is known or more precisely where so little knowledge has been documented."[30]

Though there is clearly a need to address this paradox, it is instructive that the approach of the examples in this book do not focus solely on the immediate provision of shelter, but see this as part of a chain of events, consistent with the tenets of spatial agency. Thus NGOs associated with UN-Habitat will typically attempt to engage from the start with affected community, and where possible draw upon their local knowledge of vernacular construction or else set up workshops to develop skills. They are also often involved in the longer-term reconstruction process, which necessarily involves the coordination of a wide range of services and skills. Here spatial judgment comes to the fore as a particular way of thinking that understands reconstruction to be about much more than bricks and mortar, but is clearly about the intersection of the physical and social, in which any provision has to respect the cultural and environmental context in which it is placed.[31] This sort of productive transfer of architectural knowledge from one setting to another can be seen in the humanitarian work of John McAslan + Partners, better known as commercial modernists, about which it is noted: "In that context, the architect's ability to broker and manage relationships between project funders, consultants, users and local authorities is vitally important."[32]

[Fig.2.10] Demonstration sandbag buildings at Cal-Earth Institute. Nader Khalili was an advocate for a sustainable solution to shelter by combining found materials such as earth and water with what he called "timeless building techniques": arches, vaults and domes. Khalili's agency lies both in the appropriation of "materials of war" such as sandbags and barbed wire for peaceful purposes (the application of this method is shown in the picture), as well as in his approach to create a housing solution that would be affordable and buildable by everyone and, at the same time, be not only a temporary solution in response to a disaster but a permanent place to live in.
Ph: Yvonne Magener

John McAslan's Initiative Unit is also very aware of the need to be in there for the long haul. Indeed a long-term view is essential to the success of such projects because otherwise the worst traits of short-term thinking are played out in the most vulnerable situations to tragic effect: not just those tents, but water wells installed and then not maintained, dwelling design separated from infrastructure design, and buildings designed for one place dropped in to another. Humanitarian work thus holds up a magnifying glass to the actions of spatial agency, both intensifying its productive potential and spotlighting where it may go wrong.

Ecology

The final motivation of spatial agency is a response to the ecological crisis that faces the planet. Many of the examples of such motivation that are included in the book date to before the time when global warming was an accepted term or phenomenon, and are instructive for their prescience in the way that they responded to the early signals of environmental stress. Common to the outlook of, among others, Findhorn, New Alchemy Institute, Victor Papanek and the Whole Earth Catalog, was an understanding of the interdependence of man's environment with the natural environment. [Fig.2.11] Too often in mainstream architecture, environmental issues are directly attached to the building, in terms of control and mitigation. Buildings are treated as technical devices, and design for sustainability is focussed on

[Fig.2.11] Underground Art Gallery in Cape Cod, Masachussetts, USA. Malcolm Wells (1926–2009) was one of the early advocates of environmentally responsible design and arguably the key exponent of earth-sheltered architecture, coining the term "gentle architecture". His designs, supported by his writing and teaching, were buildings with a minimal material and ecological footprint – they made use of and stored solar energy, consumed their own waste, and, by being partially buried underground, provided also a habitat to wildlife. The building pictured here was originally planned as a home and studio for Wells and his wife but they ran out of funds to build the living quarters. It functions today as an art gallery and studio space.
Ph: Katherine Williams

the optimisation of systems to reduce energy use and in the choice of materials to reduce embodied energy, both in a move towards "low carbon" solutions. Clearly these are important issues, but this limiting of environmental understanding to the technical realm alone tends to treat it as an isolated system that can be dealt with on its own terms, typically those of efficiency and control. This leads to a sense that environmental issues can be dealt with through technical fixes, but this is in fact a false sense of security because it is clear that the environment is tied into much wider networks.

As we saw in Chapter 1, spatial agency is characterised by its engagement with these networks, and in this the environment is not isolated to matters of energy reduction and efficiency, but has to be understood in relation to the social, the global and virtual realms. In their important manifesto for an *Urban Political Ecology*, Nik Heynen, Maria Kaika, and Erik Swyngedouw note that "environmental and social changes co-determine each other."[33] In this light, acting as a spatial agent motivated by ecological concerns means that one has to deal with the interchange of the social and the environmental – with how social conditions are linked with ecological conditions, as is most clearly identified in books such as Mike Davis' *Ecology of Fear*.[34] The authors of the manifesto talk of this relationship in terms of a metabolisms, recognising the cause and effect that is built into all systems, so that "while environmental (both social and physical) qualities may be enhanced in some places and for some humans and non-humans, they often lead to a deterioration of social, physical and/or ecological conditions elsewhere."[35] It is an awareness of this interdependency of systems that the ecological spatial agent brings to the table.

The Ethics of Spatial Agency

Connecting all five of these motivations is an overarching ethical intent for spatial agency. Ethics is a much used and a much abused concept in relation to architecture. Too often ethics is associated with aesthetics, as if a beautiful thing will lead to a beautiful life.[36] Our understanding of ethics in relation to spatial agency removes it from any internalised or objectified discourse and places it firmly in the messier, and less controllable, realm of social dynamics. In particular it takes Zygmunt Bauman's formulation that states that to assume an ethical stance is "to assume responsibility for the

Other."[37] As we have seen the "other" – be it the builder, user, viewer, or reviewer – should always be in the mind of the spatial agent, as their prime matter of concern, even if the final effect is intangible. In this light, the final word in this chapter on the motivation of spatial agency must go to Samuel Mockbee: "Go above and beyond the call of a 'smoothly functioning conscience'; help those who aren't likely to help you in return, and do so even if nobody is watching."[38]

1   Zygmunt Bauman, *Wasted Lives* (Cambridge: Polity Press, 2004), 114.

2   Carol Hanisch, 'The Personal is Political', (1969), http://www.carolhanisch.org/CHwritings/PIP.html

3   See Steven Brint, *In an Age of Experts* (Princeton: Princeton University Press, 1994).

4   Recent attempts to link politics to objects using Bruno Latour's theories of the interaction of the human and non-human have not got much further than stating that objects are political, and so have not yet unpacked the full social implications of the physical. See in particular Alejandro Zaera-Polo, 'The Politics of the Envelope: A Political Critique of Materialism', *Volume (Amsterdam)*, 17 (2008), 76–105.

5   Charles Jencks, *The language of post-modern architecture* (London: Academy Editions, 1977).

6   For a good unravelling of the myths associated with Pruitt-Igoe see: Katherine Bristol, 'The Pruitt-Igoe Myth', *Journal of Architectural Education*, 44, 163–171.

7   Mary McLeod, 'Architecture and Politics in the Reagan Era: From Postmodernism to Deconstructivism', *Assemblage*, 8 (1989): 27.

8   *New Architectural Pragmatism: A Harvard Design Magazine Reader*, ed. by William S. Saunders (University of Minnesota Press, 2007).

9   David Cunningham and Jon Goodbun, 'Propaganda Architecture: An Interview with Rem Koolhaas and Reinier de Graaf', *Radical Philosophy*, 2009 <http://www.radicalphilosophy.com/default.asp?channel_id=2190&editorial_id=27703>. Koolhaas' unfinished sentence, "not uncritically, but..." is completed by de Graaf with "...so as to reveal the ways in which architecture is subject to the forces of modernization and globalization."

10 Alejandro Zaera-Polo, one of the founders of FOA, writes that the Diploma Unit he ran with his partner Farshid Moussavi, was "precisely an attempt to virtualise pragmatics." Alejandro Zaera-Polo, 'A Scientific Autobiography, 1982–2004: Madrid, Harvard, OMA, the AA, Yokohama, the Globe', in *New Architectural Pragmatism*, ed. by William S. Saunders (Minneapolis: University of Minnesota Press, 2007), 10.

11 Roemer van Toorn, 'No More Dreams? The Passion for Reality in Recent Dutch Architecture... and Its Limitations', in *New Architectural Pragmatism*, ed. by William S. Saunders (Minneapolis: University of Minnesota Press, 2007), 69. Elsewhere in the same book, the critic

Hal Foster writes: "What is the difference, politically, between... postcritical affirmation (of anything goes) and the dominant neo-conservatism?", p132.

12 Roberto Mangabeira Unger, *False Necessity: Anti-Necessitarian Social Theory in the Service of Radical Democracy* (Cambridge: Cambridge University Press, 1987), 331.

13 Unger, 308.

14 The architect-politician currently with the highest international profile is the Iranian Mir-Hossein Mousavi, former Prime Minister of Iran and reformist presidential candidate in 2009. The issues he had dealt with probably overwhelmed any specifically spatial intent.

15 In the UK there is the libertarian group *mantownhuman*, whose parody of a Futurist manifesto (though apparently meant in all seriousness) was memorably described by Charles Holland of the architectural practice FAT as "The Fountainhead rewritten by Jeremy Clarkson." http://www.mantownhuman.org/manifesto.html

16 On the occasion of the award of the inaugural RIBA Lubetkin Prize for best international building, 2006, to the Red Location Building designed by Noero Wolff.

17 Mike Davis, *Planet of Slums* (London: Verso, 2006).

18 Michelle Provoost, 'Urban renewal: invention, transformation and the power of the architect', 2008 <http://www.crimsonweb.org/spip.php?article75> [accessed 10 August 2010]. First published in Daan Bakker and others, *Architecture in the Netherlands 2007–2008* (NAi Publishers, 2008). It is no surprise in the context of architecture and politics that Provoost's colleague from Crimson, Wouter Vanstiphout was appointed in 2009 by TU Delft as the first Professor of Design and Politics, a post part funded by the National Ministry of Housing, Spatial Planning and the Environment (... only in the Netherlands).

19 ibid.

20 Chantal Mouffe, "Some Reflections on an Agonistic Approach to the Public," in *Making Things Public: Atmospheres of Democracy*, ed. Bruno Latour and Peter Weibel (Cambridge, MA: MIT Press, 2005), 805.

21 A good place to start is Owen Hatherley's brilliant "SIT DOWN MAN, YOU'RE A BLOODY TRAGEDY" (http://nastybrutalistandshort.blogspot.com), whose links will take you to other like-minded places.

22 Richard Williams, 'Towards an Aesthetics of Poverty: Architecture and the Neo-Avant-Garde in 1960s Brazil', in *Neo-avant-garde*, ed. by David Hopkins (Amsterdam: Editions Rodopi B.V., 2006), 211. See also Pedro Fiori Arantes, 'Reinventing the Building Site', in *Brazil's Modern Architecture*, ed. by Elisabetta Andreoli and Adrian Forty (London: Phaidon, 2004), pp. 170–200.

23 Arantes, 193ff. One simple example is the design of metal staircases installed directly after the foundations are laid which then form the vertical access and structural spine for subsequent work, dispensing with the need for scaffold and formwork.

24 An exception is the work of Thomas A. Dutton who has been instrumental in bringing critical theory to the attention of architectural educators. Thomas A. Dutton, *Voices in architectural education: cultural politics and pedagogy*, Critical studies in education and culture series (New York: Bergin & Garvey, 1991).

25 See D. Latourell, 'The Bartlett 1969', *Journal of Architectural Education*, 23 (1969), 42–46 and M. L. J. Abercrombie, 'The work of a university education research unit', *Higher Education Quarterly*, 22 (1968), 182–196.The latter includes the wonderfully dated, but very telling quote: "The First Degree Course at the Bartlett School offers a general education in the disciplines necessary for providing an environment suitable for the needs of civilised man." For Black Mountain, see Vincent Katz and Martin Brody, *Black Mountain College: experiment in art* (MIT Press, 2003).

26 Samuel Mockbee, 'The Rural Studio', in *The Everyday and Architecture*, ed. by Jeremy Till and Sarah Wigglesworth (London: Academy Editions, 1998): 79.

27 Maurice Mitchell, *Learning from Delhi* (London: Ashgate, 2010). Unfortunately this work was not published in time for inclusion in this book.

28 'Welcome to Cybermohalla' <http://www.sarai.net/practices/cybermohalla> [accessed 30 August 2010].

29 Architectes Sans Frontières was founded in 1979 by Pierre Allard, but operated on a fairly small scale before being disbanded in 1996. One of the earliest national chapters was the Australian *Architects without Frontiers*, set up in 1999 by Melbourne architects and planners, Esther Charlesworth, Garry Ormston and Beau Beza.

30 Ian Davis, 'Emergency shelter', *Disasters*, 1 (1977): 23.

31 See, among many others: Jo Da Silva, *Lessons from Aceh: Key Considerations in Post-disaster Reconstruction* (Practical Action Publishing, 2009).

32 Chris Foges, 'John McAslan Architects: Initiatives Unit', *Architecture Today*, 2010, 48 JMP devote one percent of their overall time to work on the Initiatives Unit.

33 *In the nature of cities: urban political ecology and the politics of urban metabolism*, ed. by Nikolas C. Heynen, Maria Kaika and Erik Swyngedouw (London: Routledge, 2006), 11.

34 Mike Davis, Ecology of Fear: Los Angeles and the Imagination of Disaster (London: Picador, 2000).

35 Heynen, Kaika and Swyngedouw, 13.

36 This argument is expanded in chapter 11, 'Imperfect Ethics', of: Jeremy Till, *Architecture Depends* (MIT Press, 2009).

37 Zygmunt Bauman, *Alone Again: Ethics After Certainty* (London: Demos, 2000), 15. Bauman continues: "to act on the assumption that the well-being of the Other is a precious thing calling for my effort to preserve and enhance it, that whatever I do or do not do affects it, that if I have not done it, it might not have been done at all, and that even if others do or can do it this does not cancel my responsibility for doing it myself."

38 Mockbee.

2

THE
SITES
OF
SPATIAL
AGENCY

Having looked at the "why" of spatial agency in terms of its motivations, we now turn our attention to the "where": this chapter discusses the primary sites of spatial agency, the location in which a person's or group's work is rooted. Where, in spatial agency, is politics played out? Is it through a physical intervention, the implementation of a network, through informing, making knowledge available in a different way or through the set up of a different organisational structure? Where is professionalism challenged? Is it through working from the inside or is it by inventing new forms of practice away from the institution? What is the site for pedagogy and where does it take place, where does it take effect?

Spatial agency expands the definition as to what might constitute a site of action, seeing it as something that is spatial in the widest sense of the word – physical, social, metaphorical, phenomenal – and rarely limited by externally determined instructions and conventions. The boundaries of spatial agency materialise in social interaction, in the same way as Donna Haraway writes about bodies and their boundaries: "Objects do not preexist as such," she writes. "Objects are boundary projects. But boundaries shift from within; boundaries are very tricky. What boundaries provisionally contain remains generative, productive of meanings and bodies."[1] Spatial agency is shaped and reshaped by a complex web of social interactions, and its sites and boundaries are therefore constantly under negotiation and deeply contextual.

Because of its dynamic context, the expression of spatial agency may lie in something that is either physical – a building, an installation, an exhibition – or in something that is less tangible – a map, a network, a set of instructions – or both at the same time. To shift attention away from the building, as we discussed in the previous two chapters, is to focus on the processes that connect the different parts of the production of the built environment. We don't claim these processes and sites of spatial agency to be new "inventions": they are part of any spatial production. What spatial agency does is to acknowledge their importance, so that they assume a new significance. The engagement with these multiple processes is not seen as means to an end – the production of an artefact or knowledge for the sake of knowledge – but often constitutes the very action of spatial agency and the manifestation of a particular motivation. The sites of spatial agency are never mutually exclusive and spatial agency often starts with one site, and that site's initial boundaries, and then develops into other expressions and actions over time. Something might start as a polemical pamphlet, shift into a more structured organisation, and then may proceed, say, to self-managed design of physical objects in space.

There is a common motif for the spatial agents in this book, namely that they never take no for an answer, driven by the belief that situations in which they find themselves in can always be changed. In his seminal book *Action and Praxis*, Richard Bernstein unpicks Karl Marx's understanding of praxis and writes "[Marx] was articulating a new paradigm for describing, under-standing, and eventually changing the quality of human life. It is a paradigm shaped by his understanding of the nature, dynamics, and consequences of human activity – praxis."[2] What Bernstein in his reading of Marx alludes to, and what constitutes a key aspect of spatial agency, is the willingness to expose oneself and one's work to constant criticism and to new questions as a way of absorption in the issues at stake, and

[Fig.3.1] Front: Kunst. Kommune. Kapital. 10 Jahre K 77 (Art. Commune. Capital. 10 Years K 77) Vereinigte Varben Wawavox and Stilkamm 5 1/2 e.V. Squatting, as a global movement, questions the very notion of ownership but is also tied, particularly in the Global South, to basic housing rights and strategies of survival. In the so called Western world, squatted neighbourhoods and buildings often develop their own support structures outside of institutionalised settings: they create social and/or cultural centres, alternative childcare and play groups, communal gardens and kitchens as well as other non-monetary, low-income or informal economies. This is the case for the artist-squat K77 in Berlin, shown here, which within 18 years realised a thriving hub of self-determined and participative living and working together. Ph: Mathias Heyden

through this to develop a different perspective. The sites of spatial agency – physical reality, social and organisational structures as well as the production of knowledges – are where this takes place, where motivations are tested and experimented with, and adjusted to new situations and new contexts.

Social Structures

One of the sites for the actions of spatial agents is engagement with social structures. The emphasis here is first on the physical aspects of space, but on addressing the social (spatial) relations through seeking to found, mobilize and support social networks. As Henri Lefebvre writes "[w]hen no heed is paid to the relations that inhere in social facts, knowledge misses its target; our understanding is reduced to a confirmation of the undefined and indefinable multiplicity of things, and gets lost in classifications, descriptions and segmentations."[3] Lefebvre's is an important point: regardless of how much expertise anybody can bring to a certain project, it will be limited, and often even futile, if attention is not paid to existing and projected social

structures. Doing this is not a blueprint for a "successful" project, but taking note of, understanding, and working with inherent social structures is a necessary part of the process of the creation of spaces that have more relevance to those who use and live in them.

As many of the examples in the book show, one's perception and occupation of space is profoundly affected by the underlying ownership of that space. In the 1920s the German social democrat Walther Rathenau identified the way that the privatization of land was the key to understanding the social dynamics of space. He called for cities created free from speculation. "The new prosperity of the cities will have to have its foundation in the city soil itself," he writes, "which has not grown for either the builders who earn millions or those who have cornered the market on building ground, construction speculators, and rent tyrants... On the contrary, in a few generations the city soil on which the new constructions face will have to become the free property of the municipalities. As long as the architectural negligence of our streets exists, it will be a testimony and admonition of the negligence of our economic concepts. These concepts have granted to a monopolistic caste a right of taxation, arbitrarily augmentable by them, on the common heritage, and have made a gift of millions upon millions to the holders of urban property investments." [4]

Rathenau's desire for land to become the free property of the municipalities never materialized – in fact many municipalities and local authorities across the globe have auctioned off public land, and with it many public housing developments, to private companies for a short-term profit. However, his call to realign existing power relationships by subverting or challenging private claims to space lives on in some examples of spatial agency most obviously the various squatting [Fig.3.1] movements, or those groups inspired by the original Diggers and Levellers. Others have worked in a bottom-up manner, acting as agents for others to establish their right to land, and with it right to the city. Abahlali baseMjondolo, the movement of the militant poor in Durban, South Africa, is one such example of a grassroots organization which formed around a protest against the sale of vacant land promised to those living in a nearby informal settlement. Started as a group that organized actions, they have subsequently set up projects in the settlements such as crèches, gardens and working collectives, thereby creating new social support structures on various levels.

Another approach to the realignment of social structures comes from those groups who take a critical stance to established social and political hierarchies, which they see as restrictive to the way that certain sectors of society interact with space. Thus the Feministische Organisation von Planerinnen und Architektinnen (FOPA) emerged in Berlin in 1981 out of frustration with the way that women were in general excluded from the planning processes, and in particular from the preparations leading up to the International Building Exhibition in Berlin in 1984 and 1987. A loose grouping of feminists began to 'hijack' official meetings and later set up a formalised network, which continued to influence decision making processes throughout the 1980s and early 1990s, shifting established and unquestioned power relationships. Similar to the FOPA, the organisation Architects, Designers and Planners for Social Responsibility, set up in the early 1980s in Berkeley, USA, addresses broad issues of social justice through writings, action and advocacy. Acting as a pressure group and sounding body, they work and agitate, on behalf of disenfranchised groups, trying to ensure that

[Fig.3.2] Ideenmarkt, Halle-Neustadt, 2005. Raumlabor stress that they are not an architectural office or a company – they are a group of people with shared interests who form working groups around specific projects. Their work follows principles of constant negotiation of social and spatial territory and the testing of professional and other territories. This intent is clearly defined by Niklas Maak in the introduction to Raumlabor's book Acting in Public: "The utopian spirit of bricolage that characterises all of these projects demonstrates a new understanding of what architecture can be. Instead of being static, everlasting, inflexible and expensive, it can be removable, mobile, a stage for all kinds of scenarios." These scenarios are developed within extended social structures of "experts", who are not, academics or other professionals, but anyone with knowledge of particular local settings. In the project 'Ideenmarkt' (ideas market), pictured, Raumlabor created an "opportunity for citizens, planners and investors in Halle-Neustadt's third residential complex to gather and exchange information. Its objective was to collect development ideas, to discuss them and to publicise already planned projects." Ph: Raumlabor their wishes, but also rights, are valued and considered in planning processes. Each of these groups, and others such as Ankur and Shack/Slum Dwellers International, formed in order to address or subvert existing power relations, critically interpreting and sometimes undermining established social and political hierarchies. Often, they emerge out of some form of direct action and become a force of resistance. Thus in Paris, residents who were never before involved in politics were activated by atelier d'architecture autogérée to petition the council for land for an urban garden. Others such as Park Fiction challenge their local planning system to implement alternative planning proposals, and yet others, such as the Center for Urban Pedagogy become powerful organisations that make urban struggles visible and provide advice and support on how to enable empowering urban visions.

For other spatial agents, such as the Berlin based group Raumlabor, [Fig.3.2] new social structures can be created through the opening up and creation of innovative forms of urban space, sometimes temporary, which may be used for communication and negotiation, an approach also followed by the UK group muf. Highlighting problems inherent in existing spatial structures is also the key aim of the group City Mine(d). Whereas Raumlabor's projects are playful, City Mine(d)'s are much more politicised and intended to influence policy at a European level.

What all these groups have in common is the understanding of the significance of the connections within social structures in addressing and challenging the underlying systems of the production of space. By working with or against these connections they are able to shift seemingly predetermined and unchangeable superstructures. The key factor, however, in spatial agency's explicit engagement with the social structures is the way that that new design knowledge arises out of this engagement. The Italian design theorist Ezio Manzini argues that designers need to shift their attention to the social: "Designers must put themselves forward as those who can facilitate shared vision building by generating and proposing possible scenarios and solutions."[5] Spatial agents understand themselves to be part of, and not outside of, a complex web of social relations, because only through an approach that values these social relations as a site for action can architecture play an ultimately positive role instead of being seen as part of the social and economic problem.

Physical relations

The next site of spatial agency is that of physical relations. To concentrate on physical relations as the site of spatial agency focuses in particular on how buildings and other spatial objects are conceived, produced and occupied. As we have seen, spatial agency addresses the processes and mechanisms through which something is brought to life, and the way that those objects then evolve over time. In addressing the realities of the changing needs and desires of users, spatial agency tends towards multi-use spaces, structures that are adaptable, and projects that privilege the passage of time.

It is clear that buildings are not created in a bubble; many examples in the book confront the connections between space and power head on, understanding the creation of objects not as a matter of investment or other speculative demands of a globalised monetary economy but rather seeing buildings as some of a society's most important assets. The practice of Lacaton & Vassal [Fig.3.3] is exemplary in this. Their work challenges standards and norms, spatially and economically as well as ecologically. They negotiate exemptions from laws in order to create better and more generous living conditions. They work with the user and continue to stay involved after a building is handed over to the client and is inhabited, and they go back to visit their buildings time and time again to see and understand and learn from how they are being used. Clearly, buildings are lived in structures that only become complete through their use. Where Lacaton & Vassal's prime focus is on space and its occupation, others such as the Taiwanese practice Atelier-3/Rural Architecture Studio work with the way that buildings are put together, in order to enable people without prior knowledge and building skills to quickly understand and participate in construction processes. This approach emphasises a rethinking of commonly used construction techniques, simplifying or adjusting joints and connections between materials to make them easier to deal with. In a manner very similar to the methods employed by Walter Segal in the UK, Atelier-3 adapt DIY approaches so that the resultant buildings are not only produced more economically, but can also be easily adapted and added onto by their inhabitants. This also links to the work of people such as the Egyptian Hassan Fathy, the Iranian Nader Khalili and the Indian practice Vāstu-Shilpā Consultants, [Fig.3.4]

[Fig.3.3] Horticultural greenhouses were used to create a winter garden for apartments in the social housing at Mulhouse, France. Lacaton & Vassal oppose the idea of housing based on minimum standards but instead work with the premise to "produce quality housing that is, at equal cost, much larger than the usual dwellings that follow the norms." This 14-unit housing development in the city of Mulhouse in France is a case in point. Similar to the Chilean group Elemental, raw space provides a framework for appropriation by the residents. Their buildings work with and for the user and adapt to cyclical changes in lifestyles as well as life changes. Ph: Lacaton & Vassal

[Fig.3.4] Street scene from Aranya low cost housing at Indore. The design of the Aranya settlement (pictured), dating back to 1988 and planned for a population of 6,500 people, was based on a study and documentation of selected squatter settlements in the city of Indore where the project is based. Balkrishna Doshi describes it as a "live(d) demonstration of an integrated approach to planning." Developed by a multi disciplinary team of planners, architects, economists, environmental consultants and engineers, always in close consultation with the end users, the scheme combines appropriate building technologies with a sensitive understanding of user needs. Ph: Vāstu-Shilpā Consultants

who have refocused attention on the use of local materials and construction methods as a way to create buildings that are technically, socially and economically situated in their context. What has become known as *appropriate technology* puts an emphasis on the link between locally available and producible materials and the immediate user, making (self)builders independent from building and commercial systems beyond their control. Typically using renewable or regrowable materials such as adobe, rammed earth or cob, this approach has relevance beyond the Global South, where it has been used more extensively than elsewhere, and more generally for all those who are interested in spatial solutions that are environmental and ethical. The use of local building materials over those that have to be shipped is both environmentally and economically sustainable, strengthening as it does the local skillbase and economy, and reducing reliance on multinational conglomerates. In a world of diminishing resources, a turn to appropriate technologies, is one way of using renewables, both material and environmental, as shown in the work of the British practice Architype, the Centre for Alternative Technology in Wales or the global concept of Ecovillages. Others use waste materials to further minimize consumption as exemplified through the ecological practices developed in building the Earthships. (p.134) In all these examples, the site is not just used in the commonly accepted architectural use of the term designating a 'building site', but is extended to take into account the local engagement both with materials and with users. In the practice of the Australian office Merrima Design building sites also become training grounds for Aboriginal people, passing on some of their skills and knowledge to others in a revitalisation of the vernacular. Architecture here becomes a tool for self-help and learning.

Spatial agency in these contexts clearly doesn't discredit professional knowledge, but uses it in multiple ways. Thus in the participatory approaches as practiced by people such as Ottokar Uhl, (p.182) Eilfried Huth, (p.182) and John Habraken, the professional's role shifts from being one of sole author to that of empowering others in enabling physical relations. This needs acute spatial intelligence in designing systems and structures that enable others to participate in the processes of design and production. For Ezio Manzini, one of the primary roles of the designer is that of "upscaling" local initiatives in order that they multiply not so much in terms of size but in terms of wider dispersion. "Designers have to recognize promising cases of social innovation, to make them more visible and to better understand them," he writes, "... they have to contribute in making these promising cases more accessible, effective and reproducible".[6] Manzini posits physical relations as part of a wider set of material and resource flows, in which an understanding of the underlying systems is crucial. This can be seen in the appropriation of the everyday practices of the Global South by the Dutch practice 2012 Architecten, who propose a new role for the designer as "superuse scout", scoping out and intervening in the flows of waste materials and other available resources in any given situation.

Organisational structure

The next site for spatial agency also deals with the invisible flows of spatial production, but this time by addressing the central issues of how their own or others' organisation is structured. This approach brings attention to how the very set up of a practice or institution prescribes the parameters within which projects happen. The motivation for rethinking organisational structures often starts from dissatisfaction with received professional values, as described in the previous chapter. It is argued that these values are inscribed in the way that organisations are managed and run, and it follows that for new values and methods to emerge one has to reconsider core working practices. The site of agency here is thus in the reconfiguration of spatial practice, and refers in particular to worker and other co-operatives, to practices which work in explicitly collaborative and interdisciplinary ways, and to groups that start with an overtly political or ethical agenda.

A lot of people have speculated about what a different or alternative architectural practice might look like. Back in 1977, Tom Woolley established the "four elements of real alternative practice" as follows: a change in the relationship between all architectural workers; the establishment of new sectors of work with a broader social remit; the use of new participatory techniques not only to demystify expertise but also to help everyone understand processes more fully and, finally, a commitment to greater accountability of the entirety of the profession. He continues: "If we are to look for genuine progressive experiments, therefore, we must find examples of architectural practices which have improved relationships between management and staff, and have moved into more socially useful forms of work, or developed better ways of working with their clients. In addition, given the great degree of public dissatisfaction with the results of modern architecture, we have to look for any moves to establish greater accountability of the architect to the user and of the profession to the public as a whole.'[7] It might be argued that nothing much has changed in the field of architectural practice in the intervening 33 years since Woolley wrote this manifesto, but there are a few examples of groups that have attempted alternatives.

The first are those who have organised themselves as cooperatives. As Woolley observes with reference to Edward Cullinan Architects "[r]unning an office as a co-operative won't necessarily produce good architecture"[8] yet, if the core ideas of the co-operative model – open membership, democratic control, distribution of surplus amongst members – are also the core of a business model for a practice it is easy to see how these shared values can find expression in the production of space. A good example is the now defunct feminist practice Matrix, whose political beliefs in equality led to the establishment of a cooperative structure for the practice, which in turn informed the way that they ran projects and interacted with users and client. Whilst there are still hardly any architectural co-operatives, with the exception of practices such as URBED, (p.132) [Fig.3.5] Edward Cullinan Architects, (p.130) and Collective Architecture, (p.130) there are many examples of the co-operative structure operating elsewhere in the field of spatial production, for example the Bauhütten, which were set up by trade unions and acted as clients for government-financed housing projects, notably in Berlin under Martin Wagner in the 1920s.[9] Contemporary housing co-operatives, which are particularly strong in Latin America, often act as mediators to arrange collective loans and micro-financing for building developments or help to reinforce the rights of the members. Co-operatives remain one of the most important housing providers simply because their charters typically require them to invest any surplus back into either the continuous maintenance of buildings or into the organization; as a result rents in housing co-operatives are typically lower than in the private sector. Whilst the size of an individual co-operative might have to remain relatively small

[Fig.3.5] A meeting of the Eco Neighbourhood by design training course for residents and tenants developed by URBED and Glass House. URBED (Urbanism, Environment and Design) are an urban design and consultancy practice based in Manchester. Founded in 1976 in London, they also have a sister organisation there specialising in economic development consultancy. URBED Manchester concentrate on urban design and consultancy with a long-term commitment to a socially sustainable and equitable approach, which they translated into their own organisational structure through becoming an employee owned worker's co-operative in 2006. Through this different model of practice, URBED, demonstrate a different idea of architectural practice: one that is based on shared spatial and social values expressed through a business model, rather than the demonstration of personalities. Ph: URBED

in order to work effectively, the umbrella organizations of the Latin American Residential Organisations indicate the influence those can have on national policy developments.

Where for some spatial agents the legal form of their own practice is seen as the basis for a more equitable production of space, for others it is the form of their external engagements that is primary. These seek and form explicitly collaborative and transdisciplinary relationships, and work with ever changing constellations of people. While all architectural practice works with a variety of other disciplines in the process of the design and construction of a building, our spatial agents intentionally seek exchanges beyond the typical reference points, specifically to allow the project to be shaped by the convergence of different types of knowledge. The French architect Patrick Bouchain, for example, begins a project by bringing together diverse groups of interested people, from politicians to performers, constructors to community groups. Through this social mix, his projects are always situated in a specific context, are always developed through and by different people and enforce the social character and responsibility of architecture. This is also true for atelier d'architecture autogérée, whose work is based in the area of Paris where they live and with which they have established strong connections. While the core members of atelier d'architecture autogérée are architects by training, their collaborators involve a wide range of participants who are often equally local. The long-term engagement with the local context ensures that externally initiated projects are step-by-step handed over to local communities, with the architects retreating further and further until eventually spaces are entirely self-managed. In their own way, practices such as Exyzt, Chora, Supertanker, Mess Hall, Hackitectura and public works, also base their practice around the way that they bring others in to the process of design, and through this reconfigure normal organisational structures into networks that throw up new forms of engagement.

For yet another group of spatial agents the driving force is the empowerment of others to organize themselves. Approaches vary and include both examples from the Global South and elsewhere. The Pakistani architect Arif Hasan combines in his work the strengthening of social processes and knowledge with specific sanitation and construction techniques.

The physical infrastructure, built on the thorough understanding of the social structures, enables Hasan to truly empower the communities he is building for, but this is always complemented by his developing of associated organisational structures including the training and organisation of the thallawallas (the people who run the local construction system) and setting up of micro-finance systems to pay for the improvements. Elsewhere, the work of the Australian practice Healthabitat has established strong links between well-being and the provision of adequate housing and therefore focus their attention on the continuous improvement of housing and associated facilities. Often dealing with seemingly mundane organisational issues such as the provision of sanitation and adequate cooking facilities. This link between management and self-reliance, which is addressed by Hasan and Healthabitat in their own respective environments has also come to be the territory for an increasing number of Architectural Non-Governmental Organisations, many of which are operating under the umbrella framework of the UN-Habitat programme.

In the spirit of Marx, whose epitaph is his famous quote "philosophers have only interpreted the world in various ways; the point is, to change it"[10], spatial agency is also a call for action: for a repositioning of practice and of the way we operate internally within practice and externally with others. Different practice configurations have different spatial implications. How we position ourselves, and how and from where we operate and become part of a dialogue, has clear implications on how space is produced, used and perceived.

Knowledges

The final site of spatial agency is in the use of knowledge, and in particular in the way that knowledge may break free from the confines of professional control. The specialist knowledge of the architectural discipline is guarded as if to preserve a form of objectivity, on which professional credibility might be founded. Architectural language, as the gatekeeper to that knowledge, is extremely codified, from the technical vocabulary of the profession, through to the jargon of academia and trade magazines. All use a language (and we might be guilty of this too) that is meant for the already initiated but certainly not for a wider public. The architectural discourse is a discourse

that increasingly feeds off itself. None of this portrays the actual state of the world of architectural production, but is only a representation of a rather complex diagram of connections and power relationships that form the "inside" of architecture. In a similar way, architectural education is still most often confined to this inside. The teachers deliver architectural knowledge that remains in a defined and safe realm, and so the students, kept within known boundaries, emerge – after having been confined for a good few years – as absolute and non-negotiable experts in a certain formation of architecture.

In opposition to this, spatial agency is about a different understanding of the production and dissemination of knowledge. Architecture needs to follow Donna Haraway's advice, and allow for "partial, locatable, critical knowledges sustaining the possibility of webs of connections called solidarity in politics and shared conversations in epistemology."[11] The plural use of the word knowledge is indicative of a different understanding of what knowledge is, namely, an expression and spectrum of a variety of views. Knowledge not as a representation of supposedly unified scientific truth but knowledges in the sense of a manifestation of a multiplicity of voices. Central to the concept of spatial agency is, as argued in the first chapter, a desire to share knowledge with others. This entails opening it up to architecture's outside, through acknowledging the contribution of non-experts and through disseminating it in an accessible manner.

It also means taking seriously Haraway's call for the partial nature of knowledge, rather than making any claims to universal solutions. She writes that "only partial perspective promises objective vision. All Western cultural narratives about objectivity are allegories of the ideologies governing the relations of what we call mind and body, distance and responsibility. Feminist objectivity is about limited location and situated knowledge, not about transcendence and splitting of subject and object. It allows us to become answerable for what we learn how to see."[12] In this spirit each individual project illustrated in this book is indeed partial, each focused on its own inherent terrain and each addressing its own intrinsic conditions. But partial is not a term of weakness: the sum of all these projects provide a repository of constructive means and mechanisms of how architecture can address the spatial production in a meaningful way, giving pointers

e-flux

Clients Archive Projects Journal About Subscribe Contact RSS   Search

journal #17
06/ 2010

On the cover: Akademik Fedorov, Leningrad, black/white photograph, 48x20 cm. Author and date unknown (found in 1994 in a locker of an abandoned Russian military base near Berlin). Private collection of Marion von Osten.

*view all issues
distribution
books
contact e-flux journal
colophon*

Marion von Osten
Editorial—"In Search of the Postcapitalist Self"

An Architektur
On the Commons: A Public Interview with Massimo De Angelis and Stavros Stavrides

First, all commons involve some sort of common pool of resources, understood as non-commodified means of fulfilling peoples needs. Second, the commons are necessarily created and sustained by *communities*—this of course is a very problematic term and topic, but nonetheless we have to think about it. Communities are sets of commoners who share these resources and who define for themselves the rules according to which they are accessed and used. Communities, however, do not necessarily have to be bound to a locality, they could also operate through translocal spaces. They also need not be understood as "homogeneous" in their cultural and material features. In addition to these two elements—the pool of resources and the set of communities—the third and most important element in terms of conceptualizing the commons is the verb "to common"—the social process that creates and reproduces the commons.

Tom Holert
Hidden Labor and the Delight of Otherness: Design and Post-Capitalist Politics

[Fig.3.6] Website of e-flux journal, which is available free on-line. One of the key outlets for spatial agents is the publishing of magazines, both in hard copy form and online. Independent from multi-national publishing houses, these publications push their own agendas and views on the production of the built environment. e-flux, illustrated here, describes itself as a New York based but international network, and publish a monthly journal as part of their activities, which brings together a variety of critical views on the built environment. For example, Marion von Osten proclaims that this issue that she guest edited, "can be understood as the beginning of a debate that asks whether the (cultural) Left is still capable of thinking and acting beyond the analysis of overwhelming power structures or working within the neoliberal consensus model."

as to how to address the immediate need for intelligent social and environmental solutions to a looming climate crisis and to increasing social inequalities in the world, a need that is not addressed by any current political system.

One of the key tools for the dissemination of knowledges is through self-managed publishing, independent from the professionally endorsed routes, generating one-off papers, fanzines, more or less regular journals, books, websites, maps and so on. The motivations for the setup of these publications vary: some such as SLATE (12 issues, 1976–80) were an oppositional voice to the mainstream papers but were very limited in circulation, others such as ARse (p.90) (1969–72) were part of a wider practice of both education and the running of the Community Technical Aid Centre Support. The Whole Earth Catalog (1968–72) was an ecological trade catalogue and handbook for people who wanted to live self-sufficiently, written in an accessible manner that defused the technical complexities of the issue. More recent publications, such as glaspaper (p.90) (10 issues, 2001–7) were driven by the desire to reach audiences beyond the glossy architectural journals. The journal An Architektur (23 issues since 2002) is dedicated to a critical spatial

analysis of architecture such as migration, community design centers or the architecture of war, and public works' zines are produced quickly and cheaply to document the regular events that they hold. The Internet based journals Re-public, (p.158) Eurozine (p.158) or e-flux (p.159) [Fig.3.6] have come to be important portals for a critical and interdisciplinary discussion on the production of space beyond the standard outlets. They are peer-reviewed, yet outside the spheres of large publishing houses, and intent on reaching non-traditional and transdisciplinary audiences, and using the call-and-response mechanism that the web engenders to gather discussion and dispute. These publications and websites – together with numerous personal blogs – become important fora for topics that typically aren't discussed in the mainstream world of architectural media: the everyday, localised protests, self-initiated projects, use, critique, and so on.

Other groups are more specifically educational in their outlook, dispersing knowledges that have previously been locked up in professional circles. Exemplary of this approach is the New York based organisation Center for Urban Pedagogy. They investigate seemingly banal questions about how the city works, what democracy means in spatial terms or where the water or the electricity comes from. They devise pedagogical projects for schools and help to produce documents, pamphlets, zines that explain in simple language the processes, and then how and where to intervene. Spatial knowledge is thereby dispersed, made available and communicated to a broader public who, simply through this knowing, are empowered to engage in the urban discourse. An important part of this process is the mapping out of spatial relationships in a direct manner. In order to be able to understand the built environment and the ways in which it is produced, it is useful to visualise how people and things relate to each other. This is an increasingly difficult task in a world that shifts and moves so quickly and whose ties and links are less and less tangible.[13] The French conceptual art group Bureau d'études produce maps that make visible complex relationships, such as the entanglement of European lobby groups. In depicting the ties and web of connections, their maps become tools for action as they show how a 'system' works, but also illustrate its faults and weaknesses.

Knowing becomes a tool of empowerment since it allows everyone to evaluate and critically judge the position within which they find themselves in the world, allowing them to question, to interrogate, to intervene, to challenge and to propose other ways. Not knowing equates to not having power. It is this power of knowing that groups such as the Planners Network, a USA based organisation that has been operating since 1975, make available for others for free. Members of the Network offer their services to people who are excluded from planning processes, enabling them to engage in the complexities of the system.

Knowledge as the site for spatial agency, more so than its other sites – the social, the physical or the organizational – is concerned with the 'other': with those things that aren't told or explicated and with what is typically excluded from conventional publications. It represents a desire to create a more complete picture of relationships – in a way similar to what this book is trying to do by expanding the definition of what constitutes architectural discourse – so that architecture might come to be understood as more than just a technical or aesthetical object. A fanzine, a blog, maps and technical support are as much architecture as a building is architecture. What differentiates them is that they produce and disseminate spatial knowledge in a manner that is consciously open to others.

The Other Sites of Architecture

Of course, this division of the sites of spatial agency into four parts is artificial, because it is in the nature of all spatial production that boundaries are blurred. The four sites are by no means mutually exclusive, with many of the examples crossing over from one to another, and could surely be supplemented with others or categorised in different ways. But what they together point to is not just the possibility, but the real necessity of seeing that architecture can be played out through a multiplicity of settings, and that this gives new opportunities for architects and other spatial designers to work with. Exactly how they might do this is addressed in the next chapter.

1   Donna Haraway, 'Situated Knowledges: The Science Question in Feminism and the Privilege of Partial Perspective', *Feminist Studies*, 14 (1988): 595.

2   Richard J. Bernstein, *Praxis and Action* (London: Duckworth, 1971), 308.

3   Henri Lefebvre, *The Production of Space* (Oxford: Blackwell, 1991), 81.

4   Walther Rathenau as quoted in: Manfredo Tafuri, *Architecture and Utopia : design and capitalist development* (Cambridge, Massachusetts, and London, England: MIT Press, 1976), 70.

5   Ezio Manzini, *Enabling Solutions for Sustainable Living: A Workshop* (University of Calgary Press, 2007), xiv.

6   Ezio Manzini, xii.

7   Tom Woolley, 'Alternative Practice', *Architects' Journal*, 42 (1977): 735.

8   Tom Woolley, 'Cullinan's Co-op', *Architects' Journal*, 42 (1977): 742.

9   Magali Sarfatti Larson, *Behind the Postmodern Facade : Architectural Change in Late Twentieth-Century America* (Berkeley and Los Angeles: University of California Press, 1993), 38.

10 Richard J. Bernstein, *Praxis and Action* (London: Duckworth, 1971), 13.

11 Haraway, 584.

12 Haraway, 582–583.

13 For a very good book on historical and contemporary forms of and approaches to mapping see: Janet Abrams and Peter Hall, *Else/Where: Mapping* (Minneapolis: University of Minnesota Design Institute, 2006).

3

THE OPERATIONS OF SPATIAL AGENCY

The final section of the book is about how spatial agency can be enacted and how spatial agents operate. It aims to set out these *other ways of doing architecture* in an instructive and useful way and sits before the final part of the book, which is a compendium of individuals, groups, organisations and networks of spatial agents. This chapter is not meant to be a manual to spatial agency, nor can or should it be used as a strategic tick box list, but instead it is supposed to elaborate the concepts inherent in the operations of the groups and practices described in this book. The examples presented in this book, and the tactics and strategies employed, provide an inspirational view on the production of space. None of these other ways of doing are limited to a specific scale or to a particular position. Taken together they can be read as an attempt to permanently relocate the focus of spatial production. They should not be read as a manual on how to tackle changing economic or environmental conditions, although the global state of turmoil is making these other ways of doing even more prescient. Nor should these other ways of doing be taken as an expedient menu on how to survive a recession by refocusing the centre of a practice's attention to the "needier" parts of society. This would simply diminish the significance and importance of the examples presented here. These other ways of doing are sometimes means and sometimes techniques through which individuals and groups have shifted the focus of spatial production towards a political discussion of the inhabitation and occupancy of space and the need to talk about the relationship between created/built space and the life that goes on within it. There is no 'ideal' solution in spatial agency but a willingness to never stop questioning. Spatial agency shows that architects do have a choice and in that addresses an ethical vacuum

that seems to have appeared in many professions. The following chapter presents these choices by going through the various operations of spatial agency.

Expanding Briefs

A typical architectural project starts with being handed a brief. A local authority, an institution, a corporation or a private person owns a particular site and wants a specific building on it, or may want to extend an existing building. Institutions may want a student union or a building to house teaching facilities, a corporation may want a new office headquarter and a local authority may be looking for a masterplan for a regeneration area or for housing, commercial or any other facility. These bodies then write briefs, which set out in varying degrees of detail the kind of accommodation required, the planning requirements, and often the overall cost. They may hold an open competition to which any architectural office could submit a proposal or they invite a series of "specially qualified" architects to prepare a design. Sometimes, architects tender for a job or a particular practice might be asked directly to develop a design, usually with a client they have worked with before. In all these situations, architects take briefs and respond to them. From the very beginning this sets out a specific power relationship between the client – the person that has the money – and the architect – the person who will provide a service and will be paid for providing this service. It also tends to fix the building at a stage before the architect can contribute to the act of briefing in a creative way. Briefs are concerned with giving instructions about what can and cannot be done in a space, and are filled with explicit rules often concerned with expressions of ownership and economic imperatives.

The most unambiguous direction given in any brief usually relates to the boundaries of a site, which is presented as a delineated space – not to be crossed neither physically nor intellectually. The work of the architect, these drawn lines tell us, is to be concerned with the space within the given boundaries and ought not to go beyond. The message is that the "beyond" is not the client's concern and neither is it the architect's. Whilst many are happy to work within this set-up of, not least, economic certainty, it is this beyond and the critical interrogating of any given set of instructions that become tools for any spatial agent because this beyond is also about the context in social, political and economic terms, and about the consequences a particular development might have.

Spatial agents, therefore, understand precisely these boundaries as their territory. For Cedric Price, for example, the space between the lines of a set of given instructions was often more interesting than what the brief said. By working with the beyond, the everyday becomes an inescapable component of working in and with space simply because it propels the architect into the territory of encounter and the unfamiliar. These instances of space that are found outside the rules and regulations that typically govern the production of space

open up a more variable understanding and interpretation of space: space that is open to changing conditions and space that allows choice.

Working in such a way means deploying one's spatial intelligence outside of any given framework. It questions the "expert" role of the brief-giver and the "local" who supposedly always knows best. At the same time, however, this attitude to allow the unexpected also puts the architect into a position of constant negotiation as for example in the Sans Souci Cinema project, in which the architects set in train a series of processes that questioned exactly what would best replace the burnt down cinema in Soweto.

Briefs, in the way that they are presented as a technical fait accompli, also disguise the fact they determine social relations in a profound way. A list of rooms with sizes may be put forward as a neutral tool which presents the requirements of the client in an efficient manner, but actually such a list is very charged. Spatial agents therefore take the negotiation of the brief as a core part of their creative responsibility. Firms such as DEGW have made brief writing in collaboration with their clients a core part of their practice, understanding how the design of the brief is the first stage in the design of a set of social relations.[1]

[Fig.4.1] Villa Heerlijkheid Hoogvliet/Hoogvliet Domain, Welcome into My Backyard! 2001–2007. Crimson emphasise the importance of historical and empirical analysis as well as the use of narrative, as was the case for the regeneration plans for the Rotterdam suburb Hoogvliet. The programme, managed by them for six years, included 27 different projects – buildings as well as social and cultural projects – and were based on Crimson's conviction that "the best and most inspiring basis for the future of this postwar town was to enhance, renew and make the best use of Hoogvliet's existing characteristics and qualities, both physical and social." The book WiMBY! Hoogvliet Future, Past and Present of a New Town is an account of this engagement. Villa Heerlijkheid (pictured) is one of the many projects initiated as part of Crimson's strategy for Hoogvliet. It is a social and communal space built in a recreation park by the London based practice, FAT. Ph: Maarten Laupman

[Fig.4.2] Roof construction of the Gando primary school. Diébédo Francis Kéré initiated these school buildings in Gando, Burkina Faso, back in 1999 when he was still a student in Berlin; the project won the Aga Khan Award for Architecture in 2004. Justin McGuirk writes in a recent issue of the magazine ICON that Kéré "plays every role: community activist, fund raiser, architect and builder. Kéré treats the buildings as a form of social empowerment, using local labour and training people who can neither read nor write to translate his drawings into structures." Initiating, in Kéré's case, brings with it the responsibility for care, both for the work force as well as for the buildings and those who use them. As a consequence of this, he continues to be involved in Gando, where a library is currently built next to the existing school.
Ph: Erik-Jan Ouwerkerk

A traditional brief thus acts against the spirit of agency in so much that by setting parameters it tends to close things down and limit options. Spatial agents, on the other hand, take the brief not as a given set of instructions but as an opportunity to open up possibilities. Notable in this respect is the work of the French architect Patrick Bouchain, who in collaboration with others, often writes in his own briefs, and the Dutch collective Crimson, [Fig.4.1] who use narrative as a means of engaging with a place, and thereby fabricating a brief. As Crimson note: "being able to tell a good story, a gripping story, a touching, exciting, spectacular story is the core of designing and planning."[2]

Initiating

For many spatial agents, the project starts even before the writing of a brief, with architects and others as proactive initiators working through negotiation with others to get a project started. Exemplary of this approach are the Burkina Faso practice Kéré Architecture [Fig.4.2] and Baupiloten in Berlin. All these models of project initiation go beyond the architect-developer model, where architects simply cut out the middleman in order to generate their own business. Instead they use a range of spatial skills to unlock potential on behalf of others, opening up new social, political and economic possibilities. Thus in the work of the Rural Studio, as much effort is placed in identifying potential clients, raising funds, negotiating permissions and procuring materials as it is in the design of the buildings themselves. Another scenario is one where a group starts a project by initially raising their own money, and later supplementing these with sweat equity, governmental or other private funding, such as in the case of many small projects within the Ecovillages network.

Arguably, this process of initiation is more complex than the predominant model of architecture as service because it involves a much more multifaceted negotiation of relationships of all those involved in this process. Rather than simply answering a given set of questions, initiation is driven by a desire to inaugurate something new. Initiating an alternate direction of thinking, a new funding mechanism or a different proposal means not waiting for others to determine the makeup of the city or of space in general, but to set in motion other processes of one's own accord, as has been so powerfully shown in the work of Park Fiction. Taking the initiative stands for the power of each spatial agent to act on one's capabilities instead of letting others determine the boundaries of architecture's potential.

The economy of spatial agency

Spatial agency is not driven by classical monetary economy in the sense of the management of sheer financial resources but by the managing and administration of means such as labour, time and space. Rather than addressing questions about fees, fee structures, expenditure and the imperatives of utility and return, spatial agency often prioritises equity and self-management as demonstrated in the running of the Spanish town Marinaleda. Other examples often include non-monetary and financially non-measurable exchanges such as Local Exchange Trading Schemes, which treat the economy as an operational tool concerned with methods and processes, and the local systems of exchange initiated at Findhorn (the Eko) and Christiania (the Fed, Klump and Løn).

In other contexts, protests, petitioning and other initiatives are often prompted by a concrete situation, and action upon this is not dependent on funding of a particular person, group or activity. This often operates at the level of bottom-up initiatives, such as in the case

of the South African movement Abahlali baseMjondolo or the now global Guerrilla Gardening initiative. These and others manage on a make-do economy where labour and available resources and materials are combined to create an effect with minimal financial means: somebody's living room will become a campaign office, posters will be made from recycled card and people will give their spare time to knock on doors, real and virtual, to raise awareness of a particular cause. This is, for example, how many of the student chapters of the Architectural NGOs, and campaigns such as that run for years by the Coin Street Community Builders, [Fig.4.3] are organised. Operating in such ways therefore isn't about generating income, but about advocating common agendas that wouldn't otherwise be addressed, such as the relationship between land use and land ownership in the work of Park Fiction, or between privatisation and poverty in the work of the Planners Network. The economy of spatial agency in this instance is thereby based not on fiscal exchange but by recognising that the most valuable commodities of all in such contexts is the giving of time, the making of time, and not giving up, with the self-managed nature of both engagement and action allowing the groups to escape the limits of financial imperatives and solutions.

A different scenario within the economy of spatial agency involves groups of activists, architects or planners, often backed through governmental funding, who help to obtain financial support from outside agencies on behalf of others. The funding obtained is used for a variety of purposes, including the delivery of professional support, a feasibility study, the building of a prototype, or raising finance. The Community Technical Aid Centres and some of the North American Community Design Centers and the Australian practice Merrima Design are of note here, in which professionals deploy knowledge and skills that may not normally be required of them in a conventional architectural office, and make this knowledge and skill available to those who otherwise would not have access to it.[3] However, this economy is also heavily reliant on funding priorities defined by governmental goals and objectives and therefore highly susceptible to changes in leadership or political direction. The previously mentioned Community Technical Aid Centres, for example, ceased to exist when government funding for them dried up in the 1980s when the Conservative government in the UK moved money away from local authorities.

[Fig.4.3] The Coin Street Neighbourhood Centre provides affordable childcare and learning facilities as well as enterprise support. The example of the Coin Street Community Builders (CSCB) highlights the fact that time is one of the most valuable commodities in situations of drawn out political and spatial struggles. The process of negotiating the rights to the land and eventually developing it, saw a community action group transform itself into a community developer which bought a piece of land in South London after almost ten years of petitioning and a series of public enquiries. This clearly would not have been possible without the commitment of its members who did not seek any financial reward. The constant need for the group to creatively adapt to new circumstances, politically as well as financially, was a key factor in the project's innovative use of cross-subsidisation; for example, the public pay-and-display car park, situated underneath the IROKO housing scheme, subsidised the housing above. Ph: Tatjana Schneider

As we saw in Chapter 3 with the discussion of co-operative organisations, the internal economy of a practice can define the starting point for agency. Operating as a cooperative creates equity amongst those working within such an enterprise: often there are one-person one-vote arrangements when it comes to decision making processes. Any profit generated is invested back into new projects, accumulating social capital, which often benefits the organisations concerned. Collective Architecture (p.130) in Glasgow, for example, found that they were attracting an increasing number of clients who wanted to work with a practice that reflected their own ethical approach in working and building.

Appropriating

The next means of operation for spatial agency is that of appropriation. In cultural studies, appropriation is linked to anything from borrowing to theft of a part of a cultural manifestation such as music or prose; in economics, it can refer to the commodification of previously unowned natural resources such as water. In the context of spatial agency, however, appropriation avoids the potentially exploitative aspects of such actions.[4] Instead, it is used more positively as a means of harnessing underused resources or else unsettling the status quo. A good example of the former is the taking ownership of unused property through legal or illegal action through squatting, and of the latter the 1970s Counter Communities, in which expert knowledge (of ecology, of construction and so on) was redeployed to establish a new social order. [Fig.4.4] Christiania, the controversial Danish autonomous settlement based in Copenhagen, is one example of the appropriation of a former military site for the provision of inner city self-governed housing and was highly influential for other developments across Europe. One such development, which emerged out of both the squatter and the Autonomia movement were the Centri Sociali in Italy, with one of the longest running centres being the Centro Sociale Leoncavallo in Milan. Now legalised, the centre has been occupying an abandoned factory building since 1975 and since then has provided collective spaces for the community. Very much in the tradition of the Diggers and Levellers, these appropriations of land and property take place outside the official planning processes; illegal, or only just tolerated, to

[Fig.4.4] Entrance of the Phoenix Earthship near Taos, New Mexico. Architect, Mike Reynolds, began experimenting with Earthships in the mid-1970s, aiming to design self-sufficient dwellings using waste materials. Constructed from rammed earth and old car tyres, Earthships also utilise glass bottles, drinks cans and scrap metal. His aim was to appropriate expert knowledge in order to create a building system that could be constructed by the amateur builder. In the Garbage Warrior, a film about his mission to change the way we build, Reynolds describes one of his homes: "There's nothing coming into this house, no power lines, no gas lines, no sewage lines coming out, no water lines coming in, no energy being used... We're sitting on 6,000 gallons of water, growing food, sewage internalised, 70 degrees year-round... What these kind of houses are doing is taking every aspect of your life and putting it into your own hands... A family of four could totally survive here without having to go to the store." Ph: Kirsten Jacobsen

begin with these sites often become institutions in their own right, take on more formalised legal frameworks and, through this process, also lose some of their radical and oppositional potential. However, the physical appropriation of existing space, together with the myriad of often illegal self-building practices which simply employ the use of available resources, are an effective way to produce space in conditions of material and economic scarcity.

Appropriating becomes a tool through which private or public space can be questioned and new activities created. Whilst appropriating often leaves the true relationships of power unscathed, because many interventions are temporary, it nevertheless highlights opportunities that might exist in the longer term. The Center for Land Use Interpretation, with the compilation of their "Land Use Database", have done much to bring out both the absurdity and potential of particular plots of land. Appropriation has been enacted in a very direct manner by the mayor and citizens of Marinaleda, whose initial occupation of land led to a long term spatial and social solution. Such approaches to appropriation are open and conscious, not hidden or executed in disguise, and openly brings out fractures, conflict and contradictions of the production and use of space.

Delightful Indeterminancy

Too often, architecture, as beautified and technologised object, takes itself much too seriously. Against this, spatial agency attempts to rescue architecture and the production of space from the clutches of the determinists, the space-syntax-planners, the parametric shapers, the politics-of-the-envelope theorists and the bathetic attempts to save the world through yet another iconic building. Yet, if we take Cedric Price as an example, involving humour, pleasure and delight together with irony and a hint of ridicule when producing any form of physical or non-physical design is an effective way of challenging normative conceptions of what a room, a house, an institution or what working, living, learning might look and be like.

Being efficient in the planning of space (or life) results in approaches in which form follows function, where something like slack space cannot enter the equation because having slack space means being wasteful and uneconomical (and being economical so often is used interchangeably with profitable).[5] These efficient and determinate methods to think about and realise space, however, hardly ever take into account the everyday, the ordinary, and the mundane. It is such delightful aspects of space that are captured by the

[Fig.4.5] Exterior view of the Bauhäusle, taken in 1983. The Bauhäusle is a student hall administered by the University of Stuttgart's student services. Peter Sulzer and Peter Hübner supervised the project, which was designed and built by students in the early 1980s and prompted by the lack of student accommodation in Stuttgart. Responsibility for different parts of the project was split, which resulted in the very different characters of the block and also the realisation of different sizes and shapes of rooms. The project is a statement against determinacy in architecture, and for a certain type of beauty that comes through an acceptance of making-do. Ph: Peter Blundell Jones

Chilean practice Elemental in their social housing work for Iquique, where the houses are conceived of as unfinished frames of slack space, there to be appropriated over time by the occupants. Overdetermined spaces leave no room for their appropriation by others; instead, because these spaces are preciously designed, they tend to be hyper-controlled, scarcely leaving room for anticipation. With spatial agency, the principle of indeterminacy, becomes an indicator for pleasure as in the self-built student housing project Bauhäusle [Fig.4.5] or the work of London based 00:/ architects. Leaving unfinished, as well as defending unscripted and unprogrammed space allows others to realise a different idea of space defined through their own desires and wishes. Some spatial agents in this book, such as the Architects, Designers and Planners for Social Responsibility or Planning Action, therefore often petition and fight against overly regulated and planned spaces. Others, such as G.L.A.S., (p.132) produce graphic or agit-prop work that through the use of humour gives a twist on issues such as the privatisation of public assets. Still others, such as Hackitectura, dispute seemingly indisputable causal-rational relationships, and challenge the rule of efficiency, arguing instead for recklessness in order to realise a different idea of space or to change the terrain of spatial production.

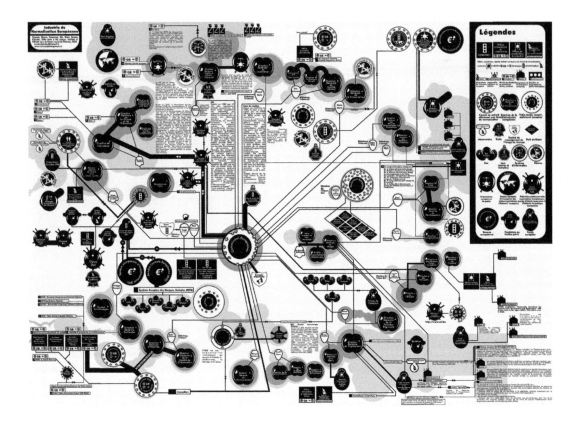

[Fig.4.6] European Norms of World Production. Image: Bureau d'études. Brian Holmes writes that the maps of Bureau d'études "aspire to be cognitive tools, distributing as broadly as possible the kind of specialized information that was formerly confined to technical publications. Yet on another level they are meant to act as subjective shocks, energy potentials, informing the protest-performances as they are passed from hand to hand, deepening the resolve to resist are they are utilized in common or alone." The map shown here named, European Norms of World Production, depicts the organisational and power structures of the European Commission (EC). The map allows the ordinary European citizen to grasp which of the hundreds of lobby groups associated with the EC deals with their particular issue. The map also reveals the three dominant sources of power to be the European Court of Justice, the European Roundtable of Industrialists and Burston Marsteller, a private consulting company who at a price can navigate for their clients the maze of bureaucracy that is the EC.

Making things visible

One of the key aims of spatial agency is the uncovering and making visible of hidden structures, be they political, social or economic. As long as the power of these structures remains largely invisible and therefore untouched, spatial agents such as Bureau d'études [Fig.4.6] or Estudio Teddy Cruz, often see it as their task to research, record, visualise and analyse the links and relationships between different nodes and actors, using maps, diagrams, drawings, talks and tours in order to explicate and often simplify otherwise impenetrable information and datasets.

Because most of our world is made up of ever more complex trans- and multinational organisational systems, it becomes much more difficult to understand how space, amongst other things, is produced or how the involvement of global players within a certain framework might impact on local conditions or vice versa. It is not surprising that much of the "making things visible" is happening online, or at least with significant aid of online applications, which allow others to enter and participate in discussions which previously could not even be had.

Networks

While the power of each participant might be limited, the conjoining of many individuals with limited power makes up a substantial force that can fundamentally alter the direction or course of an event, as happens in the contemporary phenomenon of crowdsourcing. Through such networks, individualised pockets of power located around the periphery combine to take on the otherwise so elusive centre, which would have presented a substantial barrier for each single actor within the network but not for its combined force. Spatial agency exists in the setup of these open frameworks, as can be seen in the Ecovillages, the networks of the Architectural NGOs, the Shack/Slum Dwellers International, [Fig.4.7] the large Latin American Residential networks, and the direct action or squatting networks. The invitation for participation through either action or the donation of knowledge acknowledges an incompleteness and limitation of the lone, single-disciplinary author. If you want to take on and make visible dominant power structures, as so many of the groups presented in this book do, the point of resistance often comes through a networked approach, through the convergence of mutual interests upon which the network acts.

Sharing Knowledge

The next operation concerns the way that spatial knowledge is developed and then shared, first within the academy and then in the outside world. As we saw in Chapter 2, one of the motivations of spatial agency is a reconsideration of professional educational structures, by opening up and breaking the narrative character of learning and instead practicing critical inquiry and doing. Standard architectural education is inextricably linked with the culture and growth of the profession. Entry into the studying of architecture is typically reserved for 'high achievers' at school level and is only the first hurdle into a still incredibly elitist and male

[Fig.4.7] Khayelitsha informal settlement near Cape Town. SDI, the Shack/Slum Dwellers International, is an extensive network of initiatives and organisations from across the Global South. Their stated mission is "to link poor urban communities from cities across the South to transfer and adapt the successful mobilisation, advocacy, and problem solving strategies they develop in one location to other cities, countries and regions", and through this to build cities from the bottom up. SDI facilitate exchanges on a community-to-community level, but also bring together its participating organisations to learn from each other about successful income generating projects or the replanning of an area or settlement. These processes allow participants, in SDI's words, "to see themselves and their peers as experts [and to reclaim] sites of knowledge that have frequently been co-opted by professionals." The SDI network not only involves communities, but often invites government and other officials on case study visits, thereby letting these seeming experts see and learn another perspective on development. Ph: Paul Bruins dominated profession.[6] In 1978 Hugo Hinsley, a teacher at the Architectural Association, wrote that "[n]either education nor the structure of the profession nor the design and production of buildings can be seen in abstract; they are all effected by the social, political and economic framework of our society, and a part of education is to consider and question this framework."[7] Hinsley was deeply critical of an appallingly limited view of education, the entrenchment of the profession, and against the general separation of students of architecture into, what he termed in the same article, either "bureaucracy fodder" or "master race PhD architects." Yet, at the same time there was also hope (for some time at least): some of the architecture schools in the UK – in a similar spirit to the Community Design Centers in the US – were doing community design work organising real, live and socially committed projects and doing this in an understanding that architecture was not about supposedly neutral form, but about the collaboration with others in an attempt to make architecture and architectural tools more relevant to a broader section of society. Knowledge, in these instances, therefore became a transformative tool. Contrary to the belief that knowledge gained through education is what gives architects and the professions their credibility and authority, spatial agency calls for an understanding of knowledge not as something that one can hold or own like an asset but something that emerges out of negotiation with others. Mainstream pedagogy, which is here equated with the ostensible innocent imparting of knowledge, simply produces and confirms dominant institutional and professional structures "domesticating, pacifying, and deracinating agency, harmonizing a world of disjuncture and incongruity; and smoothing the unruly features of daily existence".[8]

Against this spatial agents understand knowledge in the same way as they understand space: as a product of participative spatial encounters that cross disciplinary boundaries, such as in the early setup of Arup Associates which combined architectural, surveying and engineering services with the aim of a new and greater shared understanding. More important is the move to take a collaborative approach outside of the academy and profession, and into the relationships with others. Space is produced through a multiplicity of forces: the bank granting mortgages and loans, the various trades and builders, the innumerable disciplines involved, the inhabitants, the authorities, etc. The final

product, however, is almost always credited entirely to the architect – something that is reinforced through monograph after monograph published and self-published by architectural practices trying to secure their place in architectural history. The impact of others is very rarely acknowledged beyond the mere listing of a company's name, and interest in a building fades just before it is occupied. How buildings perform when they are finally put to use after the architect has taken his or her pictures of the untainted object is for most no longer of interest. Learning from a building's occupation is not part of the standard list of services of an architect, which does not encourage regular reflection on the performance of buildings in use. Contrary to this, spatial agency argues that a building only becomes complete through its use. In other words, the architectural process doesn't stop with the handing over of the key to the client, but only when it is lived in – and for as long as it is lived in.

Understanding space and its production as shared enterprise refers to an understanding of the built environment as collectively produced where some people might have and will have specific roles, but where processes, effects and buildings are received, designed, built and often occupied together with others. To effect the shared production of space can take a number of routes. Firstly, everyone involved in the process has a share in this process and an equal right to its conceptual or intellectual ownership. It is consistent with this that the majority of examples in the book are named as groups rather than individuals. Spatial agents operating as a collective reinforce this point through the abrogation of individual authorship as Stalker/Osservatorio Nomade, whilst others might choose to credit every single person in a specific process. Secondly, looking beyond the process of designing and/or building, spatial agents chose to understand their works beyond the initial completion of construction. They go back again and again to, for example, an inhabited space or building to understand processes of occupation, evaluating work through a continuation of relationships over time as Lacaton & Vassal do with many of their projects. The Aga Khan Award for Architecture [Fig.4.8] should also be mentioned here as the only architectural prize for which buildings can only be nominated after at least three years of use. Thirdly, there are those who provide support structures for others in order to empower a self-directed and self-managed approach

[Fig.4.8] DESI vocational school for electrical training in Rudrapur, Bangladesh. Established in 1977, the Aga Khan Award for Architecture is awarded by the Aga Khan Trust for Culture for designs that have a significant impact on Muslim societies. It is the only architecture award that takes into consideration the occupation and use of completed designs, which typically can only be nominated after at least three years of use. This transgresses standard practice of awarding prizes to recently completed buildings with no evaluation as to their operation, function and inhabitation. The Aga Khan Award shifts emphasis away from aesthetics, whilst also bringing attention to the work of lesser-known architects, who may not have a signature style, but whose work emphasises the social and cultural impact of their designs. The Meti School in Rudrapur, Bangladesh by the practice of Anna Heringer and Eike Roswag was one of the recent recipients of the award.
Ph: B. K. S. Inan

to the built environment such as Peter Sulzer and Peter Hübner in the supervision of the Bauhäusle or the Hornsey Co-operative Housing which was organised through the Community Self Build Agency and assisted by Architype using the Segal method.

Shared enterprise, however, has yet another connotation and this refers to both the deliberate sharing of resources such as equipment, facilities space or time with others, as well as the creation of a built environment that enables sharing. An office might have additional space, which might be shared with people outside of the office's network with the explicit aim to work in a cross-disciplinary and open way, as happens in the practice of public works. Space that is designed for the sharing of activities is a relatively old concept yet nonetheless still relevant. In order to create a more communal society, buildings can be designed to include collective kitchen or laundry spaces, shared gardens, facilities for children or the elderly, or technologies to allow the collective ownership of cars or electricity generating or heating systems, as in the social condenser of the Narkomfin (p.180) building, the cohousing approach and other more specific ecologically motivated projects such as BedZed housing.

Subverting and opposing

Whilst many of the *other ways of doing architecture* in this book describe tools to work within – or despite of – prevalent political systems, many practices and groups take an extremely politicised stance and radically oppose, resist and refuse to work within frameworks set by power structures set by the neo-liberal economy. In this case, actions often arise out of localised opposition to, for instance, the closure of public facilities, the privatisation of housing stock or other public land or more global issues. These often go hand in hand with a critique of professional norms, which are seen to be complicit in the status-quo. The New Architecture Movement, for example, supported and made public many campaigns through the publication of its newsletter SLATE, (p.177) which argued that a challenge to professional institutions had to be the starting point for a reconsideration of a wider role for architects.

Opposition is, in the first instance, frequently expressed through the organisation of events, writing, protest or direct action and can involve either violent or non-violent conscientious breach of the law with the aim to directly effect changes in specific policies or laws. In the second instance, opposition often becomes propositional through more concrete engagements in the public sphere. The Glasgow Rent Strikes of 1915 and 1916 and the first wave of the Berlin squatting movement in the early 1980s are examples which were extremely successful in realising changes to both Housing Acts and inner urban renovation programmes. In the first case, the rent strikes prompted the setting up of housing associations, support structures that mitigate unjust rent increases and give practical advice, but also went on to inform a series of reports and policies on social and affordable housing. The Berlin squatting movement on the other hand went beyond the 'mere' occupation of empty buildings and became an enacted solution to the city's housing crisis and a point of opposition to the demolition of tenement buildings in large inner city areas designated for wholesale demolition and rebuilding. Squatting went from being oppositional to being propositional: buildings were, to use the German term, *instandbesetzt* – they were occupied (*besetzt*) but at the same time the occupiers also improved the building's fabric (*instandgesetzt*). Eventually this achieved a complete systemic change in housing policies, from a politics of tabula rasa to an approach of careful urban renovation and a political acknowledgment of the importance and value of participation and self-organisation in the context of urban revitalization.

The discussion around radical and extremely politicised oppositional approaches in architecture probably had a high point in the late 1960s and 1970s. Groups such as the Architects Revolutionary Council called for a break with the profession. Others moved for the set-up of different educational structures, such as the HfG Ulm with its radical reform of the architectural curriculum. Still others developed a different relationship between architect and user, implemented through the setup of the Community Technical Aid Centres and Community Design Centers. Many of these approaches are still around, but have become submerged into, and emasculated by, governmental policies; thus issues such as community consultation have become a tick box exercise rather than an opportunity for the production of a radically different conception of the built environment.

As we saw in the first two chapters, in the past two decades architects and architecture became overwhelmed by the demand of the economy, leaving few points of opposition. The academic debates about the critical role of architecture were shunted into a dead-end of internalised bloodletting and so distracted attention from the wider malaise, typified by a general mode of opportunism: building at all cost became the norm – with at worst architects fighting over commissions from authoritarian and dictatorial regimes.

Counter to this, and in an attempt to rescue architecture from its seemingly inseparable entanglement with sheer speculation, many theorists have attempted to reengage the critical potential of the production of space. People such as David Harvey, Manuel Castells and Peter Marcuse, have consistently argued for the importance of a radical opposition against the standard forms of spatial production. Peter Marcuse in particular, through his background in law and planning, is one of the most outspoken critics of the increasing commodification and retreat of architecture. For him, opposition today should be directed against forms of capitalism that are destructive of human justice, and against the exploitation of the Global South and continuing sexism and racism enforced through planning.[9] For Marcuse, opposition in today's world is about a positive choice of client and about the production of alternative plans. However, it is important for architects and planners to engage in these issues collectively and also to acknowledge that the sheer scale and immensity of the issues cannot be addressed by architects and planners alone. Marcuse writes: "I don't think we need to apologize for having a limited range of professional skills, we ought to accomplish with those skills what we can accomplish, but we also need to recognise what we can't do. If we want to deal with issues of capitalism we have to use our skills in coalition with other groups, otherwise we deal only at the margins."[10]

The writings of these theorists is complemented by the actions of many of the spatial agents. One of the most important and effective forms of opposition, and one that is practiced by so many groups in this book, is active participation: testifying at hearings and participating in planning procedures, raising awareness about wider issues of planning and the distribution of resources and land, learning and listening to others and trying to implement different and more equitable systems. Together, these examples give evidence and hope that opposition to prevailing systems is not only possible, but can result in transformation. The contemporary examples do not generally call for the wholesale

[Fig.4.9] 'P L A: Public Loitering Area'. Similar to the subversion of use of space as practiced by guerrilla gardeners, or the subversion of given rules around private property in the practice of Untergunther, Adaptive Actions, a project instigated by Jean-François Prost, presents a repository of subversive "urban alterations" – of micro-scale actions that shift our perception of the environment. He notes "By observing, revealing and sharing residents' adaptive actions, this project aims at encouraging others to act and engage with their environment as well as informing designers on possible extensions to their programme." The project is an open platform to which everyone can submit their own examples of how planned space and the movements this space directs is challenged; for example as in the illustrated project, P L A (Public loitering area), which turns a fence into a sitting area. Ph: submitted by Anonymous; www.adaptiveactions.net/action/21

revolution of the 1960s, but work by opening up the cracks that inexorable dynamic of the system inevitably leaves open. This sometimes works through subversive engagement with existing regulatory frameworks, using them for ends for which they were not originally conceived. Thus, the brilliant work of Santiago Cirugeda, who takes civic rules and pushes them to the limits to create opportunities for others to claim space in inventive ways. Subversion of the norms is used here as a tactic against the dominant understanding and use of space to create communal and non-commodified space, as delightfully shown too in the set of examples brought together in the project Adaptive Actions. (p.124) [Fig.4.9]

Towards other ways of doing architecture

Spatial Agency brings up a series of fundamental questions about how and for whom the built environment is produced and probes conventional frameworks or old-established rules and regulations. Action arises out of this questioning: individuals and groups 'bypass', 'penetrate' or 'hijack' institutions or other organisational structures; they work 'open source', they work as volunteers for non-governmental organisations and charities; they understand the production of space as something that involves dialogue and always seeks the other; they recognise the radical potential of architecture and planning and work to raise awareness and to put critical and speculative ideas in the next generation;

they question the status quo; they understand making, writing and acting as tactical manoeuvres but also as informed and committed action which affects the course of events.

For spatial agency to be exercised in its fullest sense though, these actions and interventions always take place through negotiation and deliberation and ultimately bring about the empowerment of those involved. What all these *other ways of doing* have in common is that they are at the same time proactive as they are practical and they address the role that time plays in the processes of spatial production. Spatial agency shows how negotiation, tenacity, imagination, participative spatial encounters, and one's own understanding as a morally responsible actor, might together lead to a different and more ethical under-standing of spatial practice.

1   Alistair Blyth and John Worthington, *Managing the Brief for Better Design* (London: Taylor and Francis, 2001).

2   Crimson, *Too Blessed to be Depressed: Crimson Architectural Historians 1994–2002* (Rotterdam: 010, 2002), 8.

3   Further references to alternative financing include the Grameen Bank, micro-credits, feasibility grants for community organisations from The Social Investment Business, Community Development Finance Institutions (CDFI), or UnLtd, a charity that supports social entrepreneurs.

4   For a comprehensive account of different strategies in relation to the appropriation of space and participative architecture see: Jesko Fezer and Mathias Heyden, eds., *HIER ENTSTEHT: Strategien partizipativer Architektur und räumlicher Aneignung* (Berlin: b_books Verlag, 2004).

5   The concept of slack space was developed in our previous book on flexible housing and then in *Architecture Depends*.

6   The Royal Institute of British Architects has just selected its 2nd female president in over 175 years of existence.

7   Hugo Hinsley, "Education Special. What the education debate is about," *SLATE*, no. 6 (1978): 9.

8   McLaren, *Critical Pedagogy and Predatory Culture: Oppositional Politics in a Postmodern Age*, 231.

9   Peter Marcuse, 'What has to be done? The Potentials and Failures of Planning: History, Theory, and Actuality. Lessons from New York', in *Camp for Oppositional Architecture*, ed. by An Architektur (Berlin: An Architektur, 2005), 36.

10 Marcuse, 40.

4

OTHER WAYS OF DOING ARCHITECTURE

This section of the book sets out in alphabetical order some of the best examples of spatial agency. More can be found at www.spatialagency.net, which also allows sorting of entries in to thematic groups and has supplementary illustrations and references. As noted in the introduction, this selection makes no claims to be comprehensive. Its partiality will inevitably provoke questions as to what is in and what is out. We see this questioning as positive, because through it each reader will reach his or her own interpretation of spatial agency. Perhaps also provocative is the title: "Other Ways of Doing Architecture." The previous chapters have posited how this selection of examples presents a different view of architecture. What may not be so clear is why architects are equipped to engage with this broader field, especially since many of the examples do not involve architects. The answer lies in the capacity to understand relationships spatially, an attribute that is developed in architectural education and practice. The capacity is one of being able to assimilate and then synthesise a broad range of conditions – physical, material, environmental, social and political – and then make sense of them as a set of relational ecologies, which are dynamic and interdependent. Our optimism lies in the belief that architects, always working with others, are well prepared to operate in these complex spatial contexts. Our hope is that the following examples inspire the new ways of thinking and doing required to operate as such a spatial agent.

00:/

London, UK, 2005–
www.architecture00.net
00:/ is a London based co-operative practice, established in 2005 by two architects, Inderpaul Johar and

David Saxby. They describe their work as creating 'sustainable design' defining this both as an ecological and a social concern. Whilst their building designs strive for zero carbon status, their work in the field of regeneration is characterised by an emphasis on creating micro-economies through supporting small-scale businesses and non-monetary forms of exchange such as swap shops. This strategic work is combined with architectural design that creates the spatial conditions necessary for social networks to thrive, typically through making threshold and indeterminate spaces that encourage informal exchanges.

Club for social pioneers, The Hub King Cross, London. Ph: 00:/ for Blueprint / RA

Paper city, social exchange classifieds. Ph: OO:/ for Blueprint / RA

The practice places importance on empirical research and views the role of architects as also effecting change at policy level. In this they have collaborated with the think tank Demos, producing a report on the future of urban planning, and have acted as architectural advisors to CABE and the EU. OO:/ view the design of institutional, financial and social structures as the key to successful strategies of regeneration in the built environment, citing DEGW, (p.138) the Grameen Bank, which is a micro-finance community development bank in Bangladesh and the People's Supermarket, a co-operatively owned and managed supermarket as key influences. This approach is demonstrated well in their project for the Hub Collective, which aims to provide a 'global network of innovative workplaces for social entrepreneurs'. Here OO:/ designed the building as well as advising on the financial strategy for the business, creating on organisational and spatial model for encouraging small-scale community businesses.

Johar, I. (2006) 'Architecture of money: Re-building the common', *Volume* (Amsterdam), 7: 80–85.

1960s Utopian Groups

Europe, 1961–1977

The 1960s saw a second wave of utopian architecture in Europe following the social utopias imagined in the 1920s. Some of the approaches focused on emerging cultural conditions, such as mobility and flexibility, whilst others, such as those of Constant Nieuwenhuys (p.178) and Yona Friedman (p.151) saw their utopias as instruments of societal change. What often related these approaches architecturally were mega-structures that could be 'plugged-into' or 'clipped-onto', providing a framework which could be modified, adapted and extended.

The most well-known of the first group are **Archigram,** formed at the Architectural Association (p.98) in London in 1961. Using various formats including (fan)zines, comic strips, poetry and radical statements, they produced a vision of a consumerist city, made possible through a faith in technology and the optimism of a time before the oil crisis of the 1970s and the realisation of the finite nature of natural resources. Although Archigram were eschewed a directly political stance, their vision of a dynamic architecture inflecting contemporary culture influenced other groups, including those who used Archigram's systems to imagine a socially and politically engaged architecture.

One such group was **Archizoom,** whose name was a direct reference to Archigram's fourth (fan)zine issue entitled, *ZOOM! Amazing Archigram.* Founded in Florence in 1966 by four architects, Andrea Branzi, Gilberto Corretti, Paolo Deganello, Massimo Morozzi, and two designers, Dario Bartolini and Lucia Bartolini, Archizoom's work was an ironic response to Archigram's consumerist logic and their desire to detach architecture from politics. They led the Anti-design or Radical movement in Italy producing a number of projects and essays that critiqued Modernism and explored flexible and technology-based approaches to urban design. A related group, also based in Florence and formed in the same year by Adolfo Natalini and Cristiano Toraldo di Francia, was **Superstudio.** They criticized mainstream architecture for ignoring and aggravating environmental and social problems, designing polemical projects that imagined dystopian worlds, using an infinite grid as a recurring motif for a continuous and uniform environment. Also related to the Radical movement were **Gruppo Strum,** founded in 1971 in Turin by Giorgio Cerretti, Pietro Derossi, Carlo Gianmarco, Riccardo Rosso and Maurizio Vogliazzo. The group saw

architecture as a means of participating in the social and political protests of the 1960s through organising seminars and distributing free copies of their *fotoromanzi* (picture-stories).

The influence of these radical groups is seen in the shift from conceiving architecture conceived as static building alone to identifying architecture as a form of cultural critique and finally as a social and political practice.

Lang, P. and Menking, W. (eds) (2003) *Superstudio: Life Without Objects*, Milan: Skira.

Sadler, S. (2005) *Archigram: Architecture without Architecture*, Cambridge: MIT Press.

2012 Architecten

Rotterdam, Netherlands, 1997–
www.2012architecten.nl

A pavilion in Dordrecht made from kitchen sinks. Ph: John Bosma

2012 Architecten is a Rotterdam-based practice of architects Jeroen Bergsma, Jan Jongert and Césare Peeren, established in 1997. Based around a desire to reduce the use of natural resources through innovation and clever design, they have proposed the concept of 'superuse', which unlike recycling uses materials, components and objects in the form that they are found. This means that the energy wasted in the transportation, breaking down and reforming of material can be saved. By ensuring that designers are aware of what is available at the start of a project they are able to incorporate specific components within their design – for instance the superuse of five discarded rotor blades in the making of a children's playground. 2012 Architecten acknowledge that what is required for this to happen is not just creativity in design, but a change in attitudes, including innovative management practices. They have proposed a restructuring of the construction process to include a new professional: the superuse scout, a person able to gauge the opportunities and reusable potential of different objects and components.

At the start of each project, 2012 Architecten carry out an assessment of the waste and productive cycles that a given site or situation is part of, including food, water, traffic, humans, energy etc. This research informs the design process, including an overall strategy for acquiring materials, making use of competencies and skills in the locality, and finally in the design of buildings and other interventions. Through designing not just their interventions but the whole scenario of their production, 2012 Architecten empower local exchange and production with the aim of lowering dependence on goods that are not available locally. They take their inspiration from the creative use of waste material that occurs every day in conditions of scarcity across the global South, and place themselves within the self-help, DIY tradition of 1970's US and in particular the use of waste materials and ecological practices developed in building the Earthships. (p.134)

Hinte, E. V., Jongert, J. and Peeren, C. (2007) *Superuse: Constructing New Architecture by Shortcutting Material Flows*, Rotterdam: 010 Publishers.

A Civilian Occupation

Tel Aviv, Israel, 2002–2003
A Civilian Occupation is the name of a banned exhibition catalogue, which was later published as a book in 2003, edited by Rafi Segal and Eyal Weizman. The original exhibition entitled, 'The Politics of Israeli Architecture', was prepared in response to an open architectural competition organised by the Israeli

Association of United Architects (IAUA). The exhibition was to be their contribution to the International Union of Architect's congress that was held in Berlin in 2002. Segal and Weizman's response explored the role of architecture in the continuing occupation of Palestine and the politics of the Middle East. The IAUA objected to the proposal and withdrew support from the exhibition citing budgetary concerns; they also destroyed the five thousand copies of the exhibition catalogue which had already been published.

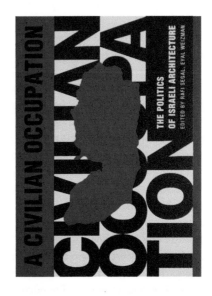

The book, *A Civilian Occupation*, finally brought this work into the public sphere. In it Israeli architects, writers, photographers, journalists and a film maker reflect on the spatial dimension of the Israeli occupation, exploring the ways in which specific architectural strategies have been used to control territory and to wield power. The essays are accompanied by maps, photographs and statistical data that reveal in detail the complicity of architectural practice in the occupation, from the strategic placement of settlements on hilltops that act as fortresses to survey the Palestinian villages below, to the role of infrastructure such as bypass roads in fragmenting Palestinian territory. The exhibition also included a map produced by Weizman, in collaboration with the Israeli human rights organisation B'Tselem, which showed for the first time all the Palestinian villages located in the West Bank alongside the Israeli settlements. The latter are usually represented as points but through mapping their precise locations, size and spatial form, the map revealed them to be carefully

Give Us Our Land Back, 2005. Courtesy Abahlali baseMjondolo

designed to achieve certain strategic goals such as bisecting a road or surrounding a Palestinian village. It also revealed how the settlements have managed to completely fragment Palestinian territory whilst only occupying a small fraction of the land.

The book thus shows clearly and in great detail how architecture is never an isolated or neutral profession and whilst the Israeli case may be an extreme example, the proliferation of urban enclaves, gated developments and evictions everywhere shows the relevance of this work to the profession in general. The interview with Thomas Leitersdorf, the architect of Ma'ale Edummim, the city which has grown to be the largest settlement in the West Bank serves as a warning to architects willing to follow their dreams to build at any cost.

Segal, R. and Weizman, E. (eds) (2003) *A Civilian Occupation: The Politics of Israeli Architecture*, Tel Aviv/London: Babel/Verso.

Abahlali baseMjondolo
Durban, South Africa, 2005–
www.abahlali.org
Abahlali baseMjondolo means 'people who live in shacks' in Zulu. It is a movement of the militant poor which began in Durban, South Africa in 2005. The grassroots organisation formed around a protest against the sale of vacant land promised to those living

in a nearby informal settlement. The movement grew rapidly from its inception and although it is mostly based in and around Durban, it claims to have mobilised tens of thousands of people and is considered to be the largest movement of the poor in post-apartheid South Africa. Although its main focus is to organise actions against local government, in recent years its members have also begun to set up projects in the settlements such as crèches, gardens and working collectives.

Shack Cinema, Motala Heights, 2007. Courtesy Abahlali baseMjondolo

Their campaigns deal directly with the living conditions of the urban poor, demanding essential services and the basic right to a home in the city. The motivations behind

Junk Jet 2 (2008)

glaspaper (2001–7)

the group's actions are rooted in the particular politics of South Africa. The shack-dwellers voted overwhelmingly for the ANC and its promise of providing adequate housing for the vast majority of black South Africans living in extreme poverty. Despite taking part in a myriad of public participation processes, they felt that they were still sold-out to the developers and were instead arrested for protesting.

Abahlali question the effectiveness of local struggles being led by foreign NGOs, academics or donors, advocating instead an approach where people act for themselves. To that end they are slowly building up a network of solidarity with like-minded associations and others in similar situations through an exchange of knowledge and experiences. Spatial agency here starts with the lived experience of the poor; Abahlali state that they want to talk about politics in the places where the poor live, at times that are suitable for them and in a manner that can include them. They see themselves as a knowledge-based as well as an action-based movement; one of the early banners proclaimed a University of Kennedy Road. Most of the intellectual work occurs in meetings and discussions, sometimes through song, continuing an oral tradition of debate. Abahlali view this as a building up of theory from below. The day-to-day

running of the organisation is also seen as an analytical exercise where the techniques of collective decision-making are continually refined and there is a meticulous system of record keeping.

Pithouse, R. (2006) *Thinking Resistance in the Shanty Town*. <http://www.metamute.org/en/Thinking-Resistance-in-the-Shanty-Town> (accessed 9 July 2010).

Alternative magazines

Alternative publishing in architecture has had a long and varied history, with two periods of prolific output, both of which have been documented in recent exhibitions: *A Few Zines: Dispatches from the Edge of Architectural Production* (2009) explores architectural zines of the nineties and their mixing of writings on the city with music, art and pop culture in general; *Clip/Stamp/Fold: The Radical Architecture of Little Magazines* (2010) focused on this phenomenon in the 1960s and the 1970s. These magazines were an alternative to the academic journals or trade magazines of the profession, whilst some provided space for the amateur and the non-professional, others were produced by specialists as an outlet for highly

Issues of *ARse* (1969–72)

specific topics and interests. Recently, blogs and other forms of output on the Internet have become a more popular means for disseminating such information, although they have not necessarily replaced the small magazines. As most fans of such publications are quick to point out, there is an 'object-ness' to these cheaply printed, stapled, DIY magazines that a blog cannot quite replace.

The motivations for alternative publishing are as diverse as the output itself, often they were terribly self-serving such as those produced by Archigram, (p.87) whilst others were highly political and part of a wider practice, for example **ARse** (1969–72) was by Tom Woolley and Peter Wild with their students at the Architectural Association. (p.98) The acronym of the title changed meaning many times from "Architects for a Really Socialist Environment," or "Architectural Radicals, Students & Educators", the AR alluding to the mainstream journal Architectural Review. The zine was produced alongside their Community Technical Aid Centre, (p.128) support, which provided architectural services to neighbourhood groups. Printed cheaply in black, white and red, *ARse* was a resolutely left-wing publication that set out to critique the architectural profession's complicity in capitalist society.

Magazines such as **Utopie** (1967–78) were research projects in their own right, produced by an editorial collective that included architects, urbanists and sociologists, whose core members were Isabelle Auriscoste, Jean Baudrillard, Michelle Guillou and Hubert Tonka. Utopie as a group came together in 1966 at Henri Lefebvre's house in the Pyrenees and his influence is felt throughout the seven issues that were produced, including theoretical texts and collages that speculated on a new practice of architecture that attended to everyday life. The collaborative nature of the publication was reflected in its format with a column reserved for comments. Alongside the publication, Utopie also produced exhibitions, pamphlets and organised related events.

Other DIY publications such as **glaspaper** (2001–7) aimed at taking the discussion around architecture and the built environment to those who would not normally have access to it. G.L.A.S. (p.132) was a collective of architecture students, teachers and designers, who produced a total of eight thematic issues on topics such as 'learning and education' and 'transport and movement'.

Whether in the form of magazines, blogs or pamphlets, alternative publishing is a means of bypassing the mainstream publishing industry. Instead, niche interests can be catered for and distribution networks created through personal contacts and overlapping interests. At a time when both the architectural profession and academia are dominated by a few big names, alternative publishing offers a way out of the homogenised discourse, offering space for a multitude of voices.

Rowe, C. (1997) *The Book of Zines: Readings from the Fringe*, New York: Owl Books.

Amateur Architecture Studio

Hangzhou, China, 1998–

Amateur Architecture Studio was founded in 1998 by Wang Shu and Lu Wenyu in Hangzhou, China. Their approach is based around a critique of the architectural profession, which they view as complicit in the demolition of entire urban areas and the transformation of rural areas through excessive building. The practice first came to wider attention in Europe with their pavilion for the 10th Venice Architecture Biennale in 2006; a comment on the on-going demolitions, their installation 'Tiled Garden' was made from 66,000 recycled tiles salvaged from demolition sites.

Xiangshan Campus, China Academy of Art. Ph: David Anthony Brown

Rather than looking towards the West for inspiration, as many of their contemporaries do, the practice's work is embedded in the history and traditions of Chinese culture. In particular they reference everyday building tactics of ordinary people and the strong vernacular tradition of building in China. The name of their practice signals this commitment to learning from

the 'amateur builder', focusing on craft skills and applying this to contemporary architecture. Wang Shu spent a number of years working on building sites with traditional craftsmen in order to learn from them. Combining this traditional knowledge with experimental building techniques and intensive research, Amateur Architecture Studio respond to the ongoing challenges of the rapidly urbanising context of China. They do so with a site-specific architecture that valorises crafts and skill over professional knowledge and expertise.

Shu, W. and Zhenning, F. (2009) 'The Outline of the Hills = Il profilo delle colline [Interview]', *Abitare*, 495: 64–73.

Amateur building tactics

Amateur building tactics refer to the myriad practices of self-building that occur across the world without the input of an architect. These practices are usually the result of need and the will to survive and are typically located in what are variously termed informal settlements, shanty towns, favelas, shacks, katchi abadi etc., settlements that are built on left-over and neglected pieces of land, on steep hillsides, by the side of railway tracks or at the edges and interstices of cities. Characterised by dense and rapid growth, informal settlements are unplanned and indicate a failure of governments to keep up with the housing needs of their citizens. Although it is difficult to define these collectively, as they occur in vastly different contexts, informal settlements are often grouped according to their legal status. This is problematic as legality is based on capitalist and neo-liberal definitions of property, which means that much of the debate around informal settlements concerns issues of land ownership. It may therefore be better to define informal settlements not through their relationship to an external system but through their own context; one such way would be to examine the different tactics involved in building and organising such settlements. For example, the *gecekondu* of Turkey take advantage of a legal loophole that means a structure cannot be removed without legal proceedings if it is already inhabited, leading to makeshift houses being built collectively overnight. The minimum required structure to qualify as a house cannot be completed alone and so requires a group of people to work together. It also means that self builders not only engage in a very fast building process but one that

Amateur building tactics. Gülensu/Gülsuyu geçekondu neighbourhoods in Istanbul. Ph: Nishat Awan

is continuous, starting with just a room and growing steadily to accommodate more people and activities, often over a number of years and generations. Another collective building practice that occurs in Brazil is named *mutirão*, meaning 'collective effort' in Portuguese, a group of family and friends get together to help build a house for one of their group; the favour being repeated for others as and when needed. The principles of *mutirão* are now also being applied to the provision of social housing across Latin America. (p.166) This type of self-building in informal settlements often occurs in a self-organised (p.197) manner with a number of services being provided within established settlements, for example the architect Arif Hasan (p.154) has supported and utilised such grass-roots initiatives in the upgrading of the *katchi abadis* of Karachi.

Whilst the standard response of many local governments has been to evict inhabitants from such areas and to relocate them to newer neighbourhoods that conform to legal and planning standards, it is now widely accepted that this is not an adequate response. It disperses established communities, with people often moved from sites close to city centres to the outskirts of the city, where there is little chance of earning a living.

In recent years, some governments are taking a more progressive attitude, looking to provide services within these communities, but due to development pressure this is still a highly contested area with many communities being evicted regularly.

United Nations Human Settlements Programme (2003) *The Challenge of Slums: Global Report on Human Settlements*, London: Earthscan, UN-HABITAT.

An Architektur
Berlin, Germany, 2002–
www.anarchitektur.com
An Architektur grew out of the loose architecture collective *freies fach*, whose work addressed the reconstruction of Berlin post the mid 1990s through actions, publications and exhibitions. Since 2002 An Architektur have worked in a number of different constellations, with various groups, including the Institute for Applied Urbanism, FAST, and Casco. Their research and projects take many forms including exhibitions, installations, actions and the designing of space for arts institutions. Critically analysing spatial relations as a form of political agency, they reflect the

original interventionist and highly political approach developed by *freies fach*.

A large part of their work is related to the production of the eponymously titled biannual magazine. Each issue is organised around a theme related to the socio-political aspects of architecture, and in particular the effects of capitalism and the neo-liberal economy on both architecture as profession and as built environment. Recent issues have discussed the increasing tensions around migration in Europe, the commodification of space, and the relationship between 'war and the production of space'. Whilst many of the chosen topics have critiqued the status quo, others celebrate grassroots successes, such as a set of issues on 'Community Design' in the context of the US, which was also presented as an exhibition. They have recently organised a conference, 'Camp for Oppositional Architecture', which brought together contemporary practices and theorists whose work presents a radical critique of current architectural practices and offers suggestions for alternative approaches.

Poster for *Camp for Oppositional Architecture* in Utrecht, 2006

An Architektur as group and publication is increasingly becoming a hub for a network of progressive research groups and projects related to a critical and highly political approach to architecture.

An Architektur (eds) (since 2002) *An Architektur. Produktion und Gebrauch gebauter Umwelt*, Berlin: An Architektur.

Mogel, L. and Bhagat, A. (eds) (2008) *An Atlas of Radical Cartography*, Los Angeles: Journal of Aesthetics and Protest Press.

Anarchitecture Group
New York, USA, 1972–1975

Based in New York in the 1970s, Anarchitecture was an artists' group whose members included artists Laurie Anderson, Tina Girouard, Carol Goodden, Suzanne Harris, Jene Highstein, Bernard Kirschenbaun, Richard Landry, and Richard Nonas, as well as the architecturally trained artist, Gordon Matta Clark (1943–78). Their name, a mixture of 'anarchy' and 'architecture', was conceived in informal conversation, one of the main ways through which the group collaborated. In 1974 they produced an exhibition of the same name, which encapsulated their critique of the modernist impulses of contemporary culture within which architecture was conceived as a symbol for that culture's worst excesses and drawbacks. Anarchitecture were very critical of the stasis in cultural attitudes and what Richard Nonas called the 'hard shell', or resistance to change, that architecture epitomised. All contributions to the show were anonymous and followed an agreed format to emphasise their collective approach. The central role accorded to architecture was perhaps a reaction to Matta Clark's own experience of architectural education at Cornell University, from where he graduated in 1968. The group as a whole tackled architecture's complicity in capitalist modes of production, using wordplay and found photographs to explore issues related to cities, ways of inhabiting buildings and the role of property.

Separately but concurrently Matta Clark also carried out the *Fake Estates* project, buying tiny slivers of unbuildable and inaccessible land, a comment on the American dream of land and ownership, his useless estate having no economic value and existing only on paper. Another project, *Food*, though not technically a part of Anarchitecture's oeuvre, included many of the same people including Girouard, Goodden and Matta-Clark. Collectively, they set up and ran the restaurant with an open kitchen which became a New

York institution. Located in Soho, it operated between 1971 and 1973, the business supported and sustained a local network of artists, becoming a social and economic hub for the area.

Later, Matta Clark went on to produce his 'building cuts' that further developed ideas of the Anarchitecture group. These were transformations of abandoned buildings, split apart, sliced through and rearranged, commenting once again on society through architecture, touching on the increasing desire for material accumulation, wealth and permanence.

Walker, S. (2009) *Gordon Matta-Clark: Art, Architecture and the Attack on Modernism*, London: I. B. Tauris & Co Ltd.

Ankur. Society for alternatives in education
Delhi, India, 1983–

Cybermohalla Lab in the Dakshinpuri settlement in south Delhi.
Ph: Nikolaus Hirsch/Michel Müller

Ankur, meaning "seedling" in Hindi, is an NGO based in Delhi which was established in 1983 to combat the sectarian divisions in Indian society and to use radical pedagogy as a means of achieving this. The organisation was founded by a group of activists, educators and artists who felt that traditional modes of teaching were failing those already marginalised in society, especially children, young people and women. Ankur work in the informal or worker settlements of Delhi and more recently also in a few other Indian cities, using education to empower these groups and as a way of equipping them with the necessary tools for living in a society full of conflicts and contradictions.

Whilst the scope of Ankur's work is diverse, including writing school curricula, developing alternative teaching resources and critiquing government policy, it is their activities in their chosen neighbourhoods that is most relevant to spatial agency. The organisation has established a series of spaces that are staffed by women from the locality, giving them an insight into the area and its particular concerns. Ankur have set up neighbourhood libraries, technology centres or media labs (which are developed in collaboration with Sarai (p.195) as part of the Cybermohalla project), spaces for young women, as well as organising events such as early morning and after-school programmes for children. These facilities and activities act as hubs in each neighbourhood, providing a space in which people from different backgrounds can meet and engage with each other. In this Ankur's experimental approach to pedagogy creates spaces for mutual learning which have the potential to empower those who are excluded from society and whose voices and experiences have been suppressed. It is interesting that this emphasis on pedagogy and especially on creativity is echoed in other urban practices that are dealing with conflict situations, such as the artist collective, **PS²** in Belfast.

Sen, S. *Building a Bridge of Empathy*. <http://www.changemakers.com/en-us/node/30042> (accessed 10 March 2010).

Ant Farm
San Francisco, USA, 1968–1978
Ant Farm was established within the counter-cultural milieu of 1968 San Francisco by two architects, Chip Lord and Doug Michels, later joined by Curtis Schreier. Their work dealt with the intersection of architecture, design and media art, critiquing the North American culture of mass media and consumerism. Ant Farm produced works in a number of formats, including agitprop events, manifestos, videos, performances and installations.

Their early work was a reaction to the heaviness and fixity of the Brutalist movement, in contrast to which they proposed an inflatable architecture that was cheap, easy to transport and quick to assemble. This type of architecture fitted well with their rhetoric of nomadic, communal lifestyles in opposition to what they saw as the rampant consumerism of 1970s USA. The inflatables questioned the standard tenets of building:

these were structures with no fixed form and could not be described in the usual architectural representations of plan and section. They instead promoted a type of architecture that moved away from a reliance on expert knowledge. Ant Farm produced a manual for making your own pneumatic structures, the *Inflatocookbook*. The inflatables thus constituted a type of participatory architecture that allowed the users to take control of their environment. Events were also organised inside the inflatables, which were set up at festivals, university campuses or conferences to host lectures, workshops, seminars, or simply as a place to hang out.

Other projects include the 'House of the Century' whose form was reminiscent of the inflatables but made from ferro cement, the video 'Media Burn' where they drove an adapted Cadillac into a wall of televisions in front of an audience hand-picked from the media. They also produced a number of utopian projects such as Convention City and Freedom Land. Finally, perhaps

their most famous work 'Cadillac Ranch', consists of ten Cadillacs in a row half-buried in the ground with their tail-fins in the air. It is both a tribute to the American car culture as well as a critique of it.

Ant Farm were heavily influenced by the likes of **Buckminster Fuller** and Archigram [p.87] and whilst creating an architecture that was utopian, their projects were also always ironic and tongue-in-cheek. Their work revealed the relationships between environmental degradation and mass industry, questioned the role of mass media and consumerism and demonstrated the use of advanced technologies with playful projects like the Dolphin Embassy. They left behind a body of research that was developed outside the privileged institutional context of universities and is still relevant today in debates around sustainable architecture, building technologies as well as public art and architecture.

Scott, F. D. (2008) *Ant Farm: Living Archive 7*, Barcelona: Actar, Columbia GSAPP.

50 x 50' Pillow, 1969; temporary installation, Saline Valley, California, for production of Whole Earth Catalog supplement, 1969. University of California, Berkeley Art Museum and Pacific Film Archive. Ph: Curtis Schreier

Poster by Architects Revolutionary Council on display at the Architectural Association

Architects' Revolutionary Council

London, UK, 1974–1980

Architects' Revolutionary Council (ARC), initially funded by the 'Rowntree Trust', was founded in 1974 by a group of students led by Brian Anson who was then lecturer at the Architectural Association. (p.98) It remained a small group who were described as 'the *enfant terrible* of the radical architecture groups – variously feared, indulged, despised, and every now and then mocked'. Very much aware of their public image, ARC announced its formation at a press conference that also called for the abolition of the RIBA. They made extensive use of graphics derived from military symbolism to produce posters that denounced the

RIBA, in order to mobilise architectural students and community groups. They believed that 'creative architecture should be available to all people in society, regardless of their economic circumstances'.

To enact their ideas, ARC members gave advice as 'community architects' on projects in Ealing, Colne Valley, and Bridgetown, as well as producing a series of community newspapers, including *The Wild Duck* and *Colne Valley News*. At the same time, ARC campaigned for 'revolutionary changes within the architectural establishment and specifically for the replacement of the RIBA by a new architectural system'. Together with the New Architecture Movement (p.177) they set out to criticise the conventional notions of professionalism

Alvin Boyarsky on front cover of Architectural Design (1972)

and the internalised structure of the profession, and in particular the system of patronage where the designer of a building has little contact with its user.

Oppositional to the core, ARC was a pressure group that also led by example. Many of their demands seem even more relevant today, such as their calls for architects to take greater responsibility for their actions and for a general acknowledgement of the class divide that still pervades the profession. ARC came to an end in 1980 following Anson's move from the Architectural Association.

Bottoms, E. (2009) *If Crime Doesn't Pay: The Architects' Revolutionary Council.* <http://www.aaschool.ac.uk/AALIFE/archive.htm> (accessed 11 Aug 2009).

Architectural Association

London, UK, 1971–1990
www.aaschool.ac.uk

The Architectural Association (AA) was founded in London in 1847 following an article published in *Builder* magazine by Robert Kerr and Charles Gray, who called upon other students to take their training into their own hands. They were unhappy with the vocational training they were receiving through being articled in private practice, a flawed system that gave highly uneven results. The AA's beginnings were modest with members and invited guests being asked to present their work at regular meetings, as well as the organisation of design sessions based on mutual critique. In 1862 the system was formalised through a voluntary exam, which was to be the start of the model of learning and testing that has contributed towards the professionalisation of architectural teaching. At this time AA also began publishing an annual prospectus, *Brown Book*, and later a monthly journal, *AA Notes*. After having discussed the admittance of female students in 1893 and 1905, the AA finally admitted women in 1918.

The contemporary history of the AA is dominated by the figure of Alvin Boyarsky who led the school out of a period of crisis following its near merger with Imperial College. Boyarsky was chairman of the AA from 1971 until his death in 1990 and under him AA became the international and globally oriented institution it is known as today. Since losing its government grant, the school had to change its student demographic from being mostly British students, mostly grant-aided, to being over ninety percent international students by the end of Boyarsky's tenure.

Boyarsky's main contribution was the establishment of the unit system, an educational model that is now followed in architecture schools across the world. Instead of a standard curriculum, the AA allowed tutors to construct their own educational structures, with students free to choose the approach that most interested them. The AA thus heralded the move from modernist orthodoxy to a much more pluralist system. Boyarsky encouraged debate, and sometimes conflict, between the units, so that work was always subjected to a variety of opinions. The AA in the 1970s and 1980s also hosted key architectural lectures and debates, becoming an international hub for the development of architectural discourse. Many of the world's most famous architects, including Rem Koolhaas and Zaha Hadid, emerged from the intense environment that the AA constructed.

Higgott, A. (2006) 'Searching for the Subject: Alvin Boyarsky and the Architectural Association School', in Higgott, A. *Mediating Modernism: Architectural Cultures in Britain*, London: Routledge.

Architectural NGOs

Architectural NGOs operate in two major areas, disaster relief and community development, with many combining the two. They operate from two main perspectives, those from the developed world working in the global South and those working within their own locality. Whilst there are many problems with the global NGO culture, not least the prevalent sidelining of local expertise and talent, they have also made a difference to the lives of many, especially in global responses to humanitarian disaster, to which architecture as a profession has been slow to respond. It was a non-architect, **Fred Cuny**, who first made a connection between disaster relief and development work in the 1970s. At the time there was no single organisation responsible for the coordination of relief efforts and the standard response to the need for shelter was the provision of lightweight temporary tents. A lack of organisation and understanding of the cultural context meant that it was common for food to rot whilst people went hungry, or for the isolated relief operations of independent charities to send unsuitable goods, such as woollen jackets to tropical countries. This situation prompted Cuny to set up his own consulting company, Fred Cuny & Associates later named Intertect.

Although Cuny and Intertect's ideas were not new, through managing to implement them they changed the way disaster management is handled, advocating better camp organisation with single family tents clustered around a communal space for cooking, laundry etc. and adjoining lavatories. This reduced outbreaks of disease, encouraged ownership and increased security, whilst also creating an atmosphere of self-help where small-scale cottage industries and other self-organised (p.197) initiatives could thrive. Other innovations included training families to build their own shelters, an approach that has influenced architects such as **Shigeru Ban**, who has designed emergency shelters made out of recycled paper cardboard tubes, a low-cost and low-tech solution that could be built by families displaced by disaster. Cuny also advocated paying local people to help in the clean-up operation so that materials could be salvaged for rebuilding efforts following a disaster.

Cuny vanished at the age of 50 on a mission to Chechnya in 1995 and the mystery of his disappearance was never solved. Yet his influence has been great, he changed the working practices of organisations such as Oxfam, whilst also being a key starting point for disaster relief and humanitarian approaches in architecture; for example, **Architecture for Humanity** (AFH) acknowledge Cuny's influence.

Whilst there are a large number of architectural NGOs operating globally, AFH can be credited for popularising disaster relief, and to some extent development architecture, in the US and European countries, especially amongst architectural students and young professionals. The volunteer non-profit organisation was founded in 1999 by architect, Cameron Sinclair, and freelance journalist and documentary producer, Kate Stohr. Formed in response to the Kosovo conflict, the pair realised that there was no organisation that coordinated the response of architects to international humanitarian crises. As AFH point out, the equivalent organisation for engineers, RedR, had at that point been in existence for twenty years. Following a meeting with UNHCR and the realisation of the scope of work involved in addressing the needs in Kosovo, AFH launched an open design competition, which has since become their preferred method of working. Rather than responding to emergencies on their own, AFH organise open calls for ideas, put architects in touch with aid organisations and NGOs that need their design services, and raise money to implement projects. The strength of response from architects to their first competition tapped into a latent desire within the profession to use their services to improve living conditions for those in need.

In 2003, this interest was consolidated in the establishment of local chapters of AFH that operate independently from the main organisation but are affiliated to it. This has led to projects being implemented not only in disaster situations but also locally based community projects, carrying out similar work to Community Design Centers. (p.126) Since 2006 AFH have organised the Open Architecture Network, an online platform that allows designers to share their ideas and resources and collaborate with each other in order to help people and communities in crisis. The network operates under a creative commons license which means that rather than each new project starting from scratch, people can build on their own experience and that of others.

Architecture Sans Frontières-UK in India. Ph: Sarah Ernst

The list of other architectural NGOs is long and includes **Architectes Sans Frontières, Habitat for Humanity International** and **Architecture & Developpement**, which are all well established NGOs, often working with the United Nations agency UN-Habitat. (p.203) Those that operate as locally based, grass-roots organisations tend to focus on community development, housing provision and other longer term solutions. Shack and Slum Dwellers International, (p.198) is one of the largest such organisations, active in Africa, Asia and South America. Others include Abahlali baseMjondolo, (p.89) a well established movement of housing related to NGOs in Latin America, the **Aga Khan Development Network, Habitat International Coalition** and many others.

Architecture for Humanity (2006) *Design Like You Give a Damn: Architectural Responses to Humanitarian Crises*, London: Thames & Hudson.

Artists and spatial practice

As architects have expanded their practice beyond the built object and artists have moved out of the gallery, so the already blurred boundaries between the two disciplines have become still more entwined within the realm of critical spatial practice. To engage with the terms of spatial agency, artistic practice must show some form of transformative potential. Although there are a large number of artists working with spatial relations, those included here influence the actual production of space or change spatial relations in some way.

Michael Rakowitz is a case in point, trained as an architect, his work straddles the divide between art and architecture. Based in New York, his most memorable project is *paraSITE* (1998), at once a critique and a making visible of the prevalent attitudes towards homelessness, whilst at the same time improving the material living conditions of those living on the streets. Rakowitz designed a series of inflatable shelters that plug into the vent outlets of buildings, creating a warm and dry space for their inhabitants. Custom designed for each individual, their oddness in the street-scape gives visibility to the homeless. In an interview, Rakowitz relates that the initial shelter was made from black plastic in the hope of providing privacy and darkness to sleep in, but upon consulting his clients, he realised that what was most important to them was to be able to see out in case of attack and a desire to be seen and acknowledged. The shelters not only comment on the situation of the homeless, but also the large amounts of energy wasted in buildings.

Marjetica Potrč's work also blurs the boundaries between art, architecture and urbanism working in diverse locations, from the informal settlements of Caracas, to the trailer parks of Florida, or in the West Bank. Trained as both an architect and an artist, Potrč's work is situated in these locations but is also displayed in galleries. Moving away from the problem solving approach of architecture Potrč tries to learn from each context through observation, developing an understanding of the micro-processes involved in order

Michael Rakowitz: Joe Heywood's paraSITE shelter (2000). Plastic bags, polyethylene tubing, hooks, tape. Battery Park City,Manhattan, NY. Courtesy the artist and Lombard-Freid Projects

to inform the eventual interventions. For example in the La Vega barrio of Caracas, Potrč worked with architect, Liyat Esakov, as part of the Caracas Case (p.114) project to design a dry toilet that responded to the lack of water. Designed in consultation with residents, rather than providing a one-off solution the toilet can be easily replicated. In another project based in Sharjah, United Arab Emirates, a small solar powered desalination device was installed in a school, in a context where

solar energy is abundant but its use is virtually non-existent. As in the work of Rakowitz, Potrč's projects simultaneously reveal uneven living conditions whilst also working to alleviate them.

The artist **Thomas Hirschhorn's** sculptural installations are participatory and collaborative in nature, and fit within an artistic tradition including the Anarchitecture Group (p.94) and Robert Smithson. Taking sculpture in its broadest sense as the manipulation of spatial

Marjetica Potrc: 'Solar-Powered Desalination Device' (2007). Energy and water-supply infrastructure Sharjah Biennial 8, Sharjah, UAE. Ph: Wolfgang Traeger and Alfredo Dancel Rubio

Thomas Hirschhorn's Bataille Monument at Documenta 11. Ph: Florian Kossak

Ursula Biemann. Still from Sahara Chronicle

conditions, Hirschhorn critiques architectural production through approximating and mimicking architectural structures. The project *Bataille Monument* (2002), named after the Surrealist writer, was located in a mainly Turkish neighbourhood of Kassel, Germany, as part of the Documenta art festival. The intervention included a television station, snack bar, an installation about Bataille and a library themed around his work. Inviting residents to participate in the installation through adding to it, the work raises questions about art and architectural practice and their relation to the production of public space.

The expanded field of spatial production is also the location of **Ursula Biemann**'s work, an artist who works between geography and art in the video format. Her work engages critically with a range of disciplines and fields of knowledge, including feminist and post-colonial theory, ethnography, cultural and media studies and urbanism. Projects such as *Sahara Chronicle* (2006–9) and *Remote Sensing* (2001) document spatial agency in unfamiliar contexts, whether it is the sub-Saharan migrations across Africa towards Europe or the territories of the global sex trade. Biemann spatialises the territorial and human relations in these situations, which are intricately linked to, and influenced by, the social and economic consequences of globalisation.

Other artists also work in fruitful collaborations with architects, such as the group of women artists and architects, **Taking Place**. Their work looks to define what a specifically feminist spatial practice could be. They have organised a number of events, from small gatherings to larger events hosted at institutions, involving students and members of the public. The events are a forum in which to discuss ideas and projects, as well as a chance for temporary transformations of space, for example lectures and talks occur in stairwells whereas lecture theatres become places to cook and impromptu performances are organised. Whether coming from an artistic or architectural point of view, Taking Place's practice is about conceptualising space as fluid, social and political, and as their name suggests, they start from the premise that 'places can simply be taken'.

Other collaborations between artists and architects include formal practices, such as muf (p.175) and public works, (p.190) or informal networks that come together around specific projects, such as those initiated by atelier d'architecture autogérée, (p.105) Crimson, (p.135) Exyzt, (p.145) Raumlabor (p.191) and others. Architectural practices such as Estudio Teddy Cruz (p.144) and collectives such as Stalker/Osservatorio Nomade (p.200) often work in collaboration with artists, whilst certain artists and artistic movements have had a large and direct impact on the practice of architecture, for example the Situationists, (p.178) who have defined new directions for architecture that emphasise the everyday and the relationships between politics and cultural practice.

Basualdo, C. et al. (2004) *Thomas Hirschhorn*, London: Phaidon.

Lundstrom, J. et al. (2008) *Ursula Biemann: Mission Reports – Artistic Practice in the Field – Video Works 1998–2008*, Bristol: Arnolfini Gallery Ltd.

Potrč, M. (2004) *Urgent Architecture*, Pap/DVD, LA: Palm Beach Institute of Contemporary Art.

Rakowitz, M. (2000) 'Parasite', in Hughes, J. and Sadler, S. (eds) *Non-plan: Essays on Freedom, Participation and Change in Modern Architecture and Urbanism*, Oxford: Architectural Press, pp. 232–235.

Thompson, N. (2004) *The Interventionists: Users' Manual for the Creative Disruption of Everyday Life*, Cambridge, MA: MIT Press.

Arup Associates

London, UK, 1963–1985
www.arupassociates.com

Ove Arup (1895–1988) founded Arup and Partners in 1946 as a firm of consultant structural engineers, based in London. Unhappy with the fragmented way in which the construction industry operated, Arup put forward his idea of 'total design'. It was a vision of a research oriented, experimental and above all collaborative endeavour, which would see architects and engineers working together on a project from its inception. Arup's education influenced this thinking, with a first degree in philosophy and mathematics followed by a brief period of study in architecture and finally a switch to a second degree in engineering.

In 1963 Arup Associates, headed by architect Philip Dowson, was founded as a multi-disciplinary firm that combined architectural, surveying and engineering services. The working method developed at the practice was necessary as it foresaw the increasingly intricate nature of modern construction and new technologies, which could not be mastered by individual professions and so required a new organisational structure based on collaboration and co-operation. Best known for a sequence of buildings in the 1970s that showed a clear integration of structure, skin and services, Arup Associates formed the blueprint for a new type of relationship between architects and engineers that stressed the mutual reliance of the two disciplines and proposed radical changes to the education and training of both architects and engineers. Despite Arup's pioneering example of the benefits of integration, the building trade and its related professions remain largely fragmented.

Brawne, M. (1983) *Arup Associates: The Biography of an Architectural Practice*, London: Lund Humphries.

Asiye eTafuleni

Durban, South Africa, 2008–
www.aet.org.za

Asiye eTafuleni is a non-governmental organisation (NGO) set up to support informal traders, and others who use public spaces for their work, by providing design and development expertise. Although street traders may have had market stalls or pitches for many years, selling a range of goods – from foodstuffs to *muthi* (traditional medicine), from clothing to electronics – they are often at a disadvantage because of their poor understanding of urban development norms that hold sway. This has made it difficult for them to stand up for themselves in the face of competition, to participate in consultation processes with city officials on equal terms, or – sometimes – to even be taken seriously. This NGO seeks to build capacity within the informal sector, so that the often fragile livelihoods of informal entrepreneurs can be buttressed by better knowledge.

Established in 2008, Asiye eTafuleni ('bring it to the table' in Zulu) emerged out of the ongoing involvement of officials, urbanists and activists working on the Warwick Junction Project, an informal market complex at the heart of Durban, South Africa. Co-founders Richard Dobson and Patrick Ndlovu saw that when traders were sympathetically consulted as part of the development processes taking place, they were able to positively engage and contribute to improved outcomes for all concerned. The NGO has sought to build on this experience, promoting a more responsive and inclusive context for development.

Better knowledge of the system, as well as knowledge of alternatives and a greater level of organising amongst the informal traders, were key steps to achieving a more equitable distribution of power, and fairer commercial opportunities. For Asiye eTafuleni, this has reinforced a belief in the principles of consultation and participation, and a concern to equip traders with the know-how and support they need. The NGO serves as a learning hub for entrepreneurs and researchers interested in local urban development and planning issues in relation to South Africa's informal economy. An innovative element of the organisation's profile is its street credibility, which has enabled multi-stakeholder engagement and

Street traders in Durban. From the publication, *Working in Warwick: Including Street Traders in Urban Plans*. Ph: Dennis Gilbert

contributed to the team's diversity: a mix of architects, social scientists, and informal traders. This mix provides a balanced and grassroots platform for any type of urban intervention.

To date, Asiye eTafuleni's main area of operation has been Warwick Junction, Durban's primary transport node, which on an average day accommodates 460,000 commuters and at least 5,000 street traders. Project work includes developing appropriate infrastructure for traders, spatial upgrading projects, and an inner city cardboard recycling project linked to tourism opportunities. The NGO has also recently been involved in evaluating responses by city officials to a proposed shopping mall – motivated by street traders whose livelihoods would be threatened by the proposed development, and who have subsequently launched a lawsuit with the assistance of the Legal Resources Centre. The case involves the street traders who work on the fringes of Warwick market, including bovine head cookers, barrow operators, and live poultry sellers, and seeks to establish their right to conduct trade in a manner that suits long established traditions and values rather than the standards associated with the formal economy.

A richly illustrated book co-authored by Richard Dobson, *Working in Warwick*, brings narratives of occupation – of the everyday practices of the street traders and their ways of interpreting and contributing to the city – into dialogue with urban policy and the debates around economic development.

Dobson, R. and Skinner, C. (2009) *Working in Warwick*, Durban: University of KwaZulu-Natal.

Atelier Bow-wow
Tokyo, Japan, 1992–
www.bow-wow.jp
Established in Tokyo in 1992 by Yoshiharu Tsukmoto and Momoyo Kaijima, Atelier Bow-wow's work includes buildings, research and art practice. Starting by documenting the unique urban reality of Tokyo, Atelier Bow-wow produced a number of publications that took the form of guidebooks, introducing the reader to the accidental, ad-hoc nature of the urban landscape. *Pet Architecture* documented tiny buildings that fill the cracks of the city and are always customised by the user, whilst *Made in Tokyo* showed instances of hybrid, cross programmed building types with unlikely juxtapositions, the result of the extreme pressure on land.

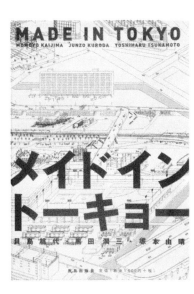

Atelier Bow-wow's approach to architecture is informed by this research and what they have termed 'micro public space', in which they attempt to recreate some of the behaviours and meetings that occur in the city in gallery installations and in their buildings. They do this through the deployment of customised urban furniture that encourages active user participation, such as their 'Furnicycle' designed for the 2002 Shanghai Biennale or the design of public kitchens and vegetable kiosks. In both their exhibition design and the design of buildings, Atelier Bow-wow construct situations rather than objects, design processes that can result in chance meetings and leaving room for users to adapt and appropriate space.

Kaijima, M., Momoyo, J. and Tsukamoto, Y. (2001) *Made in Tokyo*, Tokyo: Kajima Institute.

atelier d'architecture autogérée
Paris, France, 2001–
www.urbantactics.org
atelier d'architecture autogérée (aaa – Studio for Self-managed Architecture) is a practice based in Paris co-founded by architects, Constantin Petcou and Doina Petrescu in 2001. aaa acts as a platform for collaborative research and action on the city and much of their work is carried out with other specialists, artists, researchers and institutional partners such as universities, arts organisations and NGOs, as well as the eventual users of their spaces. Whilst the founding members of aaa remain, the practice operates as a collaborative network that forms around each project.

aaa's projects are experiments in the temporary reuse of leftover urban space through the setting up of an enabling infrastructure that is slowly taken over by local residents and transformed into self-managed spaces. Ecobox consists of a series of gardens made from recycled materials, in the La Chapelle area of northern Paris, for which they also produced a number of mobile furniture elements working with students and designers. These included cooking, media and workshop stations that can be moved around and out of the garden as needed. Over the five years (2001–6) that aaa were actively involved in its day-to-day running, Ecobox became a venue for cultural, social and economic activities, initiated by them and local residents; for example, Stalker/Osservatorio Nomade (p.200) organised a workshop and installation as part of their collaborative project 'Via Egnatia', whilst a group of residents ran a monthly market and others set up a small food business making use of the cooking module. It is at the level of this activation of social interest and action that aaa's practice is most successful; they act as curators and enablers whilst at the same time leaving enough room

Passage 56 community garden. Ph: aaa

for others to take over responsibility, to the point that residents campaigned for another site when the garden was finally evicted from its original location.

Their most recent project, Passage 56, is the transformation of a disused passageway, located in a Parisian neighbourhood noted for its density and cultural diversity, into a productive garden that minimises its ecological footprint through recycling, composting and use of solar panels. By means of a continuous participative process, the project was drawn up and constructed with minimal cost, using recycled materials collected by the residents themselves. It was carried out in collaboration with a local organisation running youth training programmes in eco-construction and was partly commissioned by local government, fulfilling one of aaa's stated aims to influence local policy towards the reuse and development of leftover spaces in the city. The Passage 56 project reinforces the idea that public space does not need to culminate in the idea of the physical construction of a designed object but is continuously developed as a social, cultural and political production. Here, the client does not precede the intervention but gradually emerges in the group of people who manage it, offering proof that everyday ecological practice can transform present spatial and social relations in a dense and culturally diverse metropolis.

atelier d'architecture autogérée (2011) *Making Rhizome: A Micro-political Practice of Architecture*, Paris: aaa.

Atelier-3/Rural Architecture Studio
Thao Village, Taiwan, 1999–
www.atelier-3.com
Atelier-3 was founded by the Taiwanese architect, Hsieh Ying-Chun, who moved his studio to rural Taiwan in the wake of the devastating earthquake of 1999. The earthquake prompted a complete rethink of architecture and construction in Taiwan and resulted in the New School Movement, which began with the rebuilding of destroyed schools using vernacular techniques. Especially affected by the earthquake were remote aboriginal communities who were living in ecologically

106

Mutual Subject – What is to be Done, Venice Architectural Biennale 2000. Ph: Julian Stallabrass

sensitive areas with a rich cultural heritage that was already under threat. These communities required help beyond the standard model of temporary disaster-relief construction. Atelier-3 proposed an architecture that was long-lasting, ecologically sound, culturally sensitive and could be built at a fraction of the cost, typically 25–50 percent below the standard. Atelier-3 developed a model for 'collaborative construction', a co-operative structure for building adapted to specific contexts; for example construction only happened in periods where farming pressures were at their lowest and surplus labour was available. They combined traditional construction techniques with 'new' technology, such as bamboo screens covered in a thin layer of cement, to make spaces appropriate to the communities involved.

In 2004, Hsieh Ying-Chun set up Rural Architecture Studio which carries out similar work in rural China, including work on the reconstruction effort following the Sichuan earthquake. Their low-key collaborative approach to architecture uses technology in a holistic way, paying attention to the preservation of environmental and cultural heritage as well as creating a sense of community. The buildings, built collectively, become guarantees for the banks allowing communities in both China and Taiwan to join a mainstream economic system that was previously completely inaccessible to them.

For Hsieh Ying-Chun, the designing of details is an act of agency, since it 'represents a real opportunity to consider and intervene in some of the most basic social and environmental issues'. He and his co-workers re-consider and re-look at commonly used construction techniques and adjust them so that they are cheaper and easier to use. Sometimes this is about simple things such as the replacing of welded constructions with screws, or of developing a system of construction that minimises the use of high-tech patented connections that are extremely expensive. This enables a DIY, 'open-architecture' which does not require the need for specialised tools or knowledge, making it possible for those with little or no prior knowledge to participate fully. But this is not where his involvement stops. In one project, he helped the local community to set up a factory in their village which now produces prefabricated steel elements that can be sold to other communities that are also in need of low-cost housing.

Ying-Chun, H. (2006) *Sustainable Construction in Community*. <http://www.naturehouse.org/english/suscom_en.pdf> (accessed 2 Sept 2009).

Bauhäusle
Stuttgart, Germany, 1981–1983
www.bauhaeusle.de
Bauhäusle is a self-build student housing scheme at the Technical University of Stuttgart. It was designed and built by students, between 1981 and 1983, under the supervision of Peter Sulzer and Peter Hübner. A number of factors came together allowing the project to occur, including strong support from the University and an

Bauhäusle exterior view. Ph: Peter Blundell Jones

A kitchen in Bauhäusle. Ph: Peter Blundell Jones

existing long running first year project where students designed their own rooms. The lack of accommodation in Stuttgart that year prompted the students to ask whether they could build their designs.

The project, which formed part of the teaching curriculum, consists of one building providing communal uses with a series of smaller buildings around it, containing three to four bedrooms each. Overall, the Bauhäusle provides space for around 30 students in rooms of 15 to 28 sq m. The buildings were constructed using the Walter Segal (p.196) timber self-build method. He was invited to teach and to help adapt the system to the specifications of the materials available in Germany, most of which were donated by the building industry. Splitting the project into a series of smaller blocks meant splitting the responsibility, with different members of staff overseeing each part. This gave a very different character to each of the blocks, but crucially for the students, also meant that negotiation and compromise had to occur at the interface where buildings met. The full participation of students in the design of their own buildings meant that they experienced the advantages of involving users in the design of their buildings, as well as learning hands-on the design, technical and constructional aspects involved. Spatial agency here is found in the process of learning through doing, the emphasis is on practical knowledge gained through experience rather than simply a professionalised or academic knowledge.

Although there are typically few to no architecture students living in the building, its repairs are still carried out by its residents and when the original permission of fifteen years ran out, the current students petitioned to extend it, with one of the original students helping out with the building permit. With its tongue-in-cheek name of 'Little Bauhaus', the project reveals how self-build methods and participation give users a sense of ownership. The two teacher/architects took a supervisory role, letting the students make their own decisions and mistakes. This resulted in the Bauhäusle having a communal atmosphere that has persisted long after the original student-builders left, and it became a precedent for many such projects in Germany, such as the ESA in Kaiserslautern or the Baufrösche, a building project using adobe in Kassel.

Sulzer, P. (2005) 'Notes on Participation', in P. Blundell-Jones, D. Petrescu and J. Till (eds) *Architecture and Participation*, London: Routledge.

Bauhütten

Berlin, Germany, 1920–1930

These were socialist building trades unions based in Germany in the 1920s, who referred to themselves as public welfare constructors. Organised co-operatively, they were led by the architect, Martin Wagner (1885–1957), who brought them together nationally. Mostly involved in building housing to address the acute housing shortage in Germany at the time, the Bauhütten adopted new building methods and materials under the influence of Wagner. They were thus popular with many of the radical architects of the time.

Wagner, M. 'Path and Goal', in Kaes, A., Jay, M. and Dimendberg, E. (eds) (1995) *The Weimar Republic Sourcebook*, Berkeley: University of California Press, pp. 460–462.

Baupiloten

Berlin, Germany, 2003–
www.baupiloten.com

Established in 2003, Baupiloten is a collaboration between Technical University Berlin and Susanne Hofmann Architekten, which allows architectural students in their fourth and fifth years to be involved in building projects. Set up in the context of a growing call within the German architectural profession for students to be more prepared for professional life, the aim of the studio is to combine education, practice and research. Susanne Hofmann Architekten are responsible for finding prospective projects and clients, whilst the changing group of students design, manage and implement the design. Supervision and support is provided by the architectural practice whose principal, Susanne Hofmann, is also part of the faculty at TU Berlin.

Kindergarten Taka-Tuka-Land, Berlin

The majority of the projects carried out by Baupiloten are for schools or kindergartens for which there is an ongoing programme of restructuring within the German school system. With schools staying open all day and kindergartens taking on explicit teaching roles, existing buildings need to be adapted. Unlike the design/build studios that are popular in the US, such as the Yale Building Project (p.213) or Rural Studio, (p.193) Baupiloten do not construct their designs, instead using professional builders. Students work in parallel on individual designs for a few weeks, placing an emphasis on involving children through workshops, drawing and modelling sessions. A final design is agreed upon collaboratively by combining elements from the various

Refurbishment of Erika-Mann Elementary School, Berlin. Ph: Jan Bitter

designs; afterwards, each student takes responsibility for a certain part of the project with Hofmann acting as mediator.

Baupiloten is one of a few examples in architectural education where students are able to work on a building project from design through to completion. The organisational structure of a separate design firm working alongside the university allows questions of liability to be handled separately, making Baupiloten a viable option for institutional clients.

Hofmann, S. (2004) 'The Baupiloten: Building Bridges Between Education, Practice and Research', *Architectural Research Quarterly*, 8(2): 114–127.

Bo Bardi, Lina
1914–1992
www.institutobobardi.com.br
Lina Bo Bardi was an Italian architect whose highly diverse and important work remains largely unknown outside of her adopted home of Brazil. This oversight is certainly due to her gender but is compounded by her positioning at the periphery of the West. Although influenced by modernist architecture, her work stands apart from it, having a playfulness and diversity not found in the work of her more famous counterparts. Unlike them Bo Bardi insisted on addressing the socio-political context of her work and rejected their grand gestures. Her oeuvre does not have a particular style and although she has built two large cultural projects, much of her work dealt with poorer communities and historic preservation. Even her heritage work is shot through with social concern: the case she made for the restoration was not about the preservation of significant historic architecture, but the 'preservation of the city's *popular soul*.' Her work is characterized by the celebration of the everyday and the ordinary, an interest that carried through from her buildings to her work as a furniture and jewellery designer, on film and theatre sets, as well as a curator and journalist.

She designed her most famous project, the Museum of Art of São Paulo, without resort to standard architectural drawing preferring instead an informal style that combined watercolours, collage and a creative way of drawing that brought the designs to life, always inhabiting her drawings with people and plants. Her other main civic building, the SESC leisure centre in São Paolo, is a testament to her desire to create democratic spaces. A conversion of an old factory, she did not try to hide the building's origins, as it spoke of its location in a working class area of Brazil. Bo Bardi's design for the SESC leisure centre created a space that combined the ambitions of both the Pompidou Centre as a free and open cultural centre and of the Barbican Centre in London as a cultural landscape.

Her work was enriched by her enthusiastic involvement in the everyday and cultural life of Brazil, she was an activist, ran a popular cultural centre which was

SESC Pompeia Leisure Centre. Ph: Patrick Skingley

closed down by the government, and also taught and wrote about architecture and the arts.

Oliveira, O. (2006) *Subtle Substances of the Architecture of Lina Bo Bardi*, Barcelona: Gustavo Gili.

Bouchain, Patrick
1946–

Patrick Bouchain is a French architect who designs situations as much as he designs buildings, taking on a number of other roles including that of developer, political advisor, site manager, fundraiser and performer. Most of his projects begin with establishing a network of interested people, collaborators, residents, local government officials, neighbourhood groups etc. Once this network is in place, the site is activated socially, usually through opening a small space that functions as a restaurant, site office and consultation area where passers-by and interested people can find out about the project, give their views, or simply watch a film. This initial phase creates relationships between the architects, builders and local people and creates uses for the site before anything permanent is built. Through such an approach Bouchain's projects are sustainable in the real sense of the word, ensuring that what is finally constructed is appropriate and useful for the site and makes good use of resources. Many of the projects are on an urban scale and include the reuse and refurbishments of old industrial buildings through minimum intervention.

With a background in theatre, circuses and urban festivals Bouchain approaches architecture as event, creating maximum impact through a mixture of illusion, clever use of materials and innovative programming. Collaborations play a large role in this type of alternative urban planning, Bouchain has worked with the artists Daniel Buren and Claes Oldenburg. On another occasion he invited Malian builders to construct an acoustic barrier from oil barrels; wherever possible, his projects employ a mixture of specialists rather than a single contractor.

Bouchain curated the 2006 French pavilion at the Venice Architecture Biennale; rather than following the standard exhibition format of words and images, the social nature of architecture was emphasised. The group Exyzt (p.145) were invited to inhabit the pavilion, constructing a scaffold-like structure inside and living in it for the duration of the biennale. The space included DJ and design studio, kitchen and sauna, underlining the fact of architecture as occupation rather than built object. This alternative approach foregrounds the role of informal networks, social space, and processes in architecture and has much in common with other European practices such as atelier d'architecture autogérée, (p.105) City Mine(d), (p.121) Raumlabor (p.191) and of course the group that Bouchain brought to international attention, Exyzt.

The French pavilion at the Venice Architecture Biennale (2006) curated by Patrick Bouchain. Ph: Florian Kossak

Bouchain, P. and Chaise, I. (2009) 'Interview: Patrick Bouchain', *Blueprint (London)*, 285: 39, 41–42.

Brodsky, Alexander

1955–
www.brod.it
Alexander Brodsky (1955–) is an architect and former member of the group **Paper Architects** operating in Russia in the 1980s, whose work centred around a refusal to take part in state sponsored architectural production of low-quality, standardised buildings. During the 1990s Brodsky produced contemporary art, moving to New York in 1996. In 2000 he returned to Russia to finally practice freely as an architect, working out of a small office in Moscow State Museum, an indication of the regard in which he is now held in his home country. Brodsky's work is characterised by a concern with traditional building, using local materials to produce an architecture that celebrates Russian

heritage whilst at the same time acting as a critique of the unregulated and corrupt building industry.

His work thus stands in contrast to the untethered development occurring in Russia, in particular in Moscow and in the threat to St Petersburg's world heritage status. Whilst Western 'star architects' are building controversial projects, Brodsky's architecture remains restrained, blurring the line between art and architecture. He has built a pavilion made completely out of discarded timber window frames from industrial warehouses, a monument to the wanton destruction of Russia's industrial heritage as well as a celebration of Russian tradition – the pavilion was designed for vodka drinking ceremonies. He has built another pavilion in the middle of a frozen lake with ice cubes, whilst his very first commission in 2002 was for a restaurant. Built on wooden stilts by a reservoir, the whole structure is tilted at an angle of 95° and infilled with wood and plastic. Brodsky's architecture combines local and reused materials to produce buildings that are both traditional and modern, his sombre buildings acting as a reminder of the fragility of the city. Although aesthetically very different, his reuse of old windows, bits of timber and glass to make new structures is similar to the approach taken by the Dutch practice, 2012 Architecten, (p.87) of recycling materials without reprocessing.

Nesbitt, L. (2003) *Brodsky and Utkin: The Complete Works*, 2nd edn, New York: Princeton Architectural Press.

Bureau d'études

Paris, France, 1998–
bureaudetudes.org
Bureau d'études are a Paris-based conceptual art group founded in 1998 by Léonore Bonaccini and Xavier Fourt. They produce maps that depict relationships and ownership ties between, for example, transnational organisations or the European Union. The maps typically reveal links between think tanks, financial firms, regulatory bodies, intelligence agencies, media groups, networks of consumer distribution, weapon makers, and satellite companies. Other maps explore anarchist positions, dissident knowledge producers, squats, and charts that relate to various forms of non-capitalist exchange. In their practice, knowledge becomes inherently political and the question of access to knowledge becomes paramount.

Refuse the Biopolice. Collective space with a wall map about surveillance and prison complex in Europe during the No border camp. Strasbourg, France, 2002. Courtesy Bureau d'études

They collaborate with the unemployed, squatter communities and the *sans papiers* [undocumented migrants] through their self-organised space in Strasbourg, the *Syndicat Potentiel*, which operates within a 'free economy', as well as the *Université Tangente* which is a project for autonomous knowledge production. These projects were set up in frustration with the art world in order to produce and disseminate work collectively, outside the institutional space of the art gallery.

Maps of the French State and its Relation to Living Bodies. This work was first shown in France in an agricultural context and is presented here in an exhibition on cartography. Zagreb, Croatia, 2007. Courtesy Bureau d'études

Bureau d'études' collaborations with the critic Brian Holmes (p.158) have produced an ongoing discourse on the possibilities of using cartography as part of social movements. Holmes describes their maps as 'subjective shocks' that through showing a totalitarian vision also highlight its weaknesses. To this end, Bureau d'études give free access to highly specialised

knowledge by producing their maps cheaply in large print runs for specific activist events, such as the European Social Forum and the No Border camp. Their maps can therefore be seen as tools of spatial agency, promoting an understanding of the highly complex workings of advanced capitalism, a necessary step towards imagining a counter-position and effective resistance. They have influenced a growing number of artists, architects and geographers who are exploring the potential of mapping as an emancipatory tool, including Hackitectura (p.153) and Counter Cartographies Collective, amongst others.

Holmes, B. (2003) 'Maps for the Outside: Bureau d'études, or the Revenge of the Concept', in U. Biemann (ed) *Geography and the Politics of Mobility*, Koln: Generali Foundation.

Canadian Centre for Architecture
Montreal, Canada, 1979–
www.cca.qc.ca

The CCA is an extensive archive and research centre that aims to promote the importance of architecture to the general public. It was founded in 1979 by Phyllis Lambert, an architect and philanthropist who has championed modern architecture, being famously involved in appointing Mies van der Rohe to design the Seagram building. More importantly perhaps, she has also campaigned against the demolition of historic buildings, organised housing co-operatives and lobbied against development schemes in her native city of Montreal. The CCA is housed in a building that Lambert saved from demolition and its extension was partly designed by her. The archive is based around her own personal collection of architectural books, drawings and pamphlets. The stated aim of the CCA, to build public awareness of the role of architecture in society and of promoting scholarly research in architecture, are also a direct result of Lambert's vision who has been its director since its inception until 1999.

The centre holds numerous exhibitions and educational programs, disseminating the work locally in Montreal as well as internationally through its accompanying catalogues. Recent exhibitions have included, Sorry Out of Gas, which looked at architectural responses to the 1973 oil crisis, as well as Sense of the City, which critically interprets the city through the senses. An onsite study centre funds visiting scholars who would benefit from the CCA archives on individual architects, their prints and drawings, as well as artefacts such as a collection on kindergarten toys. The centre also hosts public lectures and seminars, and organises outreach programs for local schools in the form of workshops and events. Spatial agency is thus found here through pedagogical means in the free and democratic access to highly specialised knowledge. It is also found in the way the institution itself has helped to turn around a deprived area of Montreal.

Early stage of the Actions exhibition and book project (2008)

Elfin Saddle play in the galleries at the 20th anniversary of the CCA (2009)

Borasi, G. and Zardini, M. (eds) (2007) *Sorry Out of Gas: Architecture's Response to the 1973 Oil Crisis*, Montreal: Canadian Centre for Architecture.

Caracas Think Tank

Caracas, Venezuela, 1993–
www.u-tt.com
Caracas Think Tank is an NGO for urban cultural research established in 1993 by Alfredo Brillembourg

and later joined by Hubert Klumpner. It is supported and partly funded by the Urban Think Tank (UTT), which consists of architects, civil engineers, environmental planners and communication specialists engaged in city policies and the discussion of controversial issues of city development in Venezuela. UTT and the Caracas Think Tank received widespread international recognition between 2002 and 2004 for the research project 'Caracas Case' (funded by the Federal German Government through the Federal Cultural Foundation) and published as *Informal City: Caracas Case*.

'Caracas Case' investigated the 'deep-rooted changes of urban realities, which are visible in the explosive growth of mega cities' with the help of invited consultants from 15 countries who engaged in the visioning of new, pioneering and alternative design ideas for the city of Caracas. This was set up in response to the incapacity of traditional planning methods to address the needs of the city's inhabitants. The book examines Caracas as well as other Latin American cities in terms of their 'barrios', 'shantytowns', or 'slums'. It assesses their validity as an architectural phenomenon in their own right and discusses these areas in terms of their own socio-economic environment. In this it differs from the official planning strategies of viewing these areas as illegal and also from the perspective of NGOs and development agencies, who view them as places for the disenfranchised. In this context it asks whether state-sponsored macro strategies might have a larger impact than micro-enterprise, market-based, small-scale solutions, and investigates which approach leads to greater socio-spatial inequalities. The publication aims to be a 'handbook of informal urban and cultural practice' and makes the case for the application of the research to other Latin American as well as African and Asian cities.

Caracas Think Tank's approach does not seek to completely rebuild and replace the informal city, but instead proposes an 'urban acupuncture' consisting of small projects such as composting toilets, public spaces and new routes inserted into the existing fabric. In their economic approach they expand the role of the architect, initially raising their own money to start a project, and later with enough interest, supplementing it with governmental funding. Here the architect's agency is that of an entrepreneur requiring a similar approach of taking initiative but also of taking risk.

Brillembourg, A., Feireiss, K. and Klumpner, H. (eds) (2005) *Informal City: Caracas Case*, Munich: Prestel.

The Center for Land Use Interpretation
Culver City, USA, 1994–
www.clui.org

Bus tour by CLUI. Ph: CLUI

The Center for Land Use Interpretation (CLUI) is a research organisation established in 1994 in Culver City, Los Angeles by Matthew Coolidge. The largely volunteer run, non-profit organisation is funded through government and private arts grants with the aim of examining the relationships between the physical landscape and its human occupation. This is carried out through an investigation into different land uses, their ownership, and the economic and cultural value associated with parts of the landscape. The work is disseminated through a variety of means including the

setting up of databases, publications, exhibitions, lectures and residency programmes, as well as the more unusual format of bus tours and the use of placards and information kiosks. Through these different methods, CLUI raise awareness and stimulate debate about the physical landscape in the US, from vast working factories to abandoned military facilities or sewage treatment works and waste incinerators. Their research uncovers the variety of unusual and often environmentally catastrophic uses that support the lifestyle that we are used to in developed countries.

CLUI's ongoing work includes the Land Use Database, a collection of material including a photographic archive on what they have termed 'exemplary' sites in the US, parts of which are available online. They are also developing the American Land Museum, which will comprise a series of sites across the US, each dealing with its own region and becoming a curatorial hub for various related programmes. CLUI prefer to present themselves as an educational organisation, taking on the role of the impartial expert relating an 'objective' view, a wry stance that allows them to highlight the problematic relationships between the economy and land-use in the US.

Coolidge, M. and Simons, S. (eds) (2006) *Overlook: Exploring the Internal Fringes of America with the Center for Land Use Interpretation*, New York: Metropolis Books.

Center for Urban Pedagogy
New York, USA, 1997–
anothercupdevelopment.org
Center for Urban Pedagogy (CUP) is a non-profit organisation based in Brooklyn, New York. It started as a loose grouping of people interested in how the city works, and who all believed that in order for a democracy to function the needs and desires of citizens have to be engaged. Their name speaks of their working method, they devise pedagogical projects for schools, young people and also for the community at large in order to allow people to intervene meaningfully within their locality. Through bringing together these diverse people CUP not only build interesting projects such as exhibitions or school curricula, but they also affect the work and thinking of the professionals through exposing them to a range of knowledges and issues that they may not normally come into contact with.

Tenant's Organisation Meeting: Launch event for Making Policy Public (2009). Ph: Rosten Woo

Their projects ask basic questions about the city such as, 'where does the water come from?' or 'where does the garbage go to?' Through these seemingly naïve questions CUP engage young people in the everyday politics of the city, for example their investigation into New York's waste disposal was a highly politicised exercise since the main landfill site of Fresh Kills had just been closed down after years of controversy. CUP also publish a series of fold-out posters that tackle various public policy issues and try to make legible highly complex and inter-related phenomena through graphic design. Recent issues include 'Social Security Risk Machine' and 'The Cargo Chain', which reveal how the local long-shore workers fit inside a highly complex and globalised shipping network.

CUP Workshop on Affordable Housing (2007). Ph: David Powell

CUP's role in these projects varies from enabling to actual intervention. As facilitators, they bring people who are interested in and knowledgeable about certain issues together with graphic designers or artists, who then visualise these questions, concerns or problems. As agents, CUP actively intervene in their environment,

working in a bottom-up manner in collaboration with others to effect transformation of existing conditions.

Menking, W. (2009) 'The Center for Urban Pedagogy (CUP)', *Architectural Design*, 79(1): 76–77.

Centre for Alternative Technology
Machynlleth, Wales, UK, 1973–
www.cat.org.uk

Located in a disused slate quarry in Wales, the Centre for Alternative Technology (CAT) started as an experimental community working towards self-sufficiency and later became an educational and information resource centre open to the public. Founded by Gerard Morgan-Grenville in 1973, CAT lead by example, promoting a lifestyle away from urban centres and without a dependence on industrial production systems. Initially twenty people lived on site communally with collective decision making. The volunteers worked hard to transform the quarry into a demonstration centre for alternative technologies and ecological lifestyles, setting up a cyclical system where waste from people, animals and crops is recycled using composting toilets and reed beds.

Community meal in the early days of the centre

Funded by donations from Morgan-Grenville's contacts, companies and manufacturers provided their products to be displayed and demonstrated in use. Wind turbines, solar panels, and innovative building products such as spray-on insulation were all used and experimented with. But as interest in environmental issues waned over the years CAT had to adapt itself. The changing political climate, especially in the highly consumerist society of the 1980s, meant that CAT had to adapt itself. It remained one of a very few initiatives still working on

Caravans sprayed with insulation serving as site offices. Courtesy CAT

environmental issues, but the counter-cultural dream that had given birth to the centre was replaced with a more pragmatic commercial and educational aim, with CAT transforming itself into a study centre and tourist attraction that provided a more stable income stream.

Today it comprises an educational centre running residential courses on eco-construction methods, renewable energy and organic food production, as well as the visitor centre giving information on sustainable living and green technologies. From its inception CAT has researched experimental construction and energy generation techniques, constructing a number of windmills, and utilising active and passive solar systems. The site is also home to one of Walter Segal's (p.196) self-build houses as an example of a low impact construction method. In its over thirty-year history, CAT has acted as spatial agent, consistently advocating sustainable development through practical example. It uses the proceeds from its various profit-making ventures to continue researching and to maintain its innovative buildings. In 1994 a graduate school was set up offering Masters and Doctoral teaching in the environmental sciences as well as a professional diploma in architecture. The school, which is affiliated to the University of East London, moved from its London location to Wales in 2000, providing opportunities for students to study at the centre.

Centre for Alternative Technology (1995) *Crazy Idealists?*, Machynlleth: Centre for Alternative Technology.

Centri Sociali
Italy, 1970–
www.leoncavallo.org

Centri Sociali flourished during the 1980s and 1990s in Italy. Born out of the squatter (p.199) and Autonomia movements, they are often self-organised (p.197) spaces which in some instances have become centres for urban counter-culture and for a radical critique of representative democracy. Many are set up as autonomous spaces, are run co-operatively and often experiment with collective forms of decision making.

The occupied buildings are usually located in the suburbs of large Italian cities and they provide spaces for collective living and a myriad of cultural, social and political activities. Established in response to increasing gentrification and a lack of affordable housing, the squatted centres provide a space that is liberated from capitalist modes of production but is also highly precarious; some centres have a semi-legal status, whilst others are regularly closed down by the authorities.

There is no clear set of activities that occur in the Centri Sociali; some have community services such as Italian language courses for migrants, drugs counsel-ling or day centres for older people, whilst others are centres for a wide variety of political campaigns, including criminal justice reform, migrant rights and anti-racism campaigns. They are also cultural spaces, being the foci of the Italian hip hop scene and other types of underground music, as well as hosting exhibitions, theatre, radio broadcasts, hacklabs and producing alternative publications. (p.90) Members of Centri Sociali usually participate in a number of loose networks and activities, and whilst the number of centres has declined recently as more are forcefully closed down, they are still regarded as important sites of activism and laboratories for cultural and political experimentation. Since the early 2000s right-wing social centres have also developed, highlighting the fact that self-organised (p.197) processes in themselves are not emancipatory, and are not the exclusive territory of the left, but are characterised instead by the political affiliations of those involved.

One of the longest running social centres is the **Centro Sociale Leoncavallo** in Milan, which was created in 1975 through the squatting of an abandoned factory located in an area of social housing, where radical left groups came together to create a self-managed space that was organised without internal hierarchies. The aim for the centre was to provide a collective space for the community and as such it incorporated a number of services, such as nurseries, counselling, exhibition spaces and communal meeting rooms. The fortunes of Leoncavallo have changed over the years but it has now achieved legal status with some inevitable forms of institutionalisation.

Wright, S. (2007) 'A Window Onto Italy's Social Centres [Articles and Interview]', *Affinities: A Journal of Radical Theory, Culture and Action*, 1(1): 12–20. <http://journals.sfu.ca/affinities/index.php/ affinities/article/view/4/46> (accessed 4 March 2010).

Chora

London, UK, 1993–
www.chora.org
Chora is the name of a research office founded in London by Raoul Bunschoten in 1993 and also of a parallel architectural office established in 1994. Combining research and practice, they have developed a methodology for working in complex urban and regional situations and have worked on projects across Europe and in the Far East. Their methodology is grounded in research, consisting of a four-step process that comprises of: a database, prototypes, scenario games, and action plans. The database collects relevant information on people, places and organisations that are somehow related to a project, whilst prototypes are

designs or organisational structures that address the issues raised in the database. Scenario games are a way of simulating and testing the different conditions in which the prototypes may function. Often taking the form of board games these are notable for the wide variety of people that Chora manage to gather together to play the games, groups of people that have overlapping and conflicting interests: residents, policy-makers, government officials, local businesses and industrialists amongst others. Here the game functions as both a platform for testing ideas and situations whilst also being a mediator, bringing together these disparate yet linked groups. Finally the action plan is a strategy for implementing the chosen prototypes and scenarios. To complement their working method, Chora have developed a complex language of diagrams and symbols that takes the large amounts of specific information gathered for each project and makes abstract notations that allow comparison and manipulation of the material. Currently Chora are also working on a project entitled Urban Gallery, a web-based tool for their methodology that is designed as an interactive environment for those working together on a long-term project.

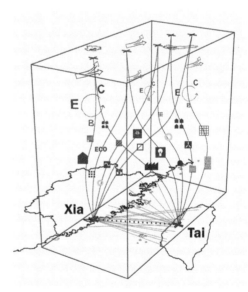

Taiwan Strait Climate Change Incubator, focusing on the cross strait relationship between the two cities of Taichung and Xiamen. Image: Chora

This method allows Chora to work at a number of different scales, drawing out unexpected and hidden links between the smallest of local details and transnational or global forces, highlighting how these may impact on each other. They see the role of the architect as that of an urban curator, a concept that Chora have developed alongside the artist **Jeanne van Heeswijk**. Rather than designing objects and buildings, Chora's urban curator designs processes, interactions and organisational structures, a way of working that allows the architect to engage a wide variety of people and to create urban strategies that can address the dynamic nature of cities.

Scenario game in progress. Ph: Chora

Bunschoten, R. and others (2001) *Urban Flotsam; Stirring the City*, Rotterdam: 010 Publishers.

Christiania

Copenhagen, Denmark, 1971–1978
www.christiania.org

Christiania is an autonomous settlement on the site of a former military barracks in Copenhagen. After the military left the site, it was fenced off but in 1971 a group of people took over parts of the site to make a children's playground. Soon after Christiania was proclaimed a Freetown with one of the original goals being to 'build up a society from scratch'. It is one of the largest 'slum communes' and was set up in direct response to the lack of affordable housing and social facilities, and as an antidote to stressful city life. The legal status of Christiania has been the source of much conflict with the Danish government and the fate of the settlement was a party political issue throughout the 1970s. However, Christiania was granted semi-legal status in 1972, following an agreement to pay a collective tax in return for water and electricity. Since then, the government's attempts to 'normalise' the settlement

seem to be driven by a desire for private development, something completely at odds with the community's founding principles of collective rights to land.

Entrance to Christiania. Ph: William Sherlaw

Although Christiania is still considered a 'Free State', the first decade of its existence was the most radical, both politically and socially. An interesting experiment in self-governance, the community devised its own rules and regulations with decisions being made collectively on the basis of unanimity; forums for the whole community discussed larger issues, whilst neighbourhood meetings were for day-to-day concerns. Social structures were also put in place at this time, such as the setting up of childcare centres and a free planning and advice service, as well as two free newspapers and Radio Christiania which served to supplement the informal communication and support systems of the community. During this time Christiania was also well known for its gay activism, parties and theatre, using performances, actions and the carnivalesque as modes of social experimentation and interaction. The context of the commune thus became a breeding ground for new social and political movements as well as functioning as a support system for those struggling in regular society such as the homeless, the unemployed and drug addicts, whom Christiania welcomed and supported.

Conroy, A. (1994) *Christiania: The Evolution of a Commune*, London: A. Conroy.

Strategies for Subversive Urban Occupation: Scaffolding – Building yourself an urban reserve (left). Skips – Taking the street (right). Images: Santiago Cirugeda/Recetas Urbanas

Cirugeda, Santiago
1996–

www.recetasurbanas.net

Santiago Cirugeda's practice is borne of the frustration that as an artist or an architect it is quite easy to transform the space of the city through obtaining permits for installations and temporary interventions, yet as a citizen it is almost impossible to take action to improve your own environment. His work therefore questions what it is to be an architect in this context and he tries to empower citizens to act in their own locality by showing how it is possible to subvert laws, regulations, and conventions. In this, his work is about the possibility for action, appropriation, occupation and use, where the citizen can act as initiator, using the guidelines and instructions set out by Cirugeda to build, display or create space. At the same time, Cirugeda's practice questions the notion of the architect as sole author-designer. His is an open-source architecture conceived as a tool kit or a user guide, distributed freely through his website *Recetas Urbanas* or 'Urban Prescriptions'. His antidotes to capitalist and commodified space are available here for anyone to replicate. Cirugeda describes his practice as 'an urban and social renovation', making an architecture that is cheap and available to all.

A substantial part of the studio's work so far has tackled those sites in cities that have been left over by demolition, lying empty or walled in – unusable for reasons of active neglect, lack of care or abandonment. One suggested action gives specific advice on how to apply to the local council for a permit to install something temporarily. This 'something' is, however, never to be taken literally, but acts as a mask for alternative actions. In the project 'Public Domain Occupation with Skips', the structure merely resembles a skip but is in fact a vehicle for citizens to occupy the urban realm through 'taking the street'. Another proposal applies for a permit to erect scaffolding for re-painting the façade of a building, but instead creates an enclosed space in a scaffold-type structure that can be used as a temporary extension or simply as a semi outdoor space; Cirugeda calls these pockets, 'urban reserves'.

Cirugeda, S. (2004) *Situaciones Urbanas*, Barcelona: Editorial Tenov.

City Mine(d)

Brussels, UK, 1997–
www.citymined.org

City Mine(d) is an NGO based in Brussels that has been in operation for over ten years and now has branches in Barcelona and London. Including artists, activists, academics, social organisations and politicians, the group came together around a series of actions in derelict buildings in Brussels in 1995 and formalised itself as an NGO in 1997, dealing with issues arising at the intersection of art and politics in the city. Through a critique of the increasing privatisation of public space in Europe, City Mine(d) describe their aims as searching for new forms of citizenship and working towards the re-appropriation of public space, virtual or otherwise. Their work takes the form of urban interventions, action research projects and they try to influence policy at a European level through localised action and through establishing a network of like-minded people and projects.

Interventions such as Ball, literally a bright orange ball of 3m diameter, are used to appropriate urban space. They describe Ball as a tool: it claims space through its sheer size and physicality, whilst also highlighting the lack of opportunities for young people to play in the city. Reminiscent of the early projects of Coop Himmelblau (p.129) and those of Haus-Rucker-Co, (p.155) City Mine(d) deliberately create temporary interventions that empower citizens and allow them to assert their presence in the city. These could be as small and simple as Ball or large-scale events such as their annual PleinOPENair festival in Brussels.

Micronomics Festival 2009: Choreography with two Cherry Pickers. Courtesy City Mine(d)

A recent action research project, Micronomics, focused on the role of small-scale economies in resisting capitalist market forces, and questioned the use of markers such as growth and productivity to measure the success of economies. The project involved local communities, academics, and specialists and included a weekly flea market, bartering schemes, as well as the Micronomics Festival. For City Mine(d) these action research projects are a means of collectively testing out

PleinOPENAir: Open air cinema on vacant land. Courtesy City Mine(d)

Tinggården cohousing, Denmark. Ph: William Sherlaw

and developing their ideas. They use networking as a basic tool to bring together residents, users, participants and city authorities, acting as a facilitator and negotiator.

City Mine(d) (ed) (2006) *Generalized Empowerment: Uneven Development and Urban Interventions*, Brussels: City Mine(d).

Cohousing

Europe and North America, 1960–

Cohousing is a housing development movement that started in the late 1960s in Denmark, where it is called *Bofaellesskaber* or 'living communities'. With increasing numbers of women working, there was a desire to reduce the burden of housework, and in particular childcare and evening meals, through shared communal services. Cohousing is also seen to improve social relations and develop a sense of community. What started as a middle-class housing solution popular with young families, is now a well established housing model for all social groups, and has spread to a number of Northern European countries where governmental policy and funding has encouraged development. It is also becoming increasingly popular in the US, Canada and New Zealand, where cohousing has a more explicit environmental agenda, sharing many similarities with ecovillages (p.142) but usually in a less radical, smaller and more urban version. Historically, cohousing has its roots in communitarian and feminist movements of the C19 and C20, including Charles Fourier's (p.150) phalanx, the co-opcrative housekeeping model developed by Melusina Fay Peirce (p.183) and Ebenezer Howard's Garden Cities (p.168) movement.

Usually purpose built, cohousing neighbourhoods consist of private homes with shared facilities, where residents own their dwellings as well as a share in the communal facilities. Neighbourhoods are self-managed through regular meetings usually operating a form of consensus decision making. The size of such developments varies in scale from 10–40 units and the ratio of common to private amenities also differs, but most tend to include private kitchens in addition to a communal kitchen. Other shared facilities can include laundry, heating, transport, open spaces and guest rooms. There are many successful cohousing schemes in Denmark, one of the older examples built in 1978 is **Tinggården**, which was the result of a design competition for alternative settlements organised by the Danish government. Designed by the architectural practice, Vandkunsten, the apartments have a flexible layout that allows families to expand or shrink their house according to need, by adding or relinquishing rooms to adjoining flats.

A recent purpose built cohousing development in the UK is located at Stroud in Gloucestershire, ranging from four bedroom houses to studio flats and consisting of thirty-two units in total. A resident driven initiative, a company was established to develop the site and own the freehold. Designed by **Architype** in consultation with future residents, the development incorporates a Common House at the centre of the site, which houses a communal kitchen where residents are obliged to cook once a month. Day-to-day decisions are made at monthly meetings of the residents' association, which includes groups who deal with the kitchen, garden, maintenance etc. Thus through a careful

Stroud cohousing. Ph: William Sherlaw

mixture of spatial design, common amenities and formal social structures cohousing is able to encourage social interaction between residents and can help create more resilient and connected communities.

Fromm, D. (1991) *Collaborative communities: cohousing, central living, and other new forms of housing with shared facilities*, New York; London: Van Nostrand Reinhold.

McCamant, K. and C. Durrett with E. Hertzman (1994) *Cohousing: a contemporary approach to housing ourselves*. Berkeley: Ten Speed Press.

Williams, J. (2005) 'Designing Neighbourhoods for Social Interaction: The Case of Cohousing', *Journal of Urban Design*, 10: 195.

Coin Street Community Builders

London, UK, 1977–
www.coinstreet.org
Coin Street Community Builders (CSCB) is a social enterprise that grew out of the Coin Street Action Group. Set up in 1977, the group was formed to resist the commercial development on a large 13-acre site on the South Bank in London. Much of the surrounding area had already been developed into commercial uses, with residents either choosing to move out due to a general lack of affordable housing or being forcefully

evicted. As the population declined sharply, schools and shops closed down and the remaining residents started to organise themselves with some help from local councillors. Eventually a 'drop-in action centre' was set up and when plans for closing a local playground were uncovered, this loose grouping formed the Waterloo Community Development Group. Later it became the Coin Street Action Group, but crucially through their earlier work they already had an identity and a strong sense of purpose. This allowed the group to carry out what was to become an extremely lengthy campaign for an alternative planning strategy based around the twin demands of affordable housing and open space.

The campaign for Coin Street lasted seven years and included two public inquiries. The first, held in 1979, was to decide the future use of the area and at which the community presented their own alternative plans. Ironically these plans were developed by the same architects who worked for the Greater London Council (GLC), which at that time supported the commercial development, but carried out in their own time as unpaid work. The inquiry rejected both plans and eventually both sides submitted revised planning applications which were also subject to a public inquiry. This inquiry too was inconclusive, approving both plans, but eventually the developers pulled out through

Coin Street Iroko social housing. Ph: Tatjana Schneider

sustained community pressure and because of the local government's eventual support for the residents.

In 1984, with the GLC facing abolition, the community acquired the land as CSCB for £1m in order to implement its development plan. Several projects on the initial site, as well as on other sites in the proximity, have been completed. These include four housing co-operative schemes, a park, a riverside walkway open to the public, as well as community facilities including a new community and sports centre. These have been funded using the profits from commercial endeavours, such as the refurbishment of the Oxo Tower, allowing CSCB to invest money back into the area. Cross-programming in each part of the scheme generates money from private ventures for use in community facilities, such as including a public car park in the basement of social housing schemes or including conference and meeting facilities in a neighbourhood centre. This careful mixture of private and public uses allows CSCB to provide a range of public facilities.

The long process that saw a community action group transform itself into a community developer is an important example of what residents can achieve even in extremely difficult circumstances. In this transition, it has been CSCB's organisational structure that has allowed it to remain accountable to its members. An affiliated housing association owns and is responsible for building the social housing, which is then leased to

independent housing co-operatives. These are fully mutual, meaning that there is no right to buy, and the day-to-day management is also the responsibility of the co-operative. New tenants are required to complete a training course which gives them a sense of responsibility and the skills required for running a co-operative. The members of the CSCB board are mainly local residents, with outsiders used to provide specialist advice. This has meant that many of the original campaigners are still on the Board, including the Executive Director, Iain Tuckett. Although helped immensely by the years of campaigning that preceded its work, CSCB has developed a successful model for implementing self-managed social housing which could be replicated elsewhere.

Tuckett, I. (1988) 'Coin Street: There Is Another Way...', *Community Development Journal* 23(4): 249–257.

Collections of alternative approaches
Berkeley, USA. 1981–
There are a number of contemporary projects that collect and collate alternative approaches to the practice of architecture. These are all projects whose curatorial approach brings together diverse practices in order to elaborate different ways of thinking and acting in relation to architecture and urbanism.

onesmallproject.com is a website and a repository of constructed and propositional projects for the world's poor by architects and architectural students. The ongoing project is described as dealing with leftovers: people who are considered leftover, such as squatters, slum dwellers and the homeless; spaces that are left over and can be put to better use; and materials that are leftover. These elements are all combined by Wes Janz, the founder of onesmallproject, to articulate a call to action for architects to take their social responsibilities seriously. The project rejects mainstream architectural practice for its complicity in propagating and maintaining unequal relations, and instead advocates small-scale charitable works carried out on a scale of one-to-one, in the hope of a quiet and incremental change. The project celebrates works that are done for others and seek to empower others, and acts as a good secondary resource for further examples of spatial agency.

Adaptive Actions gives space and visibility to alternative and marginal ways of inhabiting space. The 'actions' are intended to modify and activate the existing use and character of the urban environment,

testing the limits of what is tolerated in an increasingly privatised and surveilled public realm. Based in Montreal and initiated by Jean-François Prost in 2007, the project travels to different localities organising events, workshops, exhibitions and roundtables, but the main output is a website that collects and collates instances of small-scale ideas and actions from all over the world. The images and captions show residents, workers, passers-by taking control of their environment,

Mud pavilion made of rubble from demolished campus buildings and an earth/sand/cement mixture. CapAsia (2003) was a ten-day "build-design-build" project at the University of Moratuwa in Colombo, Sri Lanka organised with College of Architecture and Planning at Ball State University, USA. Courtesy Wes Janz/ onesmallproject.com

AA 41 All Aboard; Actor/Created by: AA; Location: Blue Wall (London 2012 Olympic site), 2007– 9. Creating extensions to the Olympic Blue Wall by painting objects found in the vicinity

Networked Cultures Dialogues. Series of debates, screenings and exhibitions on the emergence of networked cultures across Europe. Image: Peter Mörtenböck and Helge Mooshammer

which are framed and given value through a curatorial practice. It is an example of the artist or architect taking a step back and allowing the actions of others to take centre stage. Adaptive Actions gives value to the use and programming of spaces, suggesting other possibilities and other ways of engaging with the urban environment.

Networked Cultures is a project initiated by Helge Mooshammer and Peter Mörtenböck, carried out between 2005 and 2008, based at Goldsmiths College, University of London. Using sites of conflict as a starting point, the project focused on the social and cultural transformations of Europe through studying the networked spatial practices that occur in these locations and the response of architects, artists, urbanists, curators and activists. The format of Networked Cultures encouraged the further extending and nurturing of these networks through a series of interviews, talks, exhibitions and workshops.

Plate-forme Européenne de Pratiques et Recherches Alternatives de la Ville (PEPRAV – European Platform for Alternative Practice and Research on the City) was a collaborative project between atelier d'architecture autogérée (p.105) based in Paris, School of Architecture at University of Sheffield, Recyclart based in Brussels and metrozones from Berlin. Carried out between 2006 and 2007, the platform was formed

around a mutual concern for urban research and practice based in active participation and action within local and translocal networks. Their way of working included work sessions, meetings, exhibitions and public lectures that brought together the extended and evolving network of practitioners and theorists involved in PEPRAV.

aaa and PEPRAV (eds) (2007) *Urban/ACT*, Montrouge: Moutot Imprimeurs.

Mooshammer, H. and Mörtenböck, P. (2008) *Networked Cultures: Parallel Architectures and the Politics of Space*, Rotterdam: NAi Publishers.

Prost, J.-F. (2008) 'Adaptive Actions', *field:*, 1: 138–149.

Community Design Centers

USA, 1960–

Community Design Centers (CDCs) emerged in the context of the US civil rights movement and the women's liberation movement of the 1950s and 1960s, generally providing technical and design advice to communities who could otherwise not afford it. The political climate at the time led planners, architects and designers to view themselves as advocates for those excluded from the design process, and to see urban planning not as a technical or bureaucratic issue but as a political one. Paul Davidoff's concept of 'advocacy planning' was influential in this characterisation of architecture and urban planning as an engaged and participatory process of positive social change. Within architecture in particular, this concern was widespread and can be seen as a reaction to the mechanised and technological tendencies of Modernism.

Whilst state funding was available at the beginning, by the 1970s the political climate had changed and public programmes were withdrawn. Those groups who had initially relied on this now became non-profit, voluntary organisations. Today, CDCs cover a broad political spectrum, while some still have a radical politics, others are closer to the neo-conservatism of movements such as New Urbanism. CDCs share a common aim to engage local communities in the design and development process. They do so through community participation and mobilisation against imposed master-planning and regeneration strategies.

One of the first CDCs was the **Architects Renewal Committee of Harlem** (ARCH) founded in 1964, whose director was Max Bond Jnr. The group came together to fight against proposals for a new freeway in northern Manhattan, and later provided a range of services from design and technical support to training and information. Although some of its members were architects, others included a lawyer, editor and community organisers. They were associated with the Black Power movement and much of their work was concerned with the alleviation of poverty in the ghettos. ARCH was funded by grants and received contracts from various community organisations.

The climate of the 1960s also had a major influence on educational institutions resulting in many CDCs being affiliated to universities, such as the Yale Building Project (p.213) at Yale University, **Pratt Center for Community Development** at the Pratt Institute, the **Community Development Group** at North Carolina State University and the **Detroit Collaborative Design Center** (DCDC) at the University of Detroit-Mercy. These organisations combined teaching and training for students with a service to the wider community; pedagogically process was emphasised over finished product, and an increasing importance placed on practical experience. Rural Studio (p.193) based in Alabama remains one of the most influential of these university affiliated CDCs, whilst other contemporary organisations such as Design Corps (p.138) and Centre for Urban Pedagogy (p.115) are independent.

Whether affiliated to an educational institution or not, CDCs question traditional roles and power relations, such as those between the architect and user or student and teacher. Architecture and design are viewed as tools for an ethical intervention in the built

The St Joseph ReBuild Center for the homeless in New Orleans. Built by DCDC with Wayne Troyer Architects. Courtesy DCDC

environment and the transformative potential of architectural practice is underlined through a participative approach that works for those least able to afford the services of a traditional architect.

Sanoff, H. (2003) *Three Decades of Design and Community*, Raleigh: North Carolina State University.

Community Self Build Agency

Sheerness, UK, 1989–
www.communityselfbuildagency.org.uk

Community Self Build Agency (CSBA) is a non-profit organisation established in 1989 and based in Kent, UK. It promotes self-build housing initiatives for those in housing need such as the unemployed, people on low incomes and the young. They lobby local authorities and housing associations to include self-building provision within their housing strategies, secure funding for self build projects from housing corporations, liaise with training organisations to include options to gain National Vocational Qualifications, and work with architects to design housing with appropriate construction techniques.

Projects are initiated by putting people in touch with others interested in building their own home and setting up a group that can form a housing association or housing co-operative. CSBA's eventual aim is that as self-building becomes more widespread people will form their own groups. CSBA view self-building as not only providing a housing solution but also helping those involved gain skills and experience with many of their unemployed self-builders having secured jobs after completing their homes. Self-building is therefore available to those with or without building skills, who can commit the necessary time, usually 25–35 hours per week, spent at the weekends and evenings.

Housing tenure arrangements can vary according to circumstances, from outright ownership to part ownership and rental agreements. The amount of self-building can also vary by project, for example the Angell Eco Self Build group in Lambeth, London, worked on a project of ten houses completed in 2006. Designed in association with Mode 1 Architects, the structure and shell were built by a construction company, with the self-builders doing everything else, including carpentry, final electrics and plumbing, decorations etc. In other projects such as the Hornsey Co-operative Housing, also in London and completed in

2003, the ten houses were fully constructed by the self-builders using the Segal [(p.196)] method and in association with architects, **Architype**.

Broome, J. and Richardson, B. (1995) *The Self-Build Book*, Totnes: Green Earth Books.

Community Technical Aid Centres

UK, 1978–1985

Set up in the late 1970s, Community Technical Aid Centres (CTACs) arose out of the institutionalisation of the radical community architecture of practitioners such as Ralph Erskine [(p.183)] and Architects Revolutionary Council, [(p.97)] who were trying to find alternatives to the slum clearance programmes of the mid 1960s, and their consequent replacement by unpopular mass housing developments. An early precursor to CTACs was the **Neighbourhood Action Project** of 1969, where Liverpool council worked with Shelter, a charity for the homeless. Although a short-lived project, its model of setting up a local advisory office with architects, planners and social workers was highly influential.

Local communities resisting redevelopment were thus given assistance by various voluntary and professional groups but architects were prohibited from providing a free service by the RIBA's professional code of conduct. For example, **Support Community Building Design**, a co-operative set up by Tom Woolley along with students from the Architectural Association, [(p.98)] provided a very

Soft Space by Coop Himmelblau (1970), Ph: Gertrud Wolfschwenger

cheap service but could only help those groups who had managed to secure some funding. They were involved in providing planning assistance to the **Covent Garden Action Group** amongst others. Another important organisation was **Assist** related to the Architecture department of the University of Strathclyde which provided a free technical aid service for the improvement of tenements. Assist's local 'architecture shops' not only provided assistance in constructional matters but also in how to obtain funding, create neighbourhood organisations and generally petition for change. Initiatives such as these all over the UK eventually led to the introduction of **Association of Community Technical Aid Centres** (ACTAC) in 1983, which was seen by some as an alternative to the RIBA.

CTACs thus operated as local resource centres where a wide range of services were offered to individuals and community groups who wanted to have an influence on their built environment. Unlike the related service provided by the **Community Architecture Group** at the RIBA, CTACs acknowledged the diversity of professions and expertise involved in community development and therefore included organisations that advised on planning, landscaping, engineering, surveying, ecology, environmental education, financial planning, management, administration and graphics, in the belief that a combination of these skills were

required to build a community. One of the main aims of CTACs was to encourage user participation and the professionals working at these centres acted as spatial agents, enabling citizens to engage in their environment through giving specialist advice. Only those able to afford a fee were charged and although funding originally came from charitable foundations, most CTACs received governmental grants. This fitted well with the prevailing political move to transfer responsibility from a diminished local government sector to the voluntary section. An interesting twist here was that many of the CTACs funded by the state were also involved in opposing governmental redevelopment and mass housing schemes. CTACs finally came to an end in the mid 1980s as funding dried up, although many of those involved are still working in social housing.

Jenkins, P. and Forsyth, L. (eds) (2009) *Architecture, Participation and Society*, London: Routledge.

Coop Himmelb(l)au

Vienna, Austria, 1968–1980
www.coop-himmelblau.at
Coop Himmelblau was founded by Wolf D. Prix, Helmut Swiczinsky and Michael Holzer in Vienna, Austria in 1968. Their approach is similar to that of

Haus-Rucker-Co, (p.155) based on the Austrian heritage of Freud's psychoanalytic approach, which led them to explore the relationships between the architectural environment and our individual perceptions of it. Their early work leading up to the late 1970s consisted of performative installations and actions involving the spectators as participants.

A response to the work of architect, Hans Hollein and influenced by media theorist Marshall McLuhan and cybernetics in general, Coop Himmelblau produced work that explored the use of new technologies to create early versions of responsive interactive environments. The project Hard Space (1968) used the heartbeats of three people to trigger a series of explosions across Vienna, whilst Soft Space (1970) filled a street in soap bubbles. They also used inflatables and the potential of pneumatic structures for interaction in public space; these early projects exploring the city as a stage for experimental inhabitation. From the 1980s onwards the practice increasingly moved into the mainstream of architecture, with formally flamboyant buildings that appear to have lost a socially experimental edge.

Sorkin, M. (1991) 'Post rock Propter Rock: A Short History of the Himmelblau', in M. Sorkin, *Exquisite Corpse: Writing on Buildings*, London: Verso, pp. 339–350.

Co-operative practices

1844–

www.cooperatives-uk.coop

A co-operative is commonly defined as an association of people who have come together on a voluntary basis in order to work towards a common economic, social or cultural goal, as part of an enterprise that is collectively owned and often also managed collectively. This means that these are private enterprises that are as free from institutional control as possible. Co-operatives are based on values of self-help, self-responsibility, democracy, equality, equity and solidarity. They have an open and voluntary membership and are organisations that are controlled by their members who also actively participate in decision making and the setting of policies. This usually takes the form of a voting system with one member having one vote and members contributing equitably to, and democratically controlling, any capital.

The co-operative as a modern business structure originated in C19 Britain in response to the depressed economic conditions brought forth by industrialisation. The Rochdale Society of Equitable Pioneers, founded in 1844, devised the principles which have since become the model for co-operatives worldwide. A consumer co-operative, it was set up by a group of 28 weavers and other artisans whose skilled labour was less in demand due to growing mechanisation. Their store sold flour, sugar and other basic food items to its members. The 'Rochdale Principles' as they later came to be known stipulated an open membership, democratic, control, payment of limited interest on capital, distribution of surplus amongst members, cash trading only, political and religious neutrality and a promotion of education. Other than the reference to politics and religion, these principles remain intact today in the form of the International Co-operative Alliance's principles.

Architecture has been slow to take up the principles of co-operative practices. **Edward Cullinan Architects** were one of the first practices to operate as a co-operative, three years after they were established in 1968. Legally, they remained a partnership but each member looked after their own financial affairs, including indemnity insurance and all received a percentage of the fees. This informal agreement worked as all members contributed to all stages of the design work as well as to management decisions. Cullinan's still operate in a similar fashion with all permanent members of staff having the status of directors, receiving a share of the profits and having some say in day-to-day management decisions. This seems to have become the accepted model for operating as a co-operative within the architectural profession.

Collective Architecture are a Glasgow based practice that recently began operating according to co-operative principles. Originally established in 1997 as Chris Stewart Architects, in 2007 they gave equal share to each of their fourteen employees. This mutual structure is also reflected in the day-to-day running of the practice, where each architect is given complete responsibility for their project, including the design and management aspects, client liaison and fee decisions. The practice has been involved in a number of regeneration, housing and community projects across Scotland taking a sustainable approach to design. Collective Architecture's inclusive and collaborative approach to architecture is characterised both by who

Full-scale modelling of house interiors as part of Homes by Design, a training course for tenants and residents by URBED and Glass-House. Courtesy URBED

Plasticine model of neighbourhood used in the Homes by Design training course. Courtesy URBED

G.L.A.S.: Unser Berlin / Our Berlin: public and open production of an issue of glaspaper. Ph: Florian Kossak

they choose to work with: social enterprises, housing co-operatives, local manufacturers; and what they choose to build, mostly public projects including housing and community spaces. Another Glasgow based practice operating co-operatively is **City Design Co-operative**, who are landscape architects and urban designers. Their office structure is non-hierarchical with all members combining teaching and research with their professional practice.

Worker's co-operatives also exist within architecture, such as the Manchester based practice, **URBED** (Urbanism, Environment and Design). Specialising in urban design and consultancy with a long-term commitment to a socially sustainable and equitable approach, they translated this into their own organisational structure through becoming a co-operative in 2006. URBED's community involvement work acknowledges that for residents to have a meaningful input within the design process a working knowledge of the processes involved is necessary. For this they have developed training courses for tenants, devised urban interventions and organised bus tours of new and old regeneration projects, in order to empower residents to make informed decisions about their homes and neighbourhoods. Recently they have also started publishing, *Urban Scrawl*, an in-house journal that reflects on issues of urban design and regeneration, acting as a forum for more speculative work.

Architects operating outside of professional bodies can of course set up as worker's co-operatives without any legal issues, for example **Glasgow Letters on Architecture and Space** (G.L.A.S.) were a group of ex-students from the University of Strathclyde, Scotland who operated together between 2001 and 2005. Their aim was to critique the capitalist production of the built environment through design, graphic work and writings and their most notable output was *glaspaper*, a DIY publication that interrogated these issues through a series of themed issues.

Others choose to work for co-operative organisations such as **Solon**, an independent, locally-controlled and community focused housing association. Established in 1974 and currently operating in Bristol, South Gloucestershire, Mendip and the Forest of Dean, it aims at providing good quality, affordable rented housing and they are particularly involved in inner-city regeneration with a long history of encouraging resident involvement. In its early years, Solon employed its own architects,

although this was discouraged by the RIBA due to a perceived conflict of interest.

Whilst the output of the practices described in this section is diverse, they are brought together in their desire to work within an equitable environment where responsibility and gain are shared equally amongst members. Other co-operatives include Matrix, (p.171) Team Zoo, (p.201) Viennese Cooperative Garden City Movement. (p.209)

'Cooperatives in Social Development', *Social Perspective on Development Branch*, http://www.un.org/esa/socdev/social/cooperatives/ [accessed 26 April 2010].

Woolley, T. (1977) 'Cullinan's Co-op', *Architects Journal*, 166: 741–742.

Counter communities

USA, 1967–

The US has a rich tradition of utopian communities, starting with the early Puritan settlers that sailed for the New World and including the longest surviving utopian community of the Shakers, the European influenced Fourierist (p.150) settlements such as Brook Farm through to the hippie communes of the 1960s. Whilst extremely diverse in their approaches, these settlements all aimed at establishing a new social order away from the major population centres; they therefore needed to be built from scratch both physically and socially. In particular during the 1960s, many counter communities were set up in the hot arid desert landscapes of California and Arizona. Many of these projects were looking for an alternative to socially and ecologically damaging lifestyles and were usually established under the guidance of a visionary architect, artist or activist. Whilst the aim was to create a lifestyle that could be replicated, their message spreading through example, most counter communities remained as single projects. Some are still operating today in different guises, for example Nader Khalili's (p.163) vision of low-impact adobe building is still being promoted and researched by the Cal-Earth Institute.

An early example is **Arcosanti**, the brainchild of Italian architect Paolo Soleri, who envisioned a megastructure built in the middle of the Arizona desert, which could accommodate 5,000 people. Established in 1970 the project is ongoing, following Soleri's design principles, which he refers to as *arcologies*. A mixture of

Arcosanti ceramics apse (1972). Ph: Annette del Zoppo

Corner Cottage Earthship at Taos, New Mexico. Ph: Kirsten Jacobsen

architecture and ecology, the term and idea originated in science fiction and was first used by H G Wells. Soleri's *arcologies* advocate a number of extremely dense, mixed-use, self-contained and economically self-sufficient communities that promote a frugal lifestyle and are able to inhabit the planet with minimal environmental impact. Although there are some similarities to the ecovillage [(p.142)] concept, Soleri's arcologies were initially concerned with the production of an ecological architecture and did not focus on the co-operative or spiritual elements that are often also a part of the motivation for ecovillages. Arcosanti is the built testing ground for Soleri's ideas, envisioned as an alternative to suburban sprawl, it would eventually be a dense city with walking as the main mode of transport. Due to lack of funds, only a small part has been built to date and there are only 60 permanent residents. Despite this, the project is continuing with a strong pedagogical focus and over the years many volunteers from around the world have participated in its construction, workshops and seminars. The emphasis on learning through building comes from Soleri's time spent working with Frank Lloyd Wright at Taliesin in the late 1940s.

An example of a counter community that has spread beyond the US are **Earthships**, which were first designed in the mid-1970s by architect, Mike Reynolds. They aimed to be self-sufficient passive solar dwellings that were affordable, easily built without any specialist building knowledge, and using waste material wherever possible, including drinks cans, glass bottles and scrap metal. Over the years, the basic design has remained the same, with a glass façade on the sunny side and partially buried walls made from tyres rammed with earth. These act as mass heat storage devices, gaining heat during the day and releasing it at night, reducing the need for heating systems. Earthships incorporate solar panels for electricity and hot water, whilst rainwater is collected for use and greywater recycling is incorporated into the design, using the 'living machines' system first designed at the New Alchemy Institute. [(p.176)] Recently, with growing concern over climate change, Earthships have gained popularity and Reynolds is now being accepted by the professional architecture community and building regulation bodies with whom he previously had a difficult relationship; some Earthships are also being used in disaster relief situations.

Dome Village, LA (circa. 1994). Ph: Craig Chamberlain

Heerlijkheid Hoogvliet/Hoogvliet Domain, Welcome into My Backyard! 2001–7. Ph: Maarten Laupman

The Lama Foundation was established in 1967 by artists, Steve Durkee, Barbara Durkee and Jonathan Altman who moved to Taos, New Mexico to found a commune based on the goal of spiritual well-being and to live without hierarchical forms of organisation. They constructed buildings in adobe with the help of the local Native American population, whilst their friendship with Stewart Brand, founder of the Whole Earth Catalog,[p.212] led them to be introduced to Steve Baer who helped erect geodesic-type domes similar to those at Drop City.[p.141] Finally, geodesic domes were also used at **Dome Village**, founded in 1993 by activist Ted Hayes and closed down in 2006. Unique for its location in the middle of the city, in a car park next to the financial district of downtown Los Angeles, it was established as a settlement for the homeless. A self-managed community of around 35 individuals housed in 20 geodesic domes, it not only provided shelter but its organisation as a small village provided a support structure for its residents. Dome Village also organised workshops, including computer literacy, community gardening and help with job seeking. Due to its location the rent was eventually too high and Dome Village was evicted, although there are plans afoot for a second version.

Counter Communities: Projects by Paolo Soleri (Arcosanti), Lama-Foundation, Mike Reynolds (Earthships), Nader Khalili (Cal-Earth), Ted Hays (Dome Village), 2003/2009. [Film] Directed by Oliver Croy and Oliver Elser. USA: Croy and Elser.

Crimson Architectural Historians
Utrecht, The Netherlands, 1994–
www.crimsonweb.org

Crimson Architectural Historians are Ewout Dorman, Annuska Pronkhorst, Michelle Provoost, Simone Rots, Wouter Vanstiphout and Cassandra Wilkins. The group began in 1994, working between historical research, critique and architectural practice, with the contemporary city as their subject. They began with the city in which they lived, Rotterdam, unearthing another history of its post-war redevelopment which did not follow the received logic that demolition and redevelopment was the consequence of the bombing of the city during World War II. Crimson instead pointed to another narrative where the process of demolition had already begun in the thirties, and was enthusiastically continued during and after the war. This initial insight led to research on post-war cities worldwide, which dealt with how urban planning has been used as a political tool in the Cold War as well as in the current planning and building of New Towns.

Crimson view history not as a closed event in the past, but as something that can imbue the city with meaning across time, and their projects try to set this latent historical potential to work in the present. Their research on New Towns has led to a long-term engagement with the suburb of Hoogvliet in the harbour area of Rotterdam. 'Wimby: Welcome into our Backyard' was a series of proposals and policy-decisions for which

Crimson acted as spatial agent through curating and helping to implement a series of small-scale projects, such as experimental buildings, a recreational park, a festival and various artworks. During the six year project Crimson analysed, consulted and commissioned work in order to uncover and enhance the qualities of the area, and in so doing became an essential part of the regeneration process.

Their working method begins with empirical research, finding out through interviews and observations what is there both physically and socially. With this they construct a narrative for the area that is led not by the desire for commercial development but is instead a powerful and very specific story to convince people of the potential of the area. This becomes an urban strategy and in Hoogvliet this close analysis of past and present urban conditions led to highly specific proposals such as cohousing just for musicians and a park with hand-made model boats. Crimson have referred to their practice as 'painting panoramas of possibilities.'

Crimson and Rottenberg, F. (2007) *WiMBY! Hoogvliet: Future, Past and Present of a New Town*, Rotterdam: NAI.

Davis, Mike

1946–

Mike Davis is a writer and an historian who was involved in the US civil rights movement in San Diego in the early 1960s. Davis came late to academia, having worked first as an activist for Students for a Democratic Society and later as a truck driver and a union organiser. At the age of 30 he won a scholarship to study at University of California, LA with a period in the UK at University of Edinburgh and working for Verso in London. His background has informed his writings on social exclusion and poverty as well as his teaching. He taught urban theory at Southern California Institute of Architecture for a number of years, encouraging his students to explore LA through its 'social and environmental histories' and by getting involved in community projects. He has taught across a range of departments, including geography, history and political science, and is currently teaching in the Department of Creative Writing at the University of California Riverside.

Davis' books, generated from a socialist perspective, have focused on the global problem of slums and the policies of NGOs, the World Bank and the International Monetary Fund; on the decline of the American city examined through white flight, deindustrialization, housing and job segregation, discrimination, and federal policy; or the relationship between urban developments and natural ecosystems. His book *City of Quartz* is attributed as having predicted the racial tensions that led to the LA riots of 1992; and *Planet of Slums* is influential for bringing into focus the predicament of the vast majority of urban dwellers in the world today. Taking as its starting point the idea that neo-liberalism is the natural successor to colonialism, the book captures the urgency of the situation faced by the majority of the world's population. Here Davis advocates a global revolution of the working class along ecologically sound and socialist principles rather than in local reforms that bring about change through small, incremental steps.

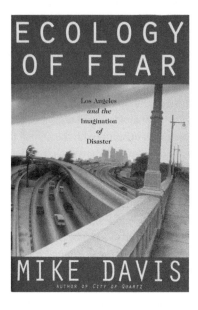

In all his work, Davis has focused on the intersection of space and politics, arguing that spatial production can only be understood through an unravelling of the underlying political forces.

Davis, M. (1998) *Ecology of Fear: Los Angeles and the Imagination of Disaster*, New York: Metropolitan Books.

de Carlo, Giancarlo

1919–2005

Giancarlo de Carlo was an Italian architect, planner, writer and educator who was one of the fiercest critics

Urbino university campus. Ph: Santo Rizzuto

of what he saw as the failure of architecture in the C20. He was one of the founding members of Team X, a group of architects challenging the modernist doctrines as set out by CIAM and was a key figure in the discourse on participation in architecture. His 1969 lecture and consequent article, *Architecture's Public*, remains a seminal text on the need for the inclusion of users in the design process and the inherently political role of the architect. De Carlo never separated architecture from politics; he was active in the Italian anti-fascist resistance as well as the post-war Italian anarchist movement, remaining an anti-establishment figure critiquing both architectural practice and academia for their preoccupation with form and glossy images over the social and lived experience.

Much of de Carlo's built work is located in Urbino, a small Italian hill town for which he proposed a master plan between 1958–64, which has slowly been implemented over the past forty years. De Carlo's interventions in the form of new buildings and renovations have been carefully inserted into the built fabric and pay close attention to the social life of the town. Combined with his social housing at Terni, an industrial town close to Rome, the built work has provided a foundation for his views on the involvement of users and inhabitants in the design process. The Terni housing was built for workers of Italy's largest steel company and for de Carlo it was not only important to discern the

wishes of the future inhabitants but to do so in company time. He insisted that workers be paid for these sessions and that management should not be allowed to attend. The steelworkers and their families were thus involved in each part of the design process with the architect assuming the role of educator and facilitator.

De Carlo's writings supported this architectural approach; he was editor of the bi-lingual journal, *Spazio e Società* published between 1978 and 2001, which covered architecture from across the world and paid attention both to high profile buildings as well as to vernacular and other more modest forms of architectural intervention. An inspiring educator, he also founded the International Laboratory of Architecture and Urbanism (ILAUD), an annual summer school that was established in 1976 and is still running. De Carlo was an intellectual who practiced architecture as a political profession that could not be separated from the context of its time: his work at Urbino and elsewhere shows an enormous respect and care for heritage whilst being open to technological advances and is characterised by an emphasis on the responsibility of the architect and the necessary relationship between practice and theory.

de Carlo, G. (2007) 'Architecture's Public', in Blundell-Jones, P., Petrescu, D. and Till, J. (eds) *Architecture and Participation*, Abingdon: Spon Press, pp. 3–22.

DEGW

London, UK, 1971–2009

www.degw.com

DEGW were established in London in 1971 as an offshoot of New York space planners JFN. The original partners were all educated as architects, with Luigi Giffone also being an engineer; Francis Duffy, John Worthington and the late Peter Ely studied together at the Architectural Association. (p.98) DEGW were one of the first practices to place an emphasis on how organisations use space and the important role that design has to play in this. They revolutionised space planning for large scale offices by placing an emphasis on the changing nature of organisations and the need for office accommodation to reflect this, incorporating ideas on mobile and remote working.

DEGW's approach to design places an emphasis on research and they combine concepts from US planning and business, such as 'time budgeting', 'activity mapping', 'advocacy planning' and the explicit use of scientific methods in building design. Their over-arching concern with time and management in architecture has produced influential work on the differing life-cycles in buildings from structural core to interior fittings, the involvement of users in the design and management of their space, the emphasis on facilities management as key to the success of large-scale building, the use of pre- and post-occupancy surveys, workshops, strategic briefing and focus group techniques. DEGW thus serve as a pioneering example of how architectural intelligence can be applied in a broad range of contexts.

A key to DEGW's approach was the combination of consultancy and design work, each challenging the other. Since their takeover by Davis Langdon in summer 2009, DEGW have closed their design services, concentrating on consultancy alone. This has arguably changed a fundamental and productive dynamic within the practice, which allowed it to test its ideas on organisational structure and management through concrete design and vice versa.

Duffy, F. (1998) *Design for Change: The Architecture of DEGW*, Basel: Birkhäuser.

Design Corps

Raleigh, USA, 1991–

www.designcorps.org

Design Corps is a non-profit organisation founded in 1991 by Bryan Bell and Victoria Ballard Bell, initially to address the severe shortage of adequate housing for migrant workers in the area surrounding Raleigh, North Carolina, where they lived. The agricultural state relies heavily on large numbers of workers from Mexico and other Central American countries, for seasonal work such as fruit picking. Due to their immigration status these workers do not qualify for healthcare or housing benefits, whilst many of the farmers on whom they depend for lodging themselves struggle financially. This has resulted in extremely poor living and working conditions and a population that is segregated. During the past ten years Design Corps have set up a Farmworker Housing Program that secures funding and tries to build culturally appropriate housing for the workers.

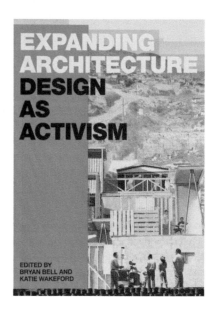

Initially, Design Corps did not wait to be commissioned but instead approached farmers, petitioning them to help build better facilities. The programme includes an application for a federal government grant which can provide 50–100 percent of the construction costs, with the remainder of the costs being met by the farmer. The buildings are subject to a ten year contract where the farmer agrees to meet certain conditions for the standard of living of the workers in return for the new building. These conditions are set by Design Corps and are the result of consultations with the workers in the form of questionnaires, interviews and workshops. Their participatory approach allows the designers to understand individual needs and problems, for example in one case, the workers were provided with bunk beds by the farmer – these proved unacceptable for older men and so a 'no bunk beds' condition was written into the contract.

Here the role of the architect is expanded: Design Corps not only propose their own projects responding to specific needs, but also secure funding, and through their contracts with the farmers they use their expertise as a bargaining chip to secure better living conditions for those in need. Design Corps' work thus shows how architects can become agents with the power to change social and physical conditions through working alongside locals who know the needs of any given community. The work of Design Corps has expanded beyond their North Carolina base, with numerous projects for other US rural communities, and the formation of a Fellowship programme that places designers in communities who would otherwise not have access to professional help. They are also initiators of the SEED (Social Economic Environmental Design) Network, which has developed a common standard to guide, evaluate and measure the social, economic and environmental impact of design projects.

Bell, B., Fisher, T. and Wakeford, K. (eds) (2008) *Expanding Architecture*, New York: Metropolis Books.

Diggers and Levellers

England, UK, 1647–

The Levellers were a loose political group that formed in England in 1647 around demands for a widening of voting rights, the toleration of religious difference and for due judicial process. The group were popularly named after the practice of 'levelling' hedges and fences, erected by landowners to keep peasants out of what used to be common land available for all to gather firewood and graze livestock. The Levellers however did not support such action and tried to distance themselves from it.

A more radical group formed in 1649 that named themselves the 'True Levellers'. Led by Gerard Winstanley they advocated an end to all property rights, a return to the state of affairs before the Norman invasion of 1066, when land was not owned by the state or the monarchy, but instead small plots of land were owned by peasants according to folk-laws or customs, which usually followed kinship principles and where each cultivated their own small holding. Over and above this the True Levellers also advocated the collective cultivation of land. In 1649, the group took over St George's Hill in Surrey and began digging the land for cultivation,

living and working in the same place. This was to be the start of a series of collective communities across England, established mostly in the south, including Wellingborough in Northamptonshire, Cox Hall in Kent, Iver in Buckinghamshire, Barnet in Hertfordshire, Enfield in Middlesex, Dunstable in Bedfordshire, Bosworth in Leicestershire, as well as a few other sites across Gloucestershire and Nottinghamshire. The activities of these groups, of digging the land for cultivation as well as the removal of hedges and fences, earned them their popular name of The Diggers. At the same time the group also published a manifesto, *The True Leveller's Standard Advance*. At its peak the movement consisted of some 100–200 people across southern and central England, but the communities were heavily persecuted by the government. They were eventually driven out by angry landowners supported by the clergy. The movement finally came to an end around 1652 the same year that Winstanley published his treatise on social reform, *The Law of Freedom in a Platform*.

Woodcut of The Declaration and Standard of the Levellers of England (1649) by William Everard

Whilst the Digger movement only lasted for a few years in the C17, heir vision of a society based on common ownership of the land has inspired many, including the

San Francisco Diggers of the 1960s whose mixture of direct action and street theatre advocated a free lifestyle, handing out free food, setting up free shops and establishing a free medical centre. **The Land is Ours** which has been campaigning in the UK since the mid-1990s references the Diggers in their call for access to land, the saving of common spaces and the participation of ordinary people in decisions about land-use and its resources. The **Diggers and Dreamers** website and publications for communal living in Britain are another offshoot from this short period of history.

Hill, C. (1972) 'Levellers and True Levellers', in C. Hill, *The World Turned Upside Down: Radical Ideas During the English Revolution*, London: Temple Smith.

Direct action

Direct action refers to protests that seek to change material conditions directly rather than through governmental politics, which are perceived to have failed or to have been inadequate. It can take many forms, from the non-violent civil disobedience advocated by Gandhi, in order to attract attention and put pressure on those in power, to using your own body as a means of protest. In the early 1900s, the suffragettes' famously protested by chaining themselves to railings, disrupting public meetings and damaging public property. Direct action has in fact been a valuable method of protest in many social movements and struggles, including the trade union movement and more recently the alter-globalisation movement, which is self-organised (p.197) in nature and has grown into a global network of grassroots groups who have created transversal links through shared goals and a desire for a different politics.

From a specifically urban point of view squatting (p.199) is a form of direct action that takes over disused buildings in order to put them to use, whilst movements such as Reclaim the Streets have temporarily transformed the urban environment in order to promote ideas of community ownership of public space over the privatisation and commodification of spaces such as those found in the City of London. The artist and activist **John Jordan** was a co-founder of Reclaim the Streets and has also worked with the social art group Platform as well as setting up the Clandestine Insurgent Rebel Clown Army and more recently the Camp for Climate Action. Jordan brings a creative approach to direct action, bringing together artistic modes with a socially engaged politics. Through organising events and working with social movements he uses art as a way of transforming social and spatial relations and not just representing them.

John Jordan with Ariadna Aston (2009) 'Think like a Forest, Act like a Meadow', *field:* 3 (1)(2009): 23–33. <http://www.field-journal.org/index.php?page=issue-3> (accessed 12 July 2010).

District Six

Cape Town, South Africa, 1966–1994
www.districtsix.co.za
District Six refers to a displaced community, the manifestations of their agency, and of how this situation and the cause it represents have been taken up by others, now representing a shared heritage or an 'urban memory' which many others beyond the members of the original community have taken to heart. The key projects related to this are the District Six Museum and its website, which also acts as an online archive and community forum. Related to this is a grand project, considered by some to be impossibly foolish and by others (such as South Africa's Land Claims Commission) to be a national obligation, to rebuild District Six. In fact implementation of this has begun (and some 24 homes have been built), although it can and will never take the form of a reconstruction of what was lost. These projects are set in the context of a history of mass defiance, campaigning, cultural and critical protest, and social mobilisation which sought and seeks to overcome the impact and legacy of the destruction of District Six.

The story of District Six is well known and well documented in South African history. Originally a city centre mixed race neighbourhood, the district was bulldozed under apartheid laws (the Group Areas Act of 1950) and 60,000 residents were moved to a new 'coloured township' – Mitchell's Plain – and other locations on the barren Cape Flats, their homes and histories taken from them by force. Since the advent of democracy in 1994, plans have been afoot to reinstate District Six through a number of built projects, urban design and other initiatives, and through various community and cultural projects. There are many books, films, and debates about District Six, including the 2009 parody science fiction film 'District Nine'.

Construction of Drop City's passive solar collector designed by Zomeworks (1967). Ph: Clark Richert

Although District Six came into being in 1867 – as the Sixth Municipal District of Cape Town, originally established as a mixed community of freed slaves, merchants, artisans, labourers and immigrants – the period in which it has been explicitly associated with resistance began in 1966, the year in which it was designated a 'white only' area. It could therefore be argued that this is the date in which the 'spatial agency' of District Six began, but of course the real story is more complicated than that. By the same token, the 'end date' given for District Six is simply provided as a point of discussion; some would say that 1994 – the year in which Mandela was elected and South Africa's rule by apartheid technically brought to an end – was simply the beginning of the end of District Six, and that the real end to the struggle will only be achieved when the community (or its memory) has been reinstated in its historical place.

Off District Six Committee Hands (1990) *The Struggle for District Six: Past and Present: A Project of the Hands Off District Six Committee*, Cape Town: Buchu Books.

Drop City

Near Trinidad, Colorado, USA, 1965–1973
www.clarkrichert.com/dropcity
Drop City was an intentional community in southern Colorado established in 1965 and abandoned in 1973. Although short lived, it was very influential and is considered as the first rural hippie commune. Filmmaker Gene Bernofsky and art students JoAnn Bernofsky, Richard Kallweit and Clark Richert bought a seven-acre plot of land in which to live and work together. Organised without any obvious hierarchies, it encapsulated a growing desire at the time to 'drop out' of mainstream life, as much a reaction to consumerist, individual lifestyles as it was to US foreign policy, in particular the Vietnam War.

During its creative heyday between 1965 and 1969, Drop City consisted of around 14–20 inhabitants whose main artistic output took the form of buildings. Inspired by the geodesic design principles of Buckminster Fuller, (p.96) a number of domes were built, a kind of DIY version of Fuller's scientific and precise method. It was the first time that geodesic domes were used for

141

domestic living; until then they had only housed exhibitions or were used for industrial and institutional applications. At Drop City, the domes were built without a systematic kit or an exact design, using waste and salvaged material, including car roofs. Mixed with vernacular building techniques, they were mutations of Fuller's ideas, and he acknowledged the community by awarding Drop City his first Dymaxion award in 1966. The award gave Drop City its place in the history of the US counter-cultural scene but also the mass media attention that eventually led to its demise. The publicity was in complete opposition to the invisibility and isolation that the original founders sought. Large numbers of young people and tourists visited the commune, its open-door policy meaning they were unable to turn anyone away. By 1969 all the original members had left and Drop City became the slightly degenerate joke that its detractors had always couched it as.

Drop City was originally envisioned as a seed that would be replicated numerous times. Whilst this never happened, it did influence a number of experimental projects and at a time when governmental funding for environmental research was scarce, it functioned as an alternative research centre. It was here that Steve Baer developed his Zome design, a flexible version of Fuller's domes, which could be added to and extended easily.

The company **Zomeworks** was an eventual offspring of Drop City, whilst other experiments were in passive solar design including the construction of a large solar collector. It is perhaps in this legacy that the agency of the short-lived experiment is most apparent; Drop City also inspired a number of counter communities, (p.132) as well as influencing the founders of the Whole Earth Catalog. (p.212)

Sadler, S. (2006) 'Drop City Revisited', *Journal of Architectural Education*, 58: 5–14.

Ecovillages
Various, 1987–
gen.ecovillage.org
Ecovillages are intentional communities that strive for a degree of self-sufficiency and a low environmental impact, often motivated by the desire to find a sustainable alternative to capitalist society. Many are part of the Global Ecovillages Network and vary in size from 50–500 members. Some have a strong spiritual dimension, for example the Findhorn Community (p.148) in Scotland and Auroville in India, whilst others focus on collaborative and egalitarian social structures. Ecovillages often experiment in social organisation, operating alternative education and social welfare systems, forms of consensus democracy, or alternative

Solar House at Crystal Waters. Ph: Max O Lindegger

Iquique Housing courtyard with additions. Ph: Cristobal Palma

economies, for example Christiania (p.119) and Findhorn Community both have a local currency and informal bartering systems. They can also be places where practical research into green technologies occurs, such as new designs for composting toilets or waste-water recycling and experiments in permaculture principles. There are currently around 500 sites in the ecovillages network, which includes large groupings of villages in Senegal and Sri Lanka, small ecotowns, sites in urban contexts such as Christiania, and educational centres such as Centre for Alternative Technology (p.116) in Wales.

One of the better known ecovillages is **Crystal Waters** located near Brisbane, Australia, which has a population of around 200 people. Initiated in 1985 as a cooperative community, in 1987 it became the first such settlement to be designed and operated wholly according to permaculture principles. The cooperative owns 500 acres of land, which was bought by a trust fund to which prospective residents contributed. Eighty percent of land is held in common, including areas for agriculture and for wildlife habitats, whilst the rest is owned privately, this includes housing and commercial property in the Crystal Waters village. The settlement aims to have a low environmental impact, to revive land quality, as well as improving the socio-economic circumstances in what is an economically depressed area. The community has a set of by-laws that ensure sustainable construction methods, govern the use of land, the types of businesses on site and levels of recycling etc. Crystal Waters does not aim for total self-sufficiency, preferring to maintain connection with surrounding communities.

Dawson, J. (2006) *Ecovillages: New Frontiers for Sustainability*, Totnes: Green Books.

Elemental
Santiago, Chile, 2000–
www.elementalchile.cl
Elemental is an architectural practice founded in 2000, which grew out of the desire to address the problem of social housing in Chile. It has since evolved into an unusual practice that is a partnership between a University (Universidad Católica de Santiago), an oil company (COPEC, the Chilean energy company) and an architect (Alejandro Aravena).

Elemental's first project located in Iquique, one of the largest port cities of Chile, brought them widespread acclaim. They were asked to rehouse a 100 squatter families on the same plot of land that they had occupied for the last 30 years, but to do this within the standard government subsidy of US$7500 per house, an amount which was to cover the land, associated infrastructure and construction costs. Their site was located in the city-centre and was therefore three times more expensive than the suburban areas normally used for social housing, which may be cheap but result in gruelling two to three hour commutes to and from work. Elemental realised that the money left over from buying the land would only allow them to build half a house and so they concentrated on building the essentials of a house: the overall structure, kitchen and bathroom. With the tradition and skills of self-building that squatter families acquire through need, they would be able to in-fill and complete the house given a well designed framework from which to start. This type of approach to the question of social housing sees it as a 'public investment rather than a public expense'. As the houses are added to over time, they gain value and their rather stark original design is softened through occupation and use.

Iquique Housing interior at handover and after. Ph: Taduez Jalocha

Elemental's insistence on referring to their housing work as urban projects is an indication of their desire to protect existing communities and design neighbourhoods, rather than individual buildings. Theirs is a participative design process that responds to the individual needs and circumstances of each community. Through acknowledging what is available both economically and socially they act as spatial agents, transforming the meagre housing subsidy into a tool that can genuinely be used to address the huge housing deficit.

Verona, I. (2006) 'Elemental Program: Rethinking Low-cost Housing in Chile', *Praxis: Journal of Writing + Building*, 8: 52–57.

Estudio Teddy Cruz

San Diego, USA, 1994–
www.politicalequator.org

Teddy Cruz's practice is situated in and informed by the Tijuana/San Diego border zone. Although the border itself is becoming more and more militarised, it remains porous through the counter-tactics of those who transgress it, tunnelling under or moving across in the cover of darkness. Whilst these 'illegal' people move northwards, all sorts of objects, large and small move southwards; the excess of US consumer society, from houses that were to be demolished to disused tyres, are moved across the border to be recycled and reused. It is in the context of this continual flow back and forth that Cruz places his own practice. Taking inspiration from the ways in which informal settlements creatively reuse 'waste' material and make flexible spaces with overlapping programmes, he creates an affordable architecture in the US and Mexico, working with NGO's and non-profit organisations on both sides of the border.

Estudio Teddy Cruz combines practice and research, with Cruz himself having taught at Woodbury University in San Diego, as well as his current position at University of San Diego California. The practice's method expands the role of the architect, carrying out research into systems and materials, socio-political phenomena, as well as engaging in the political and legal issues related to the built environment. Mike Davis (p.136) is a frequent collaborator and advisor on their urban research and has also acted as client. The practice designed an extension for the writer's house that filled the plot and built on top of the single-storey garage. The rather innocuous sounding project acted as a planning test case for one of Cruz's long-standing campaigns to increase the density of US suburban sprawl. This episode illustrates well their working method, the project began as research on migrant communities' use of the standard suburban house, a large extended family occupying space originally designed for the nuclear family, perhaps adding a business on the ground floor. These spatial practices of densification and hybrid use were not supported by obsolete planning and zoning policies, proving Cruz's point that buildings, and architecture in its traditional sense, cannot advance without the modification of political and legal structures.

The projects carried out by Estudio Teddy Cruz start with issues of scarcity and economic failure, using

Border Fence: a photographic reproduction of the US – Mexico border fence, produced by Estudio Teddy Cruz for the 11th Architecture Biennale in Venice. Ph: Lisbet Harboe

as inspiration the inventive everyday practices found in these situations of crisis. They propose bottom-up solutions in collaboration with local NGOs and other non-profit organisations in an approach that shows the emancipatory potential of architecture as well as acknowledging its inherently political context. Their work is disseminated as built-form, but also as workshops, lectures and exhibitions; they have participated in the Venice Architecture Biennale and take part in the annual **InSITE** public art programme at the Tijuana/San Diego border.

Cruz T. (2005) 'Tijuana Case Study: Tactics of Invasion – Manufacturing Sites', *Architectural Design*, 75(5): 32–37.

Exyzt
Paris, France, 2002–
www.exyzt.org
Exyzt are a Paris based collective founded by five architects, Nicolas Henninger, François Wunschel, Phillipe Rizzotti, Pier Schneider and Gilles Burban, who studied together at Paris La Villette School of Architecture. In 2002 they formed a practice around the idea of 'building and living together', an approach that means

Exyzt not only design their projects but also build them, erecting temporary structures and creating social spaces that are programmed in consultation with local user groups. Since their first project in 2003, the collective has slowly grown into a network of like minded people who come together around certain projects and include a graphic designer, plumber, DJ, photographer, woodworker, electrician, web designer, cook and writer. Exyzt have made installations and interventions in a number of cities including Paris, Venice, London and São Paulo.

Exyzt typically choose empty sites or buildings in the city, acquiring them temporarily with the permission of the owner and transforming them with simple structures and mobile units that have a DIY aesthetic and are cheap and easy to build. Although Exyzt's projects seem very informal they are heavily curated. By creating links with local inhabitants and specific user groups they design spaces that can be appropriated by them through organising specific workshops and events. Whilst projects such as the Southwark Lido and the Dalston Mill in London have been extremely popular, and opened many eyes to the wider possibilities of spatial occupation, Exyzt have so far resisted the temptation to transform these into

Metavilla kitchen. Ph: Florian Kossak/Tatjana Schneider

permanent amenities. It is in fact their temporary nature that seems to be a key component in their success, ensuring that no space is completely appropriated by one dominant user group. Exyzt's working method, and production of temporary reversible architecture informed by theatre and performance, shares many similarities with that of the Berlin based Raumlabor (p.191) collective.

Archinect (2008) *ShowCase: Southwark Lido, a Temporary Public Bath in the Heart of London*. <http://archinect.com/features/article.php? id=77268_0_23_120_M> [accessed 1 February 2010].

Fathy, Hassan

1900–1989

www.hassanfathy.webs.com

Hassan Fathy was an Egyptian architect and engineer who has been credited with bringing the vernacular architecture of Egypt to a wider audience, and for putting neglected traditional building systems to work for the poor. Set in the context of the newly independent Egyptian nation, Fathy's career encapsulates an anti-colonial stance through a rejection of modernism and the valorisation of a culturally specific architecture, which tried to accommodate traditional modes of living whilst being affordable for the majority of the population.

His approach to building was based on the Nubian mud building techniques of the Upper Egypt, where arches and vaults were used to construct roofs without expensive formwork, a technique that he feared had been lost altogether until his discovery of villagers still using the ancient methods. Fathy combined this technique with elements from the vernacular urban architecture of Cairo, incorporating into his designs elements such as the *malqaf*, a wind catcher, the *mashrabiya*, a wooden lattice screen, the *qa'a* a cool central room on the upper-storey of traditional houses with high ceilings and natural ventilation, and the *salsabil* a fountain or basin of water positioned to increase the humidity of the dry desert air. Whilst for Fathy the mixing of these very different building traditions was a way of creating a national architecture for Egypt, he has since been criticised for equating diverse cultures and for not understanding the cultural significance of certain elements, a consequence perhaps of his own westernised sensibilities.

In his book *Architecture for the Poor*, Fathy sets out his philosophy and techniques in the context of his most well-known project, New Gourna. This was a planned village commissioned by the Egyptian government in 1946 to house villagers who were to be displaced from the Antiquities Zone near Luxor, in order to stop them raiding the ancient tombs. Fathy used this opportunity

Brick making in New Gourna village. Ph: Christopher Little/Aga Khan Trust for Culture

to test his ideas on a large-scale, of providing socially and economically viable public housing that was built cooperatively by the owner-dwellers, with help and advice from architects and specialised craftspeople. The villagers were trained in adobe techniques with each house being unique to its family, having been designed in consultation with them. But ultimately the experiment failed with the refusal of the villagers to move away from the only livelihood they had known for generations, as well as their unease at moving into houses with domed roofs, which for them were only suitable for tombs.

New Gourna raises important questions for architecture, demanding that architects pay close attention to the social and cultural values of those they design for. But it also illustrates how much can be done without the involvement of real estate developers, banking and the industrial construction industry. Since New Gourna, Fathy's career was marked by the difficulties he faced in gaining commissions, being regarded as a threat against these commercial building interests. Yet, his emphasis on appropriate technology (a movement of which he is regarded as one of the founders), the use of local materials and construction methods, as well as the desire to create an architecture that was socially and economically suited to its context makes his work especially relevant today.

Fathy, H. (1976) *Architecture for the Poor: An Experiment in Rural Egypt*, Chicago: University of Chicago Press.

Feministische Organisation von Planerinnen und Architektinnen
Germany, 1981–
www.fopa.de

Feministische Organisation von Planerinnen und Architektinnen (FOPA – Feminist Organisation of Architects and Planners) has been operating since 1981, working to reduce discrimination against women in the profession and the built environment in general. The network emerged out of a protest against the organisation of the International Building Exhibition (IBA) in Berlin (1984 and 1987) which they felt excluded many women. The group 'Frau-Steine-Erde' 'hijacked' one of the first IBA meetings and held a series of lectures through which they critiqued the exclusion of women from the planning and building process, the ignorance towards female inhabitants in large refurbishment projects and the commissioning of exclusively male architects for new buildings. The first directors of FOPA were Veronika Keckstein, Kerstin Dörhöfer and Ellen Nausester; they now have regional offices across Germany, some organising lectures and seminars for the continuing professional development of women, whilst others are more research focused; they published a journal until 2004. Whilst FOPA is a German organisation, similar initiatives that promote women in architecture are present in many other countries, such as the Association for Women in Architecture in US founded in 1922, or Women in Architecture in UK, founded in 1999, amongst many others.

'Women in Architecture'. <http://www.diversecity-architects.com/WIA/wia.htm> [accessed 20 July 2010]. Spatial Agency Encyclopaedia

Ferro, Sérgio

1938–

Sérgio Ferro is a Brazilian architect and painter who was born in Curitiba (p.166) in 1938. He graduated from the University of São Paulo in 1962 but was jailed by the Brazilian dictatorship alongside his mentor, Vilanova Artigas and his colleague Rodrigo Lefèvre. Ferro was exiled for 30 years and spent a large part of this time in France teaching at the Grenoble School of Architecture. From 1960 to 1970 he was a member of **Arquitectura Nova**, a radical architecture group which he formed with Flávio Império and Rodrigo Lefèvre. The group critiqued Brazil's modernist impulse which they viewed as excluding the vast majority of Brazilians who were living in poverty. Instead they took part in urban actions and proposed strategies that would democratise access to architecture as well as the design and building process itself. They described their work as creating an 'aesthetics of poverty' and a 'poetics of economy' imagining a highly politicised approach to architecture.

Ferro in particular developed this argument of the city not as a place of aesthetic beauty, as the modernists conceptualised it, but as a place of extreme cruelty. His ideas took shape during the 1960s when he was involved in the design of Brasília, the new capital city. The disjunction between the architectural discourse of freedom and democracy that surrounded the project and the reality of the inhuman working conditions on site, were formative for Ferro and his critique of the architectural profession. He witnessed first hand the working conditions on site, the poor pay, lack of food, the dysentery that was rife, and the dangerous building practices that seemed to have no regard for the lives of the workers. Worst amongst these was the construction

of Oscar Niemeyer's showcase buildings, the National Congress whose bowl shaped chamber required a huge steel structure under which workers were crushed, and the cathedral from whose concrete ribs workers had to swing during construction. Ferro saw these working conditions as part of a system of organised repression and control, where the work camps were controlled by a constant threat of violence.

These experiences led Ferro to write extensively on architecture as the production of commodity, whose 'modern' practices demanded a division of labour in order to generate the highest profits. For Ferro, this attitude was encapsulated in the architectural drawing, whose exclusive language alienated builders, couching them as ignorant manual labour. The situation was exacerbated through isolating each part of the construction process, which effectively gave architects complete control and removed all agency from those who built their designs. In Ferro's conceptualisation of architecture, the process of designing buildings could not be separated from their construction.

Andreoli, E. and Forty, A. (2004) *Brazil's Modern Architecture*, London: Phaidon.

Findhorn community

Findhorn, Scotland, UK, 1962–
www.findhorn.org

Located in rural Scotland, the Findhorn community began in a caravan park in 1962, when the late Peter and Eileen Caddy became unemployed and moved to the park with their three children. Together with Dorothy MacLean they set out to live a more sustainable and spiritual life, starting off by growing their own food. This resulted in the highly productive Findhorn Garden, which became renowned for the quality and quantity of its produce, grown in the adverse weather conditions of northern Scotland and the sandy soil of the caravan park. The community now consists of a network of small holdings that grow organic produce, combining an ecological way of living with a strong spiritual dimension.

Findhorn has grown over the years in size and stature, from the original six it has now 300 residents living on the main site of the original caravan park, and a larger community of local businesses and organisations gathered around this main hub. They gained charitable status in 1972 as the Findhorn Foundation,

Peter Caddy in the garden at Findhorn. Courtesy Findhorn Foundation

Cabbages and the Original Caravan. Courtesy Findhorn Foundation

which is also a founding member of the Global Ecovillages Network. The network brings together communities working towards a more sustainable way of living, defined as ecological as well as economic, cultural and spiritual.

A recent study indicated that Findhorn has one of the smallest environmental footprints of any community in the industrialised world, at about half the UK average. This is achieved through its organic food production as well as through its energy independence, the four windmills on site allowing the community to sell energy back to the national grid. Findhorn also employs the 'living machine' system developed at the New Alchemy Institute, (p.176) which uses a mixture of plants and aquatic life for wastewater treatment. Other initiatives include the replacement of the original caravans with eco-friendly buildings, a local currency, the Eko, which is accepted at other Ecovillages, (p.142) as well as the many small community businesses associated with the Findhorn Foundation. These include the Findhorn Press, which has published many books on ecological and spiritual living, an organic food store and vegetable box scheme, and a complementary medicine centre. The complex also functions as a training centre running diverse courses on sustainable communal living.

Caddy, E. (1991) *Foundations of a Spiritual Community*, 2nd edn, Moray: Findhorn Press.

Fourierist communities

France and USA, 1808–1968

Charles Fourier (1772–1837) was a French social theorist who in a series of texts published between 1808 and his death in 1837, elaborated a vision for a utopian society organised along principles of sexual liberation, co-operative organisation, women's liberation and human interaction. Derived from his ideas on the different types of human personalities and the importance of all to find a partner suited to them, Fourier calculated 1,620 to be the optimum number for people living and working together. These groups of people would live communally in what he termed a *phalanstère*, consisting of a building arranged in a u-shape with a wing on either side. The *phalanstère* included large meeting rooms, private rooms and gardens and is commonly considered a forerunner to Ebenezer Howard's garden cities. (p.168) For Fourier the *phalanstères* were communities set up in direct opposition to both the industrial revolution and its attendant bourgeois society. He realised that industrial society may generate wealth but its working conditions were alienating and unjust; he advocated instead a radical vision where people would only do the work they enjoyed.

In France these ideas were put into practice by the industrialist Jean-Baptiste Godin (1817–88) who wanted to create a society where everyone had equal wealth. In 1859 Godin founded a communal settlement called the *Familistère* or Social Palace that was linked to a stove

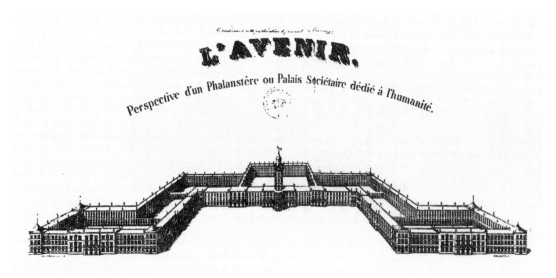

Perspective view of the phalanstère. Image: Victor Considérant

Interior courtyard at the Familistère, Guise. Ph: Melaine Lefeuvre

factory and included amenities such as co-operative shops, a wash house, nurseries, schools and a theatre. The buildings were designed according to Fourier's principles with inner courtyards and recreational gardens. Godin's experiment lasted in co-operative form until 1968, when parts of the site were sold. It is now subject to an EU funded restoration project.

Fourierism was also influential in the US where the ideas were promoted by Albert Brisbane (1809–90), who established the North American Phalanx in New Jersey in 1843 to bring community members together in varied social interactions and activities. The members themselves believed in participation in the design process, allowing buildings to be developed gradually as an expression of community, and carrying out the building work themselves. They constructed their own, locally inspired, versions of Fourier's *phalanstère* with communal spaces balanced with individual rooms and provision for families to build private cottages. The community finally came to an end in 1857 following a fire that destroyed many of the buildings on site, and which was preceded by an ideological split over women's rights, the abolition of slavery and the desire of some members to include religious affiliation for members of the phalanx.

Fourier, C. (1971) *Design for Utopia: Selected Writings*, New York: Schocken.

Friedman, Yona

Yona Friedman is a Hungarian-French architect and theorist whose utopian projects deal with issues of urban planning, infrastructure and the empowerment of the user. In 1958 Friedman published his manifesto, *Architecture Mobile*, for a new type of citizen free from the strictures of work through the growing automation of production. Friedman envisioned that the increase in leisure time would fundamentally change society and would demand a new architecture. This architecture was developed in his project *Ville Spatiale* (1958–62), consisting of temporary, lightweight structures raised above the ground which could span across existing cities, countryside, bodies of water, creating a continuous landscape that could be appropriated and inhabited by the user.

Friedman's *Ville Spatiale* has similarities with Constant's (p.178) situationist take on the utopian city, *New Babylon* (1956–69). Both are designed for the anticipated abolition of work, formally both schemes are raised above the ground on stilts, creating a network capable of spanning the globe. They also employ a similar aesthetic, one very different from the pop sensibility of Archigram (p.87); their use of collage, subdued colours and models create an atmosphere that is less exuberantly optimistic but perhaps more real. But it was Friedman's emphasis on participation

Pavement guerrilla gardening. Ph: Josef Bray-Ali

that set him apart from his contemporaries, including Constant whose *New Babylon* had a slightly authoritarian character. In Friedman's work spatial agency occurs in the valorisation of the user above the architect and the master builder, as seen in his later work (from the mid 1970s to the late 1980s) where he developed a series of self-building manuals for unskilled labourers in India, and various countries in Africa and South America. Working with UNESCO and the UN Friedman developed a language of pictograms that could communicate a system of building using local materials and convey information on dealing with issues ranging from water management and infrastructure to food policy.

Friedman's ideas frequently went beyond architecture and planning encompassing contemporary art, sociology, economics and information systems, but his work is tied together with the principle of individual freedom that he first put forward in his 1958 manifesto and with his emphasis on unpredictability, play, and the empowerment of the non-specialist and the user.

Friedman, Y. and Obrist, H. U. (2007) *Yona Friedman*, Köln: König.

Guerrilla gardening
Europe and USA
www.guerrillagardening.org
The term guerrilla gardening was coined by Liz Christy, an artist living and working in New York in the 1970s. Inner-city neighbourhoods were in decline, the middle-classes had moved to the suburbs and the lack of investment resulted in the steady decline of public spaces. Christy noticed tomato plants growing out of rubbish, the tiny plants signalling a potential; she began scattering seeds in empty spaces and planting disused tree-pits. This effort eventually culminated in a community garden, on a vacant plot located at the corner of Bowery and Houston streets in Manhattan. What started as an illicit action soon became renowned and the Green Guerrillas, as they named themselves, were invited to help start community gardens elsewhere. The original garden eventually gained legitimacy and was granted community garden status, giving it protection from development.

Richard Reynolds, a guerrilla gardener based in London and founder of the eponymous website, describes his activity as 'the illicit cultivation of someone else's land'. Although the term guerrilla gardening is mainly associated with the US and Europe, it is becoming a world-wide phenomena linked in particular through Web 2.0 technologies. In England this movement can be traced back to the Diggers' (p.139) fight for common land and the right to grow food in left-over and neglected spaces. Whilst the political ideal of common land that is owned collectively and accessed by all is reflected in guerrilla gardening, an essential difference remains. Guerrilla gardeners do not necessarily grow food, and for many it is not an act of survival, it is instead about the desire to beautify, to make a healthier environment, a communal space, to express oneself – or to simply garden.

Reynolds, R. (2008) *On Guerrilla Gardening: A Handbook for Gardening Without Boundaries*, London: Bloomsbury.

Habraken, John
1928–
www.habraken.com
John Habraken is a Dutch architect who has researched mass housing and strategies for the participation of users and residents in the building process. He is best-known for his concept of separating the physical infrastructure of buildings into support and infill, developed in the book *Supports: An Alternative to Mass Housing*, which was first published in 1961. *Supports* advocated an approach where the State provided the infrastructure on top of and between which people could build their own housing, influenced in some respects by the work of the Megastructuralists. Habraken took this further as director of the Foundation for Architectural Research (SAR) which investigated the use of industrial manufacturing in mass housing and looked at the role of architects within this.

In breaking up the provision of housing into a number of different components, each of which would be tackled separately, Habraken's solution lies between what Nabeel Hamdi (p.154) has termed the 'provider paradigm' and 'support paradigm' in his book, *Housing without Houses*. Whilst in the provider model housing is seen as a physical and technical problem that can be solved through mass production and regulation, in order to ensure quality and standards, the support model acknowledges the dispersed nature of resources in society, focusing instead on social infrastructure.

This is considered an issue of management and resource allocation, as exemplified in the work of organisations such as Habitat for Humanity (p.100) or the Community Design (p.126) movement of the US. In Habraken's method, the large-scale physical infrastructure is designed and built by the technicians – architects, engineers and construction companies – working with the State, whilst the infill is provided by a small-scale, individualised approach. This allows users to have a meaningful participation in the design of their homes, can accommodate self-building and is a highly flexible building model that can be adapted as required. Habraken's approach is complemented by those of John Turner (p.202) and Colin Ward, (p.210) both of whom focus on the social and economic aspects of housing provision with a similar model. There are also echoes of this in the work of DEGW (p.138) on office design, where they adapt the idea of support and infill to fit the life-cycles of office buildings.

Habraken, J. (1972) *Supports: An Alternative to Mass Housing*, London: Architectural Press.

Hackitectura
Seville, Spain, 1999–
mcs.hackitectura.net
Hackitectura is a group of architects, artists, computer specialists and activists founded by José Pérez de Lama, Sergio Moreno and Pablo de Soto in 1999. Their practice uses new technologies to create temporary spaces that can escape the formal structures of control and surveillance which are regulated by technological and political means in contemporary society. Inspired by hacker culture, they use free software and communication technologies to subvert established power structures through bottom-up organisation and by creating alternative connections between disparate spaces. The group often works collaboratively, carrying out research into the effects of communication and technology on physical spaces, the formation of social networks and how these can be put to work for an activist agenda.

They have collaborated with Indymedia Estrecho on mapping and creating links across the Straits of Gibraltar or *Madiaq*, the highly militarised zone that is the shortest distance between Africa and Europe. As part of a series of projects they established a network link that became a free public interface between the two continents creating an 'alternative cross-border communication space', a counter-strategy to the increasing surveillance and security regimes of the border. The project also included a series of regular events that took place on either side of the straits. Called *Fada'iat* or 'through spaces' the events included workshops, actions, and seminars bringing together migration, labour rights, gender and communication activists, political theorists, hackers, union organisers, architects and artists in a temporary media-lab that could become a permanent public interface between Tarifa and Tangiers. Combined with direct actions against the detention of migrants, for a time the event created a network of communication, action and solidarity between the two continents.

Observatorio Tecnológico del Estrecho (2006) *Fadaiat: Freedom of Movement – Freedom of Knowledge*. <http://fadaiat.net/> [accessed 2 February 2010].

Hamdi, Nabeel

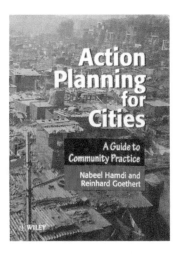

Nabeel Hamdi is one of the pioneers of participatory planning and his 2004 book, *Small Change*, has been highly influential in describing the role that informality plays in urban life. It sets out a way of thinking on cities that gives precedence to small-scale, incremental change over large-scale projects. He shows how the trickle-down effect advocated by conservatives everywhere does not produce the sort of large-scale changes that are predicted. It is instead the trickle-up effect of self-organised systems that produce the biggest

changes. He uses examples from cities in the global South, writing of how the smallest change such as the installation of a bus-stop that results in a group of people waiting, induces a whole host of small-scale economies such as people selling food or drinks, or the provision of street lighting around which children gather to complete their homework due to the lack of electricity at home, means that sweet and book sellers appear in the area hawking their wares.

Hamdi's own practice has always used the tactic of small-scale change at grass-roots level, whether in his early housing work with the Greater London Council that tested ideas on participatory design and planning, or his later work as consultant to various governmental and UN agencies. His work epitomises an approach that looks for ways to use his skills as an architect to bolster or augment already existing structures, rather than starting ab initio. It is a way of working with the given, making small changes, giving time and giving agency to those involved rather than leading the process from the outside.

As a pedagogue, Hamdi set up the highly successful Masters in Development Practice at Oxford Brookes University in 1992 as part of the Centre for Development and Emergency Practice. The MA course was one of the first of its kind and, being practice based, allows students to collaborate with practitioners in the field.

Hamdi, N. (2004) *Small Change: About the Art of Practice and the limits of Planning in Cities*, London: Earthscan.

Hasan, Arif

Arif Hasan is an architect and researcher working in Karachi, a city of more than 12 million inhabitants in Pakistan, with the associated problems of a lack of resources such as regular power cuts, water shortages and extremely high land prices. Hasan is well-known for his involvement in low-income housing especially the Orangi Pilot project, which built up a number of approaches to upgrading squatter settlements. Through research carried out in association with architecture students at Dawood College in Karachi, Hasan developed a framework for the Orangi settlement that acknowledged the central role played by the *thallawala*, someone who sets-up and manages a builders yard in the settlement. Typically, *thallawalas* make building components, give advice on building techniques, as well

A street in Orangi before and after construction of sewers. CourtesyOrangi Pilot Project Research and Training Institute

as providing water and credit loans for the embryonic settlements. The *thallawalas* therefore provide a minimum level of infrastructure required for a new settlement to be built, and the Orangi project worked by concentrating on improving the skills of the *thallawalas* and sourcing cheaper building materials for them. Spatial agency here takes account of the existing social infrastructure that allowed the settlements to be built in the first place. Hasan's approach is rare as it enhances and uses existing skills and knowledge rather than imposing other ways of doing.

Another strategy employed at Orangi was to organise the inhabitants to finance and build their own sewage systems, where each lane of the settlement took responsibility for its own part of the network. They also ran a credit programme for small businesses and health and educational programmes. During the course of the project specific sanitation and construction technology was developed which was compatible with the sociology and economics of low-income groups. Once again agency occurs through giving importance to local knowledge: the strategy of residents building their own sewage system would only have worked in the context of self-building and the existence of the *thallawalas* who provided an effective way of disseminating specialised knowledge. The emphasis on developing not only the physical infrastructure but also a social infrastructure makes the project sustainable.

This model of a micro-level planning approach is now being replicated in other settlements in Pakistan.

Hasan, A. (2002) *Understanding Karachi: Planning and Reform for the Future*, Karachi: City Press.

Haus-Rucker-Co

Vienna, Austria, 1967–1992
www.ortner.at/haus-rucker-co/de/haus-rucker.html
Haus-Rucker-Co were a Viennese group founded in 1967 by Laurids Ortner, Günther Zamp Kelp and Klaus Pinter, later joined by Manfred Ortner. Their work explored the performative potential of architecture through installations and happenings using pneumatic structures or prosthetic devices that altered perceptions of space. Such concerns fit with the utopian architectural experiments of the 1960s [(p.87)] by groups such as Superstudio, Archizoom, Ant Farm [(p.95)] and Coop Himmelblau. [(p.129)] Alongside these groups, Haus-Rucker-Co were exploring on the one hand, the potential of architecture as a form of critique, and on the other the possibility of creating designs for technically mediated experimental environments and utopian cities.

Taking their cue from the Situationists [(p.178)] ideas of play as a means of engaging citizens, Haus-Rucker-Co created performances where viewers became participants and could influence their own environments, becoming more than just passive onlookers.

155

Laurids, Zamp and Pinter with Environment Transformers (Flyhead, Viewatomizer and Drizzler) 1968. Ph: Gert Winkler.

These installations were usually made from pneumatic structures such as *Oase No. 7* (1972), which was created for Documenta 5 in Kassel, Germany. An inflatable structure emerged from the façade of an existing building creating a space for relaxation and play, of which contemporary echoes can be found in the 'urban reserves' of Santiago Cirugeda. (p.120) The different versions of the *Mind Expander* series (1967–69), consisted of various helmets that could alter the perceptions of those wearing them, for example the 'Fly Head' disoriented the sight and hearing of the wearer to create an entirely new apprehension of reality; it also produced one of their most memorable images.

Haus-Rucker-Co's installations served as a critique of the confined spaces of bourgeois life creating temporary, disposable architecture, whilst their prosthetic devices were designed to enhance sensory experience and highlight the taken-for-granted nature of our senses, seen also in the contemporaneous work of the Brazilian artist Lygia Clark. Contemporary versions of such work can be found in the pneumatic structures favoured by Raumlabor (p.191) and Exyzt. (p.145)

Rodrigo, A. (2005) *Expanded Space*. <http://www.roalonso.net/en/arte_y_tec/ espacio_expandido.php> [accessed 14 July 2010].

Healthabitat
Newport Beach, Australia, 1985–
www.healthhabitat.com
Healthabitat link environmental conditions, and in particular the provision of adequate housing, to general health and well-being. Their work has especially addressed these issues in the context of the Aboriginal

people of Australia whose living environment and health standards have been woefully inadequate in relation to white Australians. Established in 1985 by architect, Paul Pholeros, anthropologist, Stephen Rainbow and physician, Paul Torzillo, what began as a modest report on these issues for an Aboriginal controlled health service in the Anangu Pitjantjatjara Lands, is now a national programme. The initial report's aim was to find out why sickness levels in the area were so high, even with sufficient healthcare, and found correlations with the state of the housing provision.

Healthabitat's projects mostly deal with the day-to-day maintenance and improvement of housing, including the provision of adequate washing and cooking facilities, sanitation, heating etc. The success of Healthabitat's approach lies in its simplicity and their commitment that for every research phase some action or material transformation should also occur. This pledge is especially important in a context where Aboriginal communities had failed to see any major improvement in their living conditions despite numerous reports, surveys and analyses. Healthabitat's importance lies in their linking of design to health and well-being, a maybe obvious but often overlooked connection that has implications far beyond the aboriginal context.

Pholeros, P. and others (1993) *Housing for Health: Towards a healthy living environment for Aboriginal Australia*, Newport Beach, NSW: Healthabitat.

HfG Ulm

Ulm, Germany, 1953–1968
www.hfg-archiv.ulm.de
The *Hochschule für Gestaltung* (HfG – 'School of Design') was a private school of industrial design and visual communication in Ulm, Germany, which opened in 1953 and closed in 1968. The school began as a continuation of the Bauhaus experiment, under one of its former students **Max Bill**, who headed HfG until 1956 when he resigned due to ideological conflict over the teaching programme with younger members of staff. Following Bill's departure in 1957, the school took a new direction moving away from a foundation in art towards an approach that emphasised science and society, under the leadership of **Tomás Maldonado**, developing what came to be known as the 'Ulm model' of design.

The short fifteen-year existence of the school had a lasting impact on design education through its use of experimental pedagogy and through creating overt relations with industry. Much of the work produced at Ulm, alongside debates taking place within the school, were disseminated in the journal, *Ulm*, published twice yearly between 1958 and 1968.

Founded in the memory of Hans and Sophie Scholl, who were executed by the Nazis as members of the resistance, HfG Ulm was established by their younger sister, Inge Scholl with **Otl Aicher** and others. Environmental design, as a holistic approach to human habitation, combined with political education was seen as a strategy for strengthening democratic ideals within society. Set up initially with financial support from the US and Europe, the school was later reliant on governmental funding which was never quite enough. Lecturers were obliged to make additional revenue through consultancy work with industry and this was also to prove useful for the school's pedagogical strategy. Otl Aicher introduced the model of design development which tried to bridge the gap between research and teaching. Development groups were led by staff with student assistants, working with industry partners such as Braun, developing products under market conditions. Yet these collaborations also revealed some of the contradictions underlying the Ulm philosophy, on the one hand a commitment to industrial mass production and on the other a suspicion of industry, which for the need to maximise profits did not always share Ulm's goal of design that promoted social good.

HfG Ulm's experimental approach to teaching included the abolishment of departments as traditionally conceived within a university setting; instead disciplines were grouped around topics such as, Industrial Design, Visual Communication, Building, Information, and Film. The system of a large proportion of visiting faculty, four to every permanent member of staff, created an atmosphere of constant re-evaluation and critique, gaining HfG Ulm its reputation as a centre for cutting edge research and teaching in design. Its emphasis on the social responsibility of the designer also helped in the re-orientation of design as an inherently political activity. During the 1960s the school changed emphasis again towards theory, a move that Maldonado and Aicher opposed. The internal conflict finally led to the withdrawal of funding by the regional parliament and the school was shut down amid protests in 1968.

Spitz, R. (2002) *HfG Ulm. The View behind the Foreground: the Political History of the Ulm School of Design*, Felbach: Edition Axel Menges.

Holmes, Brian

brianholmes.wordpress.com

Brian Holmes is an art critic, cultural theorist and activist primarily interested in the intersections of art and political practice. His critical writings are especially useful for architects as a way into contemporary theory and art practices that critique the neo-liberal state and for introducing radical political concepts to a profession that lags far behind art practice in its engagement with issues of social and environmental justice, politics and the wide ranging consequences of 'globalisation'. His writings challenge the architecture profession's self proclaimed neutrality.

Holmes, B. (2007) *Unleashing the Collective Phantoms: Essays in Reverse Imagineering*, New York: Autonomedia.

Independent publishers

The influence of contemporary spatial agency is enhanced by access to new forms of publication and dissemination, sometimes through specialist independent publishers who are experimenting with creative modes of dissemination, often through a combination of old and new media and through utilising local networks. The types of work these publishers produce is also very different from that of commercial publishing houses and is generally more experimental in nature. Whilst alternative modes of publishing such as zines (p.90) are more geared towards self-publishing and the quick generation and distribution of material, the publishers included in this section produce peer-reviewed work.

Some self-published books also have their own internal review process and experiment with more egalitarian modes of dissemination, including the use of creative commons licenses, for example the book, *UrbanACT* by PEPRAV, was distributed through local networks and under the principle of 'one book sold/one book free' at a fixed cost. These and other initiatives, including those listed below, are working towards freeing knowledge and its distribution from the stranglehold of commercial publishing that often stifles creativity and experimentation.

A publication by b_books

b_books was founded in 1996 in Berlin as a publisher, bookshop and cultural centre that later also became involved in film production. It emerged from a network of self-managed spaces, temporary institutions and arts related organisations, including An Architektur, (p.93) sharing a common interest in issues related to the constitution of publics and counter-publics. Through a series of events, exhibitions and actions the bookshop has become an important meeting place and venue, whilst b_books continue to publish on art and urban practice and the public sphere.

Praxis (e) Press is an open access e-book publishing house, which specialises in critical works on theory and practice, including anarchist, anti-racist, environmentalist, feminist, marxist, postcolonial, poststructuralist, queer, situationist and socialist perspectives.

Re-public is a free on-line journal on contemporary politics, theory and practice which operates through open calls for thematic issues with related projects, workshops and podcasts.

Eurozine is a network of European journals that acts as a hosting site, linking partner journals and magazines. It emerged from an informal network of European journals and magazines in 1983 as a forum to exchange ideas and experiences. Since then, with the new opportunities available through web-publishing,

Eurozine was formally founded in 1998 as an independent platform for writing related to European politics and culture. The format of Eurozine allows it to combine the best of old and new media, publishing the best articles from partner journals on a free and multi-lingual site that considerably increases the exposure of those involved.

e-flux is an art journal from New York, established in 2008, which has recently started a print-on-demand service, with a network of local bookshops across a number of countries. The sellers are able to print and distribute the journal locally, either free or at a price determined according to local conditions, whilst a free on-line version of the journal remains available.

Fredriksson, C. H. and others (1998–) *Eurozine*. <http://www.eurozine.com/> [accessed 13 July 2010].

Jacobs, Jane
1916–2006

Jane Jacobs was a writer and activist who was born in the US but later moved to Toronto, Canada. Her work dealt with issues of urban planning, the decline of cities and the break up of neighbourhoods due to top-down planning policy. She is best known for her seminal book, *The Death and Life of Great American Cities* published in 1961, which was a sharp critique of urban renewal policies of the US in the 1950s. Jacobs is equally well-known for her grassroots activities, campaigning against projects that would destroy local neighbourhoods. One of the main projects she was involved in was the campaign which lasted from 1962 until 1968 and resulted in a long and protracted battle with New York master-planner, Robert Moses but eventually led to the cancelling of plans to build the Lower Manhattan Expressway in New York.

Jacobs championed the ordinary citizen and advocated an approach to planning that was situated in and centred on local communities. She often admonished planners to build cities for people and not for cars. At a time when most commentators were advocating the demolition of unsuitable post-war housing, Jacobs was one of the first to emphasise the need for adding density and diversity to the existing urban fabric. With no professional training in urban planning, she relied on her acute observation of city life, combining empirical evidence with a common sense approach. Jacobs conceptualised cities as self-organised ecosystems that interacted with their inhabitants, viewing sidewalks, parks and neighbourhoods as important elements. She advocated mixed-use urban development and above all a bottom-up approach to planning that was adopted in consultation with local inhabitants. In her later books, Jacobs suggested strategies for the economic renewal of cities through 'import replacement', a strategy for local industry to manufacture its own goods, encouraging smaller scale and more diversified economies and providing jobs locally, as well as being environmentally responsible. This approach, which was considered radical at the time is now widely recognised as a way of creating sustainable communities and of tackling climate change.

The influence of Jacobs is such that many of her most important ideas now seem everyday but at the time of their conception they were considered radical. Jacobs' lifelong activism empowered ordinary citizens and her early successes in grassroots organisation paved the way for the advocacy planning and Community Design movements (p.126) in the US.

Jacobs, J. (1961) *The Death and Life of Great American Cities*, New York: Random House.

Jersey Devil
Florida, Washington, Stockton NJ, USA, 1972–
www.jerseydevildesignbuild.com

Jersey Devil are a loose-knit group based around any combination of Jim Adamson, Steve Badanes, and John Ringel who have worked together or separately since the early 1970s. They take their name from the creature of New Jersey folklore, apparently used by a passer-by to describe one of their buildings. What brings these individuals together is their method of working: they not only design buildings, they construct them, in collaboration with other specialists and artisans. This way of working is a critique of mainstream architectural practice that separates design from construction. Instead they take their inspiration from the vernacular tradition of sustainable self-build. In this sense they do not consider their work to be 'alternative' but instead see it as a part of a mainstream that has been marginalised in the quest for greater profits. They see their work as a reclamation of this other way of building.

In Jersey Devil's projects agency derives from giving space to the work and skills of others, specialists and artisans whose craft influences the mode of

Airplane House, Colorado, under construction. Courtesy Jersey Devil

construction as well as the design. Through questioning the sequential relationship of design and construction they facilitate a creative exchange between specialised craftspeople, architects, and users. They often live on site for the duration of the project in caravans and tents, and so have the sort of relationship to the site that is impossible for architects who visit once or twice, their experience always mediated through map data and site photos. For Jersey Devil architecture is realised through the processes of designing and building rather than the provision of information and services for others to build.

Branch, M. A. and Piedmont-Palladino, S. (1997) *Devil's Workshop: 25 Years of Jersey Devil Architecture*, New York: Princeton Architectural Press.

Jorge Mario Jáuregui Architects

Rio de Janeiro, Brazil, 1994–
www.jauregui.arq.br
Jorge Mario Jáuregui Architects (JMJA) are based in Rio de Janeiro working on public interest projects, in both the 'formal' and 'informal' areas of the city and are best known for their project on the upgrading of Rio's favelas and their integration with the rest of the city. Under Brazil's military dictatorship of the 1970s favelas were demolished and their residents displaced. Since then there have been attempts at upgrading but these have been piecemeal with no clear strategy. In 1994

following Cesar Maia's election as mayor of Rio, the city established a nine year programme called *Favela-Bairro*, which is the largest squatter settlement upgrading programme in Latin America. JMJA won an open competition to lead the project and in contrast to earlier strategies they advocated a holistic approach to the favelas that builds on the existing and addresses the physical, social and economic aspects.

Translating as 'slum-neighbourhood', the city-run project tries to come up with an integrated solution where each favela is addressed separately by a team of engineers, a sociologist, legal, cultural and communication consultants, led by an architect. This ensures that each proposal is specific to its particular social and geographical conditions. Beyond providing the necessary infrastructure of water, drainage and electricity, this approach also looks to mend the social infrastructure of the area, providing schools, sports centres and community facilities that are grafted into the existing fabric. An important aspect of the projects is land tenure regularisation, the building of new roads for refuse collection and emergency services, and the upgrading of paths. Sometimes controversial ideas are employed, such as bringing tourists into the favelas; in one project JMJA proposed a funicular railway from the beach to the heart of a favela area, where local youths would be employed to act as tourist guides, a project that was eventually implemented.

160

Cable Car stations at Complexo do Alemão. Courtesy JMJA

Whilst the *Favela-Bairro* project has been criticised by some for not devolving enough power to local groups, it has been a major improvement on previous attempts at such work. JMJA's approach in particular is successful for working within the logic of the favela, recognising that established neighbourhoods have their own organisational and support structures, which should be enhanced and protected whenever possible. One of the notable features of their approach is the requirement that architects and planners involved should have a daily presence in the communities they are working with.

Machado, R. (ed) (2003) *The Favela-Bairro Project: Jorge Mario Jáuregui*, Cambridge, MA: Harvard GSD.

Kéré Architecture

Burkina Faso and Germany, 1998–
www.kere-architecture.com
Diébédo Francis Kéré is an architect from Burkina Faso who studied in Germany and now splits his time

between these two countries. In 1998 he founded the *Schulbausteine für Gando* (Stones for building schools in Gando), a non-profit organisation whose first project collected funds for the construction of a primary school in Gando, Kéré's home village. Whilst still studying at the Technical University in Berlin, Kéré launched the association asking his colleagues to donate money towards the school. Since then he has gained support from a pharmaceutical company, Hevert Arzneimittel, which has promised funding for the following ten years.

Kéré adapts technology from the industrialised world to produce low-cost buildings that are suitable to their context. Construction techniques are adapted for building without heavy machinery and an integral part of the process is the training of local people. Traditional construction methods are improved; for example in Gando the school and consequent buildings are made from compacted earth bricks using refined clay, increasing the material's performance and overcoming the perception of earth as a building material for the

Interior of primary school, Gando. Ph: Erik-Jan Ouwerkerk

School garden at primary school, Gando. Ph: Erik-Jan Ouwerkerk

Demonstration building at Calearth. Ph: Graham Burnett

poor. These are combined with other traditional methods such as a stamped earth floor and cheap materials such as a tin roof.

A sense of social responsibility drove Kéré to pursue projects first in his home village then further afield in Burkina Faso and now the practice has projects in Yemen, India and Mali. Through linking architecture with development Kéré's projects take a holistic approach and his association has expanded its remit beyond building schools to organising women's co-operatives, supporting education for girls and providing much needed employment for youth through training and projects, proving the socially transformative potential of architecture.

Slessor, C. (2009) 'Primary school, Gando, Burkina Faso: Diébédo Francis Kéré', *Architectural Review*, 226 (1352): 66–69.

Khalili, Nader
1936–2008
calearth.org
Nader Khalili was an Iranian architect who lived and worked in both Iran and USA, where he pioneered the technique known as SuperAdobe or Earthbag Construction. Designed initially in response to a NASA call for establishing human settlements on the Moon and Mars, this simple yet highly effective construction method can be used to build shelters quickly and without the need for specialist building skills. It has been used to construct emergency shelters since the first Gulf War where the technique was used in partnership with the UN Refugee Agency UNHCR to house refugees in Iran. In 1991 Khalili founded the California Institute of Earth and Architecture (Cal-Earth) to carry out technical research related to the SuperAdobe method. The non-profit organisation designs and tests prototypes in the extreme climatic conditions of the Mojave desert.

Khalili began his architecture career designing high-rise buildings with offices in Los Angeles and Tehran. Aged 39, the architect closed both offices and travelled around Iran researching appropriate technology solutions to house the poor. He spent five years studying the vernacular desert architecture and the work of Jalaluddin Rumi, the Sufi poet and philosopher whom Khalili saw as a major influence and whose work he translated into English. At this time Khalili developed the technique of *Geltaftan* (literally meaning 'clay' and 'firing' in Persian) where adobe brick buildings are fired from within to increase their durability. He used the technique to rehabilitate houses in a village close to Tehran as well as constructing a school in this method. But his technique did not gain widespread appeal, due in part to the pollution caused by the oil firing process and its relatively high cost.

The SuperAdobe method was a development of this earlier work, an attempt to adapt adobe construction for contexts where there was no prior knowledge of such building techniques. Sandbags filled with earth are laid in courses to construct a structure that has compression strength based on the structural principle of domes, whilst barbed wire placed between the bags provides tensile strength, also making it earthquake resistant. If available, a locally sourced stabiliser such as lime, cement or asphalt is added to the earth. The appeal of this system is that it does not require skilled labour and is built entirely from readily available, local and environmentally friendly material. The structures can be adapted both in form and spatial layout and the flexible system can either be used temporarily or made permanent with a waterproof finish applied to the exterior. This option to convert a temporary structure into a permanent shelter is especially useful in disaster relief situations and in refugee camps where host countries may not prefer permanent structures but the realities of war can demand otherwise. Rather than employing contractors for specialist work, these shelters can be built by the refugees themselves including women, children and the elderly. It also encourages local economies rather than relying on large globally operating construction companies. Khalili's humanitarian architecture thus gives agency to those most in need, being able to construct their own

homes restores a sense of dignity to refugees and even if the shelters are only constructed for temporary use, the solidity of the buildings can give an air of permanence to fragile lives in a way that standard emergency solutions such as tents cannot.

Khalili, N. (1996) *Ceramic Houses and Earth Architecture: How to Build Your Own*, Hesperia, CA: Cal-Earth Press.

Lacaton & Vassal
Paris, France, 1987–
www.lacatonvassal.com
Established in Paris in 1987 by Anne Lacaton and Jean-Philippe Vassal, the practice have designed commercial, educational, cultural and residential buildings. A connecting thread across their work is the desire to find what is essential in each situation and to create a modest language of architecture based on an economy of means. Whether it is their celebrated conversion of the Palais de Tokyo or their social housing refurbishments, Lacaton & Vassal make intelligent re-use of the existing, minimising new building through innovative design, and through an appreciation of the transformative possibilities in each situation. They maintain that ninety percent of what is required for most projects is already available on site. Philippe Lacaton traces this attitude to five years spent in Niger

Social housing, Mulhouse, France. Ph: Philippe Ruault

Palais de Tokyo, Paris, France. Ph: Philippe Ruault

which he describes as a formative experience, where he witnessed first hand what could be achieved with very little through the innovation and creativity of those living in scarcity.

The practice have recently published a book, *PLUS: Large Scale Housing Development – an Exceptional Case*, on the transformation of social housing in the Parisian suburbs that demonstrates their design approach well. Here they make the case for alterations and remodelling rather than the demolition advocated by local authorities. Lacaton & Vassal maintain that demolition is not an environmentally friendly option, regardless of how green the replacement building may be. Instead they outline an approach for remodelling the dysfunctional buildings from the inside out, starting with the needs of the users and letting this dictate their form and look. Walls and façades are removed, balconies are added, communal spaces created, alongside the addition of a lightweight structure for a winter garden. These changes occur building by building with the ability to transform the character of the entire neighbourhood. Through a careful phasing of work, their approach also has the advantage of not displacing and scattering established groups of residents. The practice is currently implementing this strategy on a sixteen-storey block of flats in the 17th arrondissement of Paris and a housing block on a high-rise estate in La Chesnaie, Saint-Nazaire, France.

Lacaton & Vassal state that the first task of the architect is to think, and to decide whether to build or not. They see their role as extending far beyond just building, creatively engaging with the legal and regulatory aspects of each project. Famously, they often manage to stretch budgets far beyond the norm to create spaces that, whilst not according to accepted niceties of finish and surface, are incredibly generous. For example, their social housing project in Mulhouse, France provides twice the normal area by reducing costs through a careful handling of the construction programme and by using unusual construction methods, but to achieve this the architects also had to engage with tax regulators and housing law in order that tenants were not overtaxed. Horticultural greenhouses were erected on top of a concrete frame, with users adapting the raw aesthetic in huge variety of ways, and architects enjoying this apparent loss of control with relish.

Ruby, A., Ruby, I. and Steiner D. (eds) (2007) *Lacaton & Vassal* (2G Books), Barcelona: Gustavo Gili.

Latin American Residential Organisations

Latin America, 1960–

Much of the social housing in Latin America is built through housing cooperatives which can arrange collective loans and can organise micro-financing. Most follow *autogestión* principles, meaning that they are self-organised and managed through autonomous, grassroots, and democratic decision making. Construction is usually carried out according to mutual self-help principles and although some co-operatives allow residents to sell their properties, others only allow them to be passed down to the next generation.

Chile in particular has a strong movement where over 20 percent of low rent housing has been built by housing co-operatives. In 1906, it was one of the earliest national governments to subsidise housing, and later the state became the second largest mortgage lender and largest housing provider in the country. However, the housing subsidy was inadequate and the export of this model to other countries has sometimes been used as an alternative to equitable housing policies. The low subsidy has led to some innovative housing solutions such as the model developed by Elemental (p.143) at Iquique, or through the government working alongside international organisations, such as Habitat for Humanity, (p.100) which provide organisational and technical assistance.

Several Latin American housing cooperatives are part of **Secretaria Latinoamericana de Vivienda Popular (SeLVIP)**, an organisation set up to discuss alternatives to capitalist housing and planning systems; co-operatives representing Argentina, Bolivia, Brazil, Colombia, Cuba, Ecuador, Mexico, Uruguay, Paraguay, Peru, Republica Dominica and Venezuela are part SeLVIP. Established in 1990, it organises annual meetings and its co-founder, the architect Nestor Jeifetz, is a leading figure in the debate on low-cost housing provision. Jeifetz also founded the **Movimiento de Ocupantes e Inquilinos (MOI – Movement of Squatters and Tenants)** in 1998, an organisation with roots in the squatter movement of Buenos Aires, Argentina. MOI takes over unused buildings to act as temporary accommodation for co-operative members whilst their own homes are being built. These are realised through mutual aid contributions, constructed collectively and are self-managed. MOI's other role is to campaign for housing rights and it seeks to influence housing policies.

In Uruguay, housing co-operatives were established in the late 1960s as part of the National Housing Plan which provided the legal framework for the co-operative ownership of property and created a national fund to which every employee must contribute one percent of their pay with employers obliged to match. Shortly afterwards, in 1970, the **Uruguayan Federation of Housing for Mutual-Support Cooperatives (FUCVAM)** was established. It is a national umbrella organisation which grew out of an established labour movement and is now one of the largest and most organised social movements representing 300 separate housing co-operatives and 200,000 families. FUCVAM provides legal and accounting services, has a technical department, training centre, sports and youth facilities, as well as campaigning to lower the interest rates and increase the housing fund, changes that were enacted under the twelve-year dictatorship of 1973–1985.

FUCVAM has thus defended co-operatives in Uruguay through difficult times, ensuring that the legal framework set up during the 1960s remains in place. They are now extending their model across South America, through supporting local struggles and offering their expertise to, for example, groups in Bolivia and Venezuela. It is also a member of **Habitat International Coalition**.

There are a whole host of similar organisations across Latin America, some who help organise and implement the actual construction and management, such as **Centro Experimental de la Vivienda Economica** in Córdoba, Argentina, **Fedevivienda** in Bogota, Colombia, and **Centro de Asesoramiento y Estudios Educativos, sociales y Urbanos** in Montevideo, Uruguay. Others concentrate on training and political reform so that better housing policies are adopted, such as **Red Nacional de Asentamientos Humanos** in Cochabamba, Bolivia.

Fox, M. (2007) 'Building Autonomy, One Co-op at a Time', *Yes! Powerful Ideas, Practical Actions*. Available. Online HTTP: <http://www.yesmagazine.org/issues/liberate-your-space/building-autonomy-one-co-op-at-a-time> [accessed 20 April 2010].

Lerner, Jaime

www.jaimelerner.com

Jaime Lerner is an architect and urban planner who was mayor of Curitiba, in southern Brazil, and also

Bus shelter, Curitiba. Ph: Luciano DeSouza

Curitiba From Barigui Park. Ph: Rodrigo

Main pedestrian thoroughfare, Curitiba. Ph: Lee Pruett

elected twice as governor of the state of Paraná at various times between 1971 and 2002. His tenure of mayor between 1971–5, 1979–84 and 1989–92, transformed Curitiba into one of the greenest cities in the world with a 70 percent recycling rate and an efficient and fairly priced transport system that has been replicated successfully in Bogotá, Los Angeles and Panama. One of the key moves that allowed Lerner to achieve this success was the establishment of the Urban Planning and Research Institute of Curitiba (IPPUC) by his predecessor, Ivo Arzua Pereira (1962–6). The creation of an independent agency that could

supervise and implement planning ensured the continuity of city plans. The unique approach adopted by IPPUC addresses urban problems with inventiveness and simplicity, invariably costing much less than orthodox solutions, for example the use of herds of sheep to trim grass in municipal parks, a tactic that has been replicated in many cities across the world.

Starting out as a practicing architect and planner, Lerner was part of a local team from the Universidad Federal do Paraná which responded to a city call for a plan for the renewal of Curitiba in 1964. Known as the Curitiba Master Plan, it was adopted in 1968 and recommended the establishment of IPPUC. Following his appointment as mayor in 1971, Lerner took this work forward, with his first big achievement being the pedestrianisation of the main shopping thoroughfare. This task was carried out in just 72 hours, the speed of conversion giving no time for shop-keepers to oppose the plans; although causing some controversy, with the subsequent increase in trade the scheme was accepted as a major improvement to the city's environment.

Lerner's best known urban project is Curitiba's integrated bus transit system, the Rede Integrada de Transporte (RIT), which carries as many passengers as a large-scale metro but at a fraction of the cost. Dedicated and exclusive bus lanes, innovative shelters, and a flat-rate which subsidises travel to the outskirts of the city where the poorest citizens live, mean that the RIT is regarded as one of the most efficient and cheapest transport systems in the world. Other problems were also solved in ways that show a thorough understanding of the city and its inhabitants, combined with the power to implement radical plans, for example the problem of collecting rubbish and encouraging recycling in the favelas where the streets are far too narrow for garbage trucks to pass. Here arrangements were made for trucks to visit the favelas at a set time each week, with bags of sorted rubbish being exchanged for bus passes or tickets to see a show or football match. School children were also encouraged to collect rubbish in exchange for toys; the unemployed and homeless were employed in recycling plants and retrained on salvaged computers. As governor, Lerner implemented a scheme where fishermen were paid to collect rubbish from the water, thereby supplementing their income and cleaning the bay at the same time. In Curitiba, rather than building expensive canals to divert flood water, floodplains were turned into parks with overspill areas becoming boating lakes. This has boosted green space in the city and costs much less than building expensive levees.

The initiatives put in place by Lerner show how creativity and lateral thinking can create sustainable and user-centred cities without the need for massive investment. Here spatial agency is encapsulated in understanding the connections between city-wide implementation and local conditions, but it is also a testament to the leadership and charisma of one man who has managed to bring about large-scale change in relatively short periods of time. Lerner's decision to pursue politics is perhaps of most importance; it is difficult to imagine how these achievements could have occurred without such an involvement and highlights how closely space is connected to politics.

Kroll, L. (1999) 'Creative Curitiba', *Architectural Review*, 205 (1227): 92–95.

Letchworth Garden City
Letchworth, UK, 1903–
www.letchworth.com

Letchworth Garden City started in 1903 in Hertfordshire, UK was one of the first new towns and is an early example of urban planning considered alongside strategies of community management and economic sustainability. The brainchild of Ebenezer Howard (1850–1928) it was based on ideas first disseminated in his book, *To-morrow: a Peaceful Path to Real Reform* (1898) reissued as *Garden Cities of To-morrow* (1902), which outlined a model for self-sustaining towns combining the convenience of urban life with the advantages of a countryside location, surrounded by an agricultural greenbelt that provided jobs and food. The book generated a lot of interest, enabling Howard to found the Garden Cities Association in 1899 and raise enough money for Letchworth to be delivered entirely by private enterprise.

Although now best known for the design principles of the Garden City, Howard's most radical contribution is probably in the way he developed the social and economic structures of the Garden City. He formed a company, First Garden City Ltd (FGC), to construct the town with the intention that residents would purchase the estate after seven years. However, FGC remained in ownership until 1945 and following two Acts of Parliament the residents have been able to keep control of their land, with the estate now being owned by Letchworth Garden City Heritage Foundation. FGC originally leased plots for homes and farms with rental income being invested back into the town. Since all citizens were shareholders, they had a say in how the money was used. The company faced many challenges, not least the creation of new homes, and its single most effective marketing strategy was the staging of a national housing design competition and exhibition in 1905 for the design of an innovative home for no more than £150.

Today, the community management of Letchworth still broadly follows Howard's principle of 'rate-rent',

S 6396   SOLLERSHOTT E. LETCHWORTH GARDEN CITY

Westholm Green, Garden City, Letchworth

Postcards showing cottages on Eastholm and Westholm Green designed by Parker and Unwin for Garden City Tenants in 1906.

where residents pay for their services (rates) and those who invested in the initial development receive a return (rent), which is in this case is reinvested back into the town. This system has enabled the Heritage Foundation to develop a range of services and amenities including a hospital, museum, parks, minibus and shopmobility service, whilst also operating a number of businesses to supplement its income. Recently, the town has reached its target population of 30,000 and has also paid off its debts. With the system finally breaking-even, Letchworth has partly fulfilled Howard's original vision by becoming economically self-sustaining.

After Letchworth, Howard established Welwyn Garden City in 1920 and since then the garden city movement has been hugely influential in the UK and around the world, though mainly for its formal characteristics and not its social innovations. Letchworth was also pioneering for its two schemes, Meadow Way Green and Homesgarth, which included co-operative house-keeping (p.183) arrangements that challenged traditional ideas of domestic work. Homesgarth, built between 1909 and 1913, was a thirty-two flat housing development designed for professional people looking to reduce the burden of housework. Meals were cooked in a central kitchen and could either be taken in your own flat or a communal dining room. Howard himself was a great advocate of such co-operative schemes, living in Homesgarth until his move to Welwyn Garden City.

Howard, E. (1902) *Garden Cities of To-Morrow*, 2nd edn, London: Swan Sonnenschein.

Manzini, Ezio

www.sustainable-everyday.net
Ezio Manzini trained as an architect and is currently teaching industrial design at the Milan Polytechnic. His

research focuses on strategic design and social innovation as a way of responding to the environmental and social challenges of the contemporary world. Manzini describes social innovation as occurring in the everyday as a response to social problems and often making use of new technologies that have not yet been absorbed into mainstream society. Here Manzini sees the role of the designer as enabler, who creates the right conditions for such creativity to emerge by designing systems and processes rather than products and objects. Scenario making techniques are one of the key methodologies that Manzini identifies for a designer acting in such a way.

Manzini cites many small-scale, localised and grass-roots initiatives of such social innovation, services that people themselves have created to make intelligent use of resources, including time banking, carpooling, nurseries at home and restaurants in living rooms. People thus create collaborative clusters around the need for certain services and the design of such strategies and tactics is what Manzini refers to as 'service design'. For architects and urbanists this means viewing the city first and foremost as an organisation of people rather than the usual way of describing it as an organisation of buildings and infrastructure.

A grassroots project that takes a similar approach of 'service design' is the **Maker Faire Africa** project. Established in 2009 by Emeka Okafor and entrepreneur and supported by co-organisers Nii Simmons (co-founder of Afrobotics), Henry Barnor (co founder of GhanaThink), Eric Hersman (co-founder of AfriGadget) and Mark Grimes (Founder Ned.com) and others, the project is an extension of the US Maker Faire magazine and annual events for DIY technology enthusiasts. The African version acts as a platform that brings together innovators from across the continent, with a focus on designing bottom-up technologies and making prototypes that are useful for the specific developmental challenges of Africa. Working alongside local institutions, their main partner is Ashesi University College in Ghana, Maker Faire Africa's main task is to provide the infrastructure to supports local innovation through organising annual events, offering a matchmaking service for designers on their website and raising money for and awareness of local talent. This approach of combining vernacular and craft techniques with new technologies is similar to that adopted in India by Sanjeev Shankar (p.209) and by Anna Heringer (p.209) in her work in Bangladesh.

Manzini, E. and Jégou, F. (2003) *Sustainable Everyday: Scenarios of Urban Life*, Milan: Edizioni Ambiente.

Marcuse, Peter
www.marcuse.org/peter/peter
Peter Marcuse is a lawyer and planner who has written extensively on social housing, housing policies, the history and ethics of planning, the legal and social aspects of property rights and privatisation, as well as on questions of globalisation and space.

His writing is concerned with the defensiveness in the professions of architecture and town planning, the separation between architecture as design and planning as only dealing with the use of space and the built environment. At the same time, Marcuse highlights the growing resistance to the commodification of architecture and planning and the means by which this can be accomplished. One of the examples he refers to in terms of a different form of working and a different type of organisation is the Planners Network, (p.185) of which he was an early member. Lately, Marcuse has collaborated with the Right to the City alliance, putting critical urban theory to work for grass-roots organisations, and working around his own central thesis that in order to imagine an alternative city, those who are 'deprived', the poor, the homeless and the exploited should be supported by those who are 'discontented' with society, artists, intellectuals etc. Here the role of theory is to build mutual understandings between the two groups.

Marcuse, P. (1991) *Missing Marx: A Personal and Political Journal of a Year in East Germany, 1989–1990*, New York: Monthly Review Press.

Marcuse, P. and R. van Kempen (2000) *Globalizing Cities: A New Spatial Order?*, Oxford: Blackwell Publishing.

Marinaleda
Marinaleda, Spain, 1989–
www.marinaleda.com
Marinaleda is a town in the province of Seville, Spain with a population of 2,700 and has been run as a farming cooperative (p.130) since 1989. The town became a focal point for the struggle of landless workers in the

area under the direction of the mayor Juan Manuel Sánchez Gordillo, who was first elected in 1979 as a representative of the United Workers' Collective. Until the 1980s the majority of land in the region was owned by aristocratic landlords who farmed olives and cotton on a large industrial scale. During the 1970s the area suffered from very high unemployment rates, reaching 75 percent in Marinaleda, with most of the available work being on farms as seasonal day labourers, a precarious existence that led many families to move away in search of better employment. This situation was addressed in Marinaleda through the formation of a coalition between the council and the local agricultural union, following the election of Gordillo as mayor. Together they aimed at acquiring the land for a farmers' cooperative through a series of direct actions (p.140) and campaigns, including land occupations and hunger strikes. The eleven-year campaign finally ended with surrounding privately owned farm land being sold to the Andalucian government, who eventually handed it over to the town.

A village assembly in Marinaleda. Ph: Sylwia Piechowska

Since then Marinaleda has become a model for a co-operatively run settlement consisting of olive groves and a 3,000 acre farm which produces a number of labour intensive crops without the ecologically damaging practices of agri-business. A co-operatively run factory was also established to provide further jobs in the processing of the produce into products such as olive oil.

New housing was built partly with government subsidies and partly by self-building which provided a form of sweat equity in order to achieve the local rents of around €15 a month. Those who apply for a house are given land to build on for free as well as the services of

an architect and other specialists, providing they do not own property elsewhere. The town also provides a number of social services, including free home help for the elderly, cheap nurseries and various sporting facilities, including a swimming pool, which are financed through the co-operatively run farm and factories. Overall Marinaleda pays very low taxes to central government since certain services such as rubbish collection and street cleaning are carried out collectively on what are named 'Red Sundays'.

Although Marinaleda is very much associated with the figure of its mayor, it operates a form of direct democracy through organising village assemblies that vote on all matters concerning the management of the town, including a system of participatory budgeting that allows local people to influence council investments and expenditure. Since the early struggle to secure land and the setting up of the farms, factories and basic services, participation in the village assemblies has declined as the new generation finds less reason to join in. Yet, whilst the rest of Spain struggled in the recent housing and economic crisis, Marinaleda has been flourishing, an example of how much can be achieved following the principle of collectively owned land that is co-operatively managed and financed.

Laboratory of Insurrectionary Imagination (2007) 'A Utopian Detour', *Les Sentiers de l'Utopie/Paths Through Utopia*. <http://www.utopias.eu/paths/> [accessed 8 March 2010].

Matrix Feminist Design Co-operative
London, UK, 1980–1995

Matrix Feminist Design Co-operative was set up in 1980 as an architectural practice and a book group that grew out of the Feminist Design Collective, itself an offshoot of the New Architecture Movement's feminist group. They were one of the first architectural groups in Britain to take an overtly feminist stance in their way of working and designing, and in the projects they took on. The practice was run as a workers' co-operative (p.130) with a non-hierarchical management structure and collaborative working. Their work explored issues surrounding women and the built environment, but also the relationship of women to the architectural profession and to the procurement of architecture. One of their first moves as a group was to publish the book, *Making Space: Women and the Man Made Environment*, where they explored the socio-political context of designing the built environment, and traced the implications of feminist theory and critique on urban design, such as the viewing of domestic work also as a form of labour. In the book they set out one of the fundamental guiding principles of their work, the idea that 'because women are brought up differently in our society we have different experiences and needs in relation to the built environment'.

Matrix: a leaflet describing the work of Matrix, for client organisations. Courtesy Julia Dwyer

Matrix worked in two main areas, design projects that were all publicly funded social projects and technical advice. During the late 1970s and early 1980s governmental funding was available for voluntary organisations in the form of technical aid, which could be used for advice on design and other technical issues related to the built environment; Matrix was heavily involved in this, operating as a Community Technical Aid Centre. (p.128) This work resulted in a number of publications produced for community groups, such as A Job Designing Buildings, that addressed women in the construction industry. Here Matrix acted as spatial agents by giving advice to women's groups and individual women that allowed them to take control of their own environment. This could take the form of small meetings to identify sources of funding or the production of large-scale feasibility studies.

As an architectural practice, Matrix developed participatory design methods, acknowledging that architects' ways of working needed to be adapted in order to make the design process more understandable

and engaging for clients and users. For example, they tried to adapt the conventional architectural drawing and made use of models that resembled doll's houses. Publications also arose out of this work such as Building for Childcare, which was the result of a consultation process. Here again Matrix's work was about empowering women through deliberately choosing to research and design the sorts of spaces that had been ignored by a male-led profession, such as women's centres and nurseries, and also by developing tools which could involve women in the design process itself.

Matrix (1984) *Making Space: Women and the Man Made Environment*, London: Pluto Press.

Merrima Design

Sydney, Brisbane and Coffs Harbour, Australia, 1995–
www.communitybuilders.nsw.gov.au/building_stronger/ inclusive/merrima.html
Merrima Design was established in 1995 as Merrima Aboriginal Design Unit within the Australian government's Department of Public Works in Sydney. It was founded by the architect Dillon Kombumerri, later joined by architect Kevin O'Brien and interior designer Alison Page. The first of its kind, Merrima's aim was to design public buildings in rural Australia which could include and respond to indigenous needs and desires. Since 2000, the three designers have worked separately but have founded an association of indigenous architects, Merrima Design, 'committed to the struggle for self-determination through cultural expression in the built environment'. Kombumerri remains in Sydney within the aboriginal design unit, whilst O'Brien practices in Brisbane and Page in Coffs Harbour.

The early attempts at addressing the issue of aboriginal needs in architecture was focused on the design of public buildings whose iconographic language incorporated cultural references and symbolism. But this approach proved problematic since many different indigenous communities are involved in a single project, raising questions of whose icons and symbols are given preference. This is especially significant since the depiction of Ancestral Beings is related to questions of custodianship, meaning that a particular group can claim rights over a place, object or building that displays their symbols. Consequently, in more recent projects Merrima have taken a different approach viewing the inclusion of Aboriginal people in decisions regarding their environment as key. Having a sustained dialogue with the communities involved creates an architecture that respects Aboriginal cultural practices, pays close attention to the significance and meaning of places, and makes spaces that respond to their cultural needs. The fact that all staff at the design unit are indigenous gives Merrima a deep understanding of the social and cultural issues involved.

Another strategy that Merrima employ is to use their projects to create jobs for Aboriginal peoples and as a training opportunity. For the Wilcannia Health Service project they set up a training scheme for craft workers and labourers to make baked mud bricks. In another project, Girrawaa Creative Work Centre, they set up a design competition for prison inmates to design the building. In all these interventions, Merrima's work seeks to empower those who have been deliberately excluded from any form of political representation through creating a design process that can address their social and cultural needs, using architecture as a tool for self-help and learning.

O'Brien, K. J. (2006) 'Aboriginality and architecture: Built projects by Merrima and unbuilt project on Mer', unpublished thesis, University of Queensland.

Mess Hall

Chicago, USA, 2003–
www.messhall.org

Mess Hall is an experimental cultural centre based in Chicago, and founded in 2003 as a temporary project. It acts both as host for exhibitions, discussions, film screenings, workshops, concerts, campaigns and meetings, as well as a place for radical politics, visual art, applied ecological design and creative urban planning. The centre operates out of a shop unit, a rent free space donated by the landlord, and the project in its current state is dependent on this arrangement for its survival. The space enables Mess Hall to be a completely free resource for the local community, one of the fundamental principles on which it was founded. It does not have regular opening hours but opens for scheduled events, with an on-line calendar and mailing list. This means that in order to engage with Mess Hall, local residents and visitors have to take some responsibility for finding out about events – you can't just turn up. Presently there are eight 'keyholders', people who

have keys to the space, and who are responsible for its day-to-day running and the organisation of events, exhibitions etc. They give their time and resources for free, and although they have gained some funding in the past, the centre mostly runs on their generosity.

One of Mess Hall's "FREE" bins (2008). Ph: Samuel Barnett

Mess Hall library (2008). Ph: Justin Goh

In recent years Mess Hall organised numerous events including: workshops on sewing, where people could learn how to produce their own garments in order to encourage recycling, renovation and the reuse of textiles; an event on waste stream diversion which was about the reclaiming and reuse of surplus and wasted material; a book launch of *Trashing the Neoliberal City: Autonomous Cultural Projects in Chicago From 2000–2005*; an event with the Institute of Infinitely Small Things, which conducts participatory and creative research into how to temporarily transform public space dominated by non-public agendas; a presentation of 'The Library of Radiant Optimism for Let's Re-make the World'; and, a series of discussions on the changing nature of work.

Interface of Spatiality' used by people in a vacant lot to create a temporary space to enjoy the view of the city. Ph: MOM

Through this diverse programme of events Mess Hall acts as spatial agent by providing both the space and the support structure for local interactions and exchanges to occur outside of the commodified spaces of cafés and shops or the institutionalised spaces of galleries and libraries. Nonetheless, Mess Hall remains a curated space and events are organised around the interests of the 'keyholders'.

Hall, M. and R. Hollon (2007) 'Surveilling Crime Control', *Area Chicago: Art/Research/Education/ Activism*. Available. Online HTTP: <http://www.areachicago.org/p/issues/issue-4/surveilling-crime-control/> (accessed 31 Dec 2009).

Morar de Outras Maneiras
Belo Horizonte, Brazil, 2004–
www.mom.arq.ufmg.br
Morar de Outras Maneiras (MOM – Living in Other Ways) is a research group based in the School of Architecture at the Federal University of Minas Gerais in Belo Horizonte, Brazil. Their work is concerned with everyday spaces such as dwellings or simple public facilities. MOM try to empower others, seeing architecture as an open process, starting from the design through to building and use. There are no buildings in this work but rather something they call 'instruments' or

'interfaces' that are designed to help all actors involved in the building process realise their own space.

Practice and research in this process are interrelated; one doesn't exist without the other. Their work with people in informal settlements, helping them to build their own homes, happens in conjunction with the organisation of seminars and workshops around the same issue. The architect as one actor within this process is facilitator and mediator, knowledgeable about where to intervene, with whom, but also knowing when to retreat again and when to let go. This is particularly evident in their work with self-builders in the informal settlements of Belo Horizonte. Through their research they have identified a gap between the types of building materials available and the construction techniques that the self-builders use: building products are designed to be used with specialised and expensive equipment on a large scale, not by the individual self-builder. It is in the bridging of this gap that MOM place their own practice, assuming the role of mediator between the self-builder, who has very rarely chosen to build their own home but does so through necessity, and the types of knowledge required to complete a building. Since none of the self-builders would have come to an architect for help, it required MOM to take a proactive approach. Agency here is generated through their going out, realising and researching a certain condition, criticising and questioning the relations of production and their offering of practical advice.

MOM's interventions thus take on a political and ethical meaning: they influence processes by stepping in and affecting their cause through deliberation and negotiation. This is not about the solving of problems, but about posing problems so that all actors involved in the process develop their own power to critically perceive and transform their built environment.

MOM (2008) 'Architecture as Critical Exercise: Little Pointers Towards Alternative Practices', *field:* 2(1): 7–29.

muf architecture/art

London, UK, 1994–
www.muf.co.uk
Founded in London in 1994, muf officially coins itself as 'a collaborative practice of art and architecture committed to public realm projects'. The practice was set up defiantly and explicitly as an alternative to what the founding members, Liza Fior, Katherine Clarke and Juliet Bidgood, saw as mainstream practice. As the clearest defining set of principles in setting up muf, Liza Fior mentions the 'bringing together of interesting women'. Feminism is not openly mentioned, yet there is an underlying and often explicit tenet of feminism within their work, in particular the notion of collaborative practice signals a commitment to 'mutual knowledge', and the context of the public realm indicates a social (spatial) ambition beyond the fixity of the building as object.

muf's work includes urban design, buildings and strategic documents where the processes of planning are left open to include the voices of others; they are, in fact, all about the voices of others. Spatial arrangements and material resolutions are treated as the negotiation of interests that come about through consultation between public and private, communal and individual; often, muf suggests frameworks for action rather than determining specific outcomes. Decisions are guided by intuition, aspirations, rows; methodology comes out of doing and then reflecting at the end of doing. The idea of non-imposition informs all

Folly at Barking town square. Ph: muf

Roots and wings, Liverpool. Ph: muf

their work, with a continuous deliberation and conversation between process and product, and an implicit questioning of given briefs.

This approach allows muf to support marginal claims to space and they often privilege a multiplicity of small, modest proposals to an over-arching solution. They give emphasis to the specificities of each situation, whilst openly acknowledging that an architect's research methods leave out much, meaning that a project can hinge upon a chance encounter. Here the practice of the architect shifts from claiming complete authority to being a more reflexive and intuitive endeavour. On many occasions, muf have advised their clients not to build, an ethical position that may lose them work in the short-term but in the long-term results in lasting relationships that can engender more work. In recent years, muf have collaborated on large-scale regeneration schemes and have trod a difficult line between working with commercial developers and keeping true to their methods. Here muf's subtle subversions and persuasive powers have allowed them to cajole developers and council officials alike into providing much more than they had bargained for.

muf (2001) *This Is What We Do: A Muf Manual*, London: Ellipsis.

New Alchemy Institute
Cape Cod, USA, 1969–1991
www.vsb.cape.com/~nature/greencenter
The New Alchemy Institute was a research centre founded by John Todd, Nancy Jack Todd and William McLarney in 1969. It grew out of a critique of modern industrial agricultural processes, researching instead energy efficient, integrated systems of living that could operate in harmony with the planet. Their aim was to create self-sufficient, regionally autonomous communities without a dependence on fossil fuels. Since John

Cape Cod Ark. Courtesy John Todd

The Zweig Pond, hydroponics in solar ponds, Cape Cod Ark. Courtesy John Todd

Todd and William McLarney were both marine biologists the work took inspiration from wetland ecologies creating micro-environments or what they called 'living machines'.

Their research on agriculture focused on intensive organic farming techniques and types of planting that did not rely on machinery. 'Aquaculture' was fish farming in ponds that could happen on a small-scale in people's gardens and back yards. 'Bioshelters' were essentially large greenhouses adapted for food production that created an artificial environment for the ponds and planting, allowing food to be grown year round. From the humble beginning of a small inflatable pool covered with a plastic dome, bioshelters became highly sophisticated and specialised environments that could maintain a productive ecosystem. A number of these were realised, including the Ark for Prince Edward Island (PEI Ark) in Canada, built in 1974 and funded by the Canadian government. It became the site for testing many of the principles of 'living machines'.

Much of the research was published in the Journal of the New Alchemists as detailed guides and manuals in the hope that others would recreate their experiments. It was a radical vision for changing the way we live and crucially connecting humans back into the ecosystem, rather than trying to solve the problems of unsustainable lifestyles. The New Alchemy Institute closed in 1991 but its archives can be accessed via the Green Centre, also based in Cape Cod. John and Nancy Todd later founded the Oceans Ark International which continues with similar work.

Many of the ideas developed at the New Alchemy Institute are now seen as standard ecological design practice, such as the use of composting toilets, water purification using plants, solar collectors, or composting greenhouses that use the heat generated from compost to warm the greenhouse-a modern adaptation of the centuries old French method of heating glass cloches with horse manure. The New Alchemists combined a political anarchist view of self-sustaining, self-organising (p.197) society, with an environmentalism that rejected urban life and saw humans inhabiting the earth with minimal impact. Spatial agency is located in this radical vision but more importantly perhaps in the production of practical research that made possible this other way of living. The work they produced is especially relevant in the current climate as the world once again focuses on ecologically sensitive design.

Todd, N. J. (1977) *The Book of the New Alchemists*, New York: Dutton.

New Architecture Movement
London, UK, 1975–1980

The New Architecture Movement (NAM) was founded in 1975 and arose out of a conference organised by the more tightly knit Architects' Revolutionary Council. (p.97) NAM also took an explicitly oppositional stance to normative architectural practice: it set out to criticise the conventional notions of professionalism and the internalised structure of the profession, and in particular the system of patronage where the designer of a building has little contact with its user. NAM also called for the unionisation of architects, claiming that the RIBA failed to represent the majority of architects working within the private sector, dominated as it was (and still is) by private practice principals rather than their employees.

Front cover of SLATE 9

Much of this discussion was presented in SLATE, the newsletter of the NAM, published between 1976 and 1980, which ran articles on local authority housing, education, women in construction, the Schools of

Architecture Council, and features on 'What It Means to Architecture'. SLATE argued that architecture could not be separated from its political implications and social obligations, and that architecture as promulgated by the RIBA, had become an apologia for architects that was not accountable to the people who have to live in and with the architects' work.

'Working for what?' cartoon from SLATE

SLATE ceased publication in 1980 and NAM moved into different existences, including 'Women in Construction', one of the working groups within NAM, which was the starting point for Matrix, (p.171) one of the first explicitly feminist architecture practices in the UK. However, by the mid 1980s most of the initial energy of these groups had been dissipated, overwhelmed, one suspects, by the ascendant values of the Thatcherite era. NAM's unapologetic critique of professional norms and the political structures that shape those norms is as relevant now as it was then, and SLATE, by turns acerbic, aggressive, witty and serious, remains an inspirational source.

New Architecture Movement (1976–1980) *Slate: the newsletter of NAM*, London: NAM.

Nieuwenhuys, Constant
1920–2005
Constant Nieuwenhuys was a Dutch artist and one of the founding members of the Situationist International formed in 1957. He is also known for his utopian project,

New Babylon, started in 1956 and on which he worked for nearly twenty years. Constant was one of the theoretical drivers behind the Situationists alongside Guy Debord (1931–94) and it was a widening gulf between their two positions that eventually led Constant to leave the group in 1960.

The Situationists were an overtly political group whose critique of the alienation of capitalist society has had a lasting effect on contemporary culture. They saw modern society as a series of spectacles, discrete moments in time, where the possibility of active participation in the production and experience of lived reality were eluded. The rift between Constant and Debord focused on the structuralist tendencies of the former; through his explorations of 'unitary urbanism', Constant focused not only on the atmosphere and social interactions of the Situationist city, but also on the actual production of the city as built space. The project *New Babylon*, is today considered an exemplary expression of the Situationists' take on the city.

Designed around the abolition of work, *New Babylon* was a city based on total automation and the collective ownership of land. With no more work, citizens were free to move around, with *New Babylon* inspired by a gypsy encampment and designed to facilitate such a nomadic lifestyle. Divided into a series of interconnected sectors, the city operated on a network of collective services and transportation. Through a large number of models, drawings and collages, Constant explored the various sectors, floating above the ground on stilts, interconnected with bridges and pathways; above and below traffic flowed whilst the inhabitants travelled the sectors by foot. Whilst the city's physical reality was explored through drawings and maquettes, architecture itself was conceived as social relations in which Constant elaborated a critique of bourgeois, utilitarian society. The degree to which the details of the city had been worked out and Constant's own discourse showed that he viewed this as a concrete proposal for a future city rather than just a polemical project.

New Babylon focused on the social construction of space with every aspect of the city controllable by its citizens in order that they could construct new atmospheres and situations within the given infrastructure. It was a dynamic environment that could easily be adapted and changed, allowing inhabitants to explore their creativity through play and interaction. That the

Inkwenkwezi Secondary School, Du Noon Township, Cape Town. Courtesy Noero Wolff Architects

whole of *New Babylon* rested on a technological dream that can no longer be fulfilled has been commented on often, but as Francesco Careri of the group Stalker/ Osservatorio Nomade (p.200) has commented, perhaps a change in thinking is required that sees *New Babylon* as already existing within the voids and fissures of the contemporary consumerist city.

Wigley, M. (1998) *Constant's New Babylon: The Hyper-architecture of Desire*, Rotterdam: 010 Publishers & Witte de With.

Noero Wolff Architects

Cape Town, South Africa, 1985–
www.noerowolff.com

Established in Johannesburg in 1985 as Jo Noero Architects, the practice was named Noero Wolff Architects in 1998 when Heinrich Wolff joined; it is currently based in Cape Town. Their work has always reflected the belief that grass-roots projects involving the local population have the ability to transform lives. In the early 1980s, Noero, a long-time ANC member and anti-apartheid activist, worked in Soweto and other townships surrounding Johannesburg, having been appointed diocesan architect by Archbishop Desmond Tutu. Working alongside black community activists, Noero was involved in training local people to build their own homes using cheap and readily available materials. Since then, Noero Wolff have built projects that span the full range of buildings types, whilst sticking to their principles of not working for clients whose political views they disagree with.

Their projects in the townships always strive to expand the remit of the brief, as they point out opportunities to build there are so few that each project must do several things at once. They also involve local people in the design process as much as possible. Thus in one of their most challenging and successful projects, the Red Location Museum of Struggle in Port Elizabeth, Noero Wolff set up an advisory group from the local area to oversee the project, which eventually led to the setting up of an oral history project. Conceived as a new kind of museum for people who had historically been prohibited from visiting such cultural institutions, it is located in a shack settlement that had been a prominent site of resistance. Rather than following the typology of museum architecture, it borrows from the visual language of factories, places that acted as

Narkomfin Building, Moscow. Ph: Florian Kossak

organisational hubs in the struggle against apartheid. In Noero Wolff's practice architecture has been used both as a form of resistance and later as a transformative practice that manages to empower and to provide hope in a context where buildings and urban design have been put to such oppressive use.

Noero, J. (2003) 'Architecture and Memory', in Krause, L. and Petro, P. (eds) *Global Cities: Cinema, Architecture, and Urbanism in a Digital Age*, Piscataway, NJ: Rutgers University Press.

Ob'edineniye Sovremennikh Arkhitektorov

Moscow, Russia, 1925–1930
Ob'edineniye Sovremennikh Arkhitektorov (OSA – Union of Contemporary Architects) was founded in 1925 in Moscow by Moisei Ginzburg, Leonid Victor and Aleksandr Vesnin. From the outset OSA attempted to change the modus operandi of the architect by arguing that architectural skills were central to the definition and construction of social questions and to new ways of life and living. Through the use of architectural knowledge and expertise the members of OSA advanced the concept of the application of theoretical work to real problems and the notion of the architect as an 'organiser of building'. Their endeavour for new social building typologies, known as social condensers, pervades the group's theoretical as well as practical work.

In 1926, OSA founded the journal *Sovremennaya arkhitektura* ('Contemporary Architecture'), which was used as a vehicle to promote their views on methods of design, theoretical and operational questions and the social, economic and national conditions of the Soviet situation. In the first issue Ginzburg set out how the development of ideas worked in the 'Functional Method', in which processes 'would be open to scrutiny' both in terms of 'data and decision making, and thus publicly accountable'. Ginzburg saw the aim of contemporary architecture as one where the 'consumer' had a specific contribution to make, where construction was a collective act, it was participatory, and both the public and the specialists would make specific contributions. Most clearly he saw the architect's role as synthesising different positions without overwhelming them.

Seen in the context of the time where design was typically dictated by either an architect or developer, Ginzburg's approach seems radical; he understood architecture as something that works for and with the users. Architecture is presented as a discipline that is socially aware, acts with intent but nevertheless acknowledges production as a continuous process.

Khan-Magomedov, S. O. (1987) *Pioneers of Soviet Architecture: The Search for New Solutions in the 1920s and 1930s;* trans. Alexander Lieven, London: Thames and Hudson.

Papanek, Victor

1927–1999

Victor Papanek was a designer and educator who promoted ethical design that was socially and ecologically responsible. His ideas encompassed both design and architecture, based in his practical experience in industrial design and also influenced by his interest in anthropology. Papanek spent time studying and living with Navajos, Inuit and Balinese communities, where he explored the relationships between different societies and their tools. He admonished developed societies for designing products that were not suited to their task and being far too concerned with aesthetics.

Papanek was also a vocal critic of multi-national corporations and the consumer culture that was causing large-scale damage to the environment, calling for an increased awareness of environmental issues in industrial design practices and construction. He published a number of highly influential books on the topic including *Design for the Real World* (1971) and *The Green Imperative* (1995) both of which are user-centred takes on design and the ethical responsibilities of the designer.

Papanek, V. (1985) *Design for the Real World: Human Ecology and Social Change*, 2nd edn, Chicago: Academy Chicago Publishers.

Park Fiction

Hamburg, Germany, 1994–2005
www.parkfiction.org

Park Fiction is a project that began in 1994, evolving out of a campaign by a resident's association against the development of a site in the harbour area of Hamburg, Germany. The work of the *Hafenrandverein* (Harbour Edge Association), prevented the execution of a housing and office development for this highly prominent site. Instead, in a parallel planning and design process, the association drew up plans for a public park that they managed to get initiated. Although Park Fiction was a collective and participatory planning project, there were a number of key figures that led the process, negotiated with the local officials and organised the campaign, including the artist Christoph Schäfer, the film-maker Margit Czenki, and Ellen Schmeisser who was later employed by the city to liaise with the residents.

The project is based in the St Pauli neighbourhood of Hamburg, an area which has a history of dissent with the squatter movement of the 1980s being especially prominent. In the context of the prolonged neglect of the area by the city authorities and the relative wealth of much of West Germany, this local activism developed into a demand for a public amenity rather than private development. Highly embedded in its context, the Park

Event at Park Fiction Ph: Olaf Sobczak

Fiction project would be difficult to replicate elsewhere, although the methodologies and tools developed during the incredibly lengthy process can be applied in other situations. One of the most successful strategies was to not only protest for a public space but to act as if one already existed. To this end, the group organised a series of public events in the site, including talks, exhibitions, open-air screenings and concerts. Schäfer points out that this continual use of the 'park' by residents and visitors made it a 'social reality'.

The initial phase of the project, financed by funds from the 'art in public space' programme of the city's culture department, developed the idea of a 'collective production of desires'. Throughout the process, Park Fiction developed special tools and techniques to make the planning process more accessible. This included the temporary events organised in the park, as well as the installation of a 'planning container' on site which could be moved around the neighbourhood to collect residents' wishes. A film by Margit Czenki, 'Desire will Leave the House and Take to the Streets', was produced and a game about the planning process was developed to make transparent the opaque workings of bureaucracy. Other strategies included presenting the project at international art and music events, including Documenta 11 to which the 'planning container' was taken, and an event in St Pauli where groups involved in similar initiatives were invited to present their experiences. Such exposure ensured that Park Fiction was widely known and made it difficult for the authorities to block the proposals. The park was finally realised in 2005.

Schäfer, C. (2004) 'The City is Unwritten: Urban Experiences and Thoughts Seen Through Park Fiction', in Bloom, B. and Bromberg, A. (eds) *Belltown Paradise/ Making their own Plans*, Chicago: White Walls Inc., pp. 38–51.

Participation

During the 1970s the failures of the Modern Movement were becoming increasingly apparent to many architects who looked for ways to redress the balance of power between the architect and the user. A number of different approaches were developed including methods to involve future users in the design process, using workshops, consultations and through establishing neighbourhood offices. Others chose to self-build so that users could be involved not only in the design of their dwellings but also in their construction, and finally there was a move towards flexible layouts that could adapt to users needs. Whilst their methods differed the architects shared a common aim of empowering users to take control of their dwellings in a manner that allowed for their creative input whilst not reducing the role of the architect to that of a mere technical facilitator.

One of the pioneers of the participation movement of the 1970s was **Lucien Kroll**, a Belgian architect who became well-known for the Maison Médical student accommodation at the University of Louvain (1970–6). Students approached Kroll for an alternative to the monotonous design proposed by the university and conducted a successful campaign for its adoption. Developed in intense consultation with students and others who would use the building, an evolving physical model became a record of the design process. The resulting building has a fragmented look, as it was split into sections with each part handed over to a separate team of architects within the office. Kroll's adopted method of separating the overall framework of the building, including the structure, from the infill is similar to that of John Habraken, (p.153) allowing him to create a highly customised architecture.

The image of the Maison Médical became synonymous with a certain type of architecture and influenced others to adopt participatory techniques within their work. One such architect was the Austrian, **Eilfried Huth**, who having produced utopian designs similar to those of Yona Friedman, (p.151) in the early 1970s changed direction to a more practical and grounded architecture that looked to transform the material living conditions of ordinary people. Huth practices participatory architecture in the context of self-help housing including self-build, recognising that through being involved in the design and building of their homes, residents would also create a strong community. The radical nature of the projects is revealed in their time span, the first project was a small development of sixteen houses which took sixteen years to complete, with the future inhabitants forming an association and being involved in each stage of the design including the choice of contractors.

Self-build can act both as a form of participation as well as a pedagogical technique, for example in the project Bauhäusle, (p.107) architecture students as part of their course designed and built their accommodation using the construction system designed by Walter Segal, (p.196) and more recently the Community Self Build Agency (p.128) facilitates such projects in the UK by providing training for people to build their own homes.

A well-known example of participation as community architecture and related to the British Community Technical Aid (p.128) movement is **Ralph Erskine's** (1914–2005) social housing project, Byker Wall. Based in Newcastle upon Tyne, it was built between 1969 and 1975 to rehouse those working in the shipyards and factories along the banks of the River Tyne. Erskine set up a community office in the neighbourhood in a disused funeral parlour and had an open door policy, inviting local residents to drop in and share their views. This elicited a dialogue on topics ranging from vandalism to leaking pipes as well as the design of the final project. A pilot scheme, Janet Square, was built in 1972 with forty-seven families volunteering to take part in the project. Their input also served to highlight the complex relations and hierarchies amongst the residents of Byker, which was reflected in the final design. Erskine's grassroots approach to participation required a long-term commitment from the architect, who became a part of the local neighbourhood for the duration of the project.

Byker Wall. Ph: Carol McGuigan

Another UK practice that pioneered community architecture was Hunt Thompson, whose partner Edward Burd was a key figure in the move towards tenant empowerment in the design process. The practice was formed in 1971 and their involvement with tenants' groups began in 1982 with the renovation of Lea View House in Hackney, London. Their approach of treating tenants in exactly the same way as private clients was rare at the time and raised the standard of social housing. In 1999, Burd retired and the practice changed name and direction.

Finally, **Ottokar Uhl**'s take on participative architecture was to design dwellings that were highly flexible, allowing users to adapt them according to their needs. Flexible housing allowed Uhl to create an architecture that could break down the fixed hierarchies between designer and user and his systems building approach led to collaborations with John Habraken (p.153) on how to design buildings that could be adapted and upgraded for changing use. Uhl was thus concerned with designing buildings across their whole lifespan, considering how they could accommodate a changing demographic and their living patterns, as well as considering the eventual demolition of the building, a concern he shared with Cedric Price. (p.189)

Peirce, Melusina Fay
1836–1923

Born in Burlington, Vermont, Melusina Fay Peirce developed a model for carrying out housework collectively, designed to free women from their daily chores in order to pursue other interests. She was motivated by what she characterised as the daily drudgery of women's lives and men's patronising attitudes towards those who tried to do other things. Another driving force was her belief that her mother, a skilled musician, died prematurely due to the pressures of housework which did not allow her to follow her ambitions fully. Peirce thus laid out a detailed critique of the domestic economy of the home, being as critical of bourgeois women's 'laziness' as she was of men. She coined the term 'cooperative housekeeping' for her proposal, which was published in the journal Atlantic Monthly from 1868 to 1869.

A group of 15–20 women would organise and run a co-operative to carry out the common tasks of cooking, laundry and sewing. These would be done by skilled women on a wage, the goods and services being sold to members at a fair price with profits also being shared. Whilst women from richer backgrounds like her would act as managers, it was the poorer women who would carry out the work. Although Peirce's scheme kept class divisions intact, it was radical for its time, bringing together women from hugely different backgrounds. It also did away with house-servants and she hinted at the working women eventually being allowed to become full members of the co-operative. However tentative, this was a suggestion at a classless society pioneered by women. In fact, her ideas on cooperative housekeeping were akin to the labour movements of the time, who had implemented consumer cooperatives such as farmers and mechanics stores. Peirce's contribution was to extend such thinking to the domestic realm and for the benefit of women.

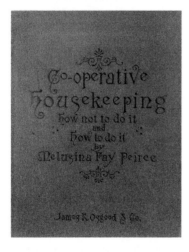

Forming the Cooperative Housekeeping Association in Boston in 1870, Peirce tried to put her ideas into practice, but her experiment was short lived undermined by husbands not allowing their wives to participate fully. A communal kitchen was planned but it was never implemented and the collective buying of goods did not become profitable. Although the experiment failed, Peirce carried on with her theoretical work, imagining the consequences of her proposals on the design of houses. As the increase in land values made even bourgeois families consider living in apartment blocks, Pierce translated her initial proposal for communal kitchens and laundries from neighbourhoods of detached houses to apartment blocks. The precedent for such thinking came from Charles Fourier (p.150) who had identified Parisian apartment blocks as an intermediate step between the individual family dwelling and the phalanstery. For Peirce, the changes to the home and neighbourhoods were something that women were best placed to design and in 1903 she patented her own design for a co-operative apartment building with

communal kitchens. Her pioneering work later inspired others to imagine communities of collectivised domestic work, such as the Ruskin colony, or community dining clubs and kitchens.

Peirce, M. F. (1884) *Co-operative Housekeeping: How not to do it and How to do it*, Boston: J.R. Osgood and Co.

Philanthropic housing
UK, 1800–1900
Industrialisation in C19 Britain led to a rapid growth of towns, resulting in a severe lack of housing and unsanitary conditions. Whilst government initiatives were slow to respond, acute inequality saw the rise of charitable endeavours. The Victorian model of philanthropy was tied to religious and social morality, designed to help those who were deemed worthy of salvation, but it usually did not cater for the very poorest in society. In contrast, the self-help model tried to empower the poor and saw the eventual development of the co-operative movement (p.130) and friendly societies.

Almshouses are one of the earliest examples of philanthropic housing that started before the Victorian era and continue today. Providing subsidised rental for those who could not afford standard rates, the first almshouse was built in the C10 in York. Since then, a total of around 30,000 almshouses have been built in the UK, of which only a few hundred still serve their original purpose. Up to the C19, almshouses provided for a wide demographic but as the general standard of housing improved, they were reserved for the elderly. Today they are usually managed by local charities that decide on the eligibility of tenants.

Much of Victorian philanthropic housing was provided by industrialists who wanted better living conditions for their workers. One of the earliest and best known examples is **New Lanark** village in Scotland, built between 1800 and 1829 by Robert Owen. He took over the existing textile mill and transformed it into a working example of how he thought a healthy, co-operative community should be organised. New Lanark changed working practices through emphasising encouragement and supervision over punishment. Although much of the housing was already built when Owen arrived, he enlarged the properties, provided better sanitation and built communal facilities, such as a purpose-built school. Owen's social and welfare

West Hackney House in London still functions as an almshouse. Ph: Nishat Awan

programmes were as important as the buildings: he restricted child and women's labour, was the pioneer of nursery provision in Britain and organised sheltered housing for the elderly. The New Lanark store was a precursor to the co-operative movement, (p.130) establishing a fair trading system, and using profits to benefit the whole community; for example teacher's salaries were paid with this money.

Other examples of industrial model villages include **Bournville** near Birmingham, built in 1893 by Quakers, George and Richard Cadbury. They moved their factory to a greenfield site away from the town centre in order to provide better and healthier living conditions for their workforce. Pensions were pioneered here, a joint workers committee set up, and there was also a staff medical service. Similarly Port Sunlight in the Wirral was built between 1899 and 1914 by industrialist, William H. Lever. Organised as a garden suburb with an emphasis on recreation, modern housing was built as well as an open-air swimming pool, art gallery, schools, concert hall and allotments, all funded by the profits from the factory.

Some Victorian philanthropists addressed housing for the poor: for example **Octavia Hill** (1838–1912) worked towards providing good quality rental housing for the poor. Based in London, she was opposed to the prevalent view that slums should be demolished and rebuilt, as she believed that such developments excluded the very people they were trying to help. Instead, Hill preferred renovation and repair combined with a strict enforcement of rent and tenancy conditions. This she believed would encourage a responsible attitude amongst the poor and she trained her tenants in housing management. Hill persuaded wealthy benefactors to buy property for her to manage and rent out, including John Ruskin who bought her three houses to manage in 1863. During the same period in London, **George Peabody** set up the Peabody Donation Fund in 1862, using his private fortune to provide housing for those who could afford only the lowest rents. The modest three percent return was ploughed back into the housing, which took the form of flats in dense blocks that are still highly popular in London.

Whilst philanthropic housing had many problems, not least that it did not provide for the very poorest in society, the people and projects described above contributed towards establishing the social housing movement in the UK and pioneered a model that has been followed in many other countries.

Owen, D. E. (1964) *English Philanthropy, 1660–1960*, Cambridge, MA: Harvard University Press.

Planners Network
USA, 1975–
www.plannersnetwork.org
The Planners Network has its origins in Planners for Equal Opportunity, an organisation that was formed in 1964 around the civil rights movement in the United States and specifically around the rent strikes of New

Progressive Planning covers (2009). Courtesy Planners Network.

York. In 1975 as a replacement for the recently disbanded Planners for Equal Opportunity, Chester Hartman established the Planners Network by sending out newsletters to radical planners as a way of keeping in touch and sharing information. This format has since remained an integral part of Planners Network's activities and from 2002 they have also published a quarterly magazine, *Progressive Planning*. Currently the network consists of around 500 members, which includes professionals, students and academics as well as community activists from areas in which the network has been active. Based at Cornell University in Ithaca, New York State, it has local branches in a number of the major US cities, as well as being active in Canada as Planning Action (p.186) and having a related organisation in the UK.

At the outset the central aim of the group was to make their services as volunteers available to community groups, tenant groups and neighbourhood organisations, in order to serve those who were excluded from the mainstream planning process, particularly dealing with issues affecting women and the consequences of racism and segregation. In these concerns, Planners Network overlaps with Community Design Centers, (p.126) which were also formed in the context of the civil rights movement and the women's liberation movement. Since then, the concerns of Planners Network have grown to include issues around gay rights, migration and the effects of the neo-liberal economy on urban and rural environments. Much of their work is carried out through local branches who act independently and organise themselves around local issues, mobilising campaigns and facilitating discussions. Planners Network have recently published a *Disorientation Guide* for planning students who want to combine activism with their academic studies, and provide a help and support system for those studying in an academic environment that does not valorise such work. They also organise regular conferences which are deliberately independent of the professional organisations, recognising the need to work outside of existing structures in order to include voices from neighbourhood groups, women's groups, people from labour unions, representatives from labour unions – all people who are involved directly in issues of the built environment but not as 'professionals'.

Planners Network (quarterly from 1997)
Progressive Planning: The Magazine of Planners Network, New York: Planners Network Inc.

Planning Action
Toronto, Canada, 2001–
Planning Action is a Toronto-based non-profit organisation whose members include urban planners, architects and activists. They came together following the Planners Network (p.185) conference of 2000 in Toronto, as a group of graduate students who had helped to

co-ordinate the event but were unsatisfied by the outcomes. They founded Planning Action with the intention of being a more explicitly activist organisation engaged in local issues. They are organised as a number of workgroups, each dealing with a very specific issue such as developing 'alternative' plans for the Toronto waterfront, or investigating the impacts of global decisions on local planning, or offering planning, design and advocacy services to local communities. They not only critically challenge the status quo but also act propositionally, suggesting other ways of imagining the city.

Toronto University [Dis]Orientation tour with Planners Network (2003). Courtesy Planning Action

Public meeting. Courtesy Planning Action

They have modelled themselves on the CTACs [(p.128)] of the UK and other similar organisations, but unlike these, Planning Action also acts as a pressure group. They have campaigned against the Official Plan for Toronto in 2002, which they saw as catering only to the needs of property owners and developers and have also critiqued the lack of participation in the planning system. Using their expert knowledge, they have intervened in planning committees, written articles in community publications, and organised public meetings to try to open up the discussion beyond the narrow confines of the planning profession.

Hammett, K. (2006) 'Voices of Opposition', *Designer/Builder*, 13(2): 11–14.

Plotlands

South-east England, UK, 1870–1939

Plotlands refers to small pieces of land laid out in regular plots on which a number of self-built settlements were established in the southeast of England from the late 1800s up to WWII. Characterised by the fact that they were largely built outside the conventional planning system, Plotlands were tolerated by local councils but eventually replaced with new towns and garden suburbs through compulsory purchase orders. Very few traces of the original communities remain, though Jaywick Sands in Essex has evaded development through its geographic and economic marginality. Reaching its peak in the period between the 1920s and 1930s, the Plotland phenomenon was interrupted by WWII and the planning regulations that followed.

The result of a specific set of circumstances, Plotlands were a peculiarly English phenomena, tied in large part to the desire to own a piece of land, no matter how small. The agricultural decline of the 1870s, brought on in part by increased imports from British colonies, resulted in farms becoming bankrupt and their land being sold off cheaply in small plots by developers. Farmers in marginal areas that had vulnerable sea-side locations or where the soil was not very fertile, such as the clay soils of Essex, were worst hit. With an increase in holidaying, buying a small plot of land to build a holiday home or set up a small holding became a popular and cheap option for Londoners wanting to escape the cramped conditions of the city.

These self-built, self-reliant settlements were often without basic services such as water and sanitation, with the owners having to petition councils, and to sometimes contribute financially towards their provision, which lead to a strong sense of community.

An old show wagon, trellis and other salvaged materials used to build homes in the Plotlands (1971–2).
Ph: Stefan Szczelkun

Due to the relaxed planning regulations, the Plotlands took on a character of their own, some converted boats and railway carriages, whilst others built summer-houses; anything from discarded bits of mahogany joinery to sections of garden trellis were used. Over time people from these settlements were relocated to new towns or the areas upgraded so that they have slowly become part of the encroaching suburbia.

Dennis Hardy and Colin Ward (p.210) gave a definitive account of the Plotlands in their book, *Arcadia for All*, where they also made the point that increasing planning and building regulations which demand houses to be fully finished before moving in, combined with the difficulties of obtaining a mortgage, has put an end to such self-help housing in the UK. But with the lack of affordable housing and a genuine desire for self-building (p.196) today, the model of the Plotlands seems increasingly relevant.

Hardy, D. and Ward, C. (1984) *Arcadia for All. The Legacy of a Makeshift Landscape*, London: Mansell Publishing.

Prawoto, Eko

Eko Prawoto is an Indonesian architect and educator who combines contemporary design with local knowledge, commenting that he views his buildings as social entities as much as physical objects. Through using locally sourced and often recycled materials, his designs are not only environmentally sensitive but also reduce building costs so that builders' pay can be maximised. When building in remote rural areas, he carries out resource surveys to establish what building materials are available and works alongside local craftsmen and builders.

Bamboo construction at Community Learning Center in Ujung Alang, Cilacap (2005). Ph: Eko Prawoto Architecture Workshop

Prawoto has researched earthquake resistant buildings made from materials such as bamboo, straw and coconut wood and is working to reintroduce these to the general public. However, there is a preference in

Indonesia for more modern concrete buildings which signal affluence, a similar situation to that in Colombia, where Simón Vélez and Marcelo Villegas (p.206) are also pioneering contemporary bamboo construction. In contrast to Vélez and Villegas' approach, Prawoto's buildings are usually more modest in scale and therefore require less specialist training making them more suitable for self-building, a quality that allowed Prawoto to use his expertise in the reconstruction efforts following the 2006 earthquake, in which he helped villagers to rebuild their homes as earthquake resistant structures as cheaply as possible, and before the slow handout of governmental assistance for which not all can wait.

The swampy conditions and soil erosion problems demanded special construction techniques. Ph: Eko Prawoto Architecture Workshop

Typical of many spatial agents, Prawoto's practice expands beyond architecture, including collaborations with artists, exhibiting (including at the Venice Architecture Biennale), teaching and advocacy.

Gunawan Tjahjono (2010) 'Context, Change, and Social Responsibility in the Work of Eko Prawoto', *Journal of Architectural Education*, 63(2): 147–152.

Price, Cedric
1934–2003
Cedric Price was an architect whose oeuvre though mostly unbuilt, has had a marked influence on contemporary architecture. Through his drawings, teaching and writing Price questioned architecture's identification with building alone, which was tied in part to his suspicion of institutions and their desire to use buildings as a means of consolidating power. Instead, Price proposed a time-based approach to architecture conceived as a series of interventions that were both adaptable and impermanent. He was a harsh critic of the tendency in the UK to list and preserve buildings endlessly and, alongside others proposed the influential idea of **Non-plan**, a critique of overbearing and outdated planning regulations that called for control to be handed back to citizens in order to allow self-organised (p.197) processes to occur.

The aviary at London Zoo. Ph: Tatjana Schneider

Whilst the Aviary at London Zoo (1961) is one of a few built projects, realised in collaboration with the engineer Frank Newby and the photographer Lord Snowdon, it is the unbuilt projects such as Fun Palace (1960–1) and Potteries Thinkbelt (1964) that cemented Price's reputation. Both projects took an innovative approach, addressing the new economic and social context of post-war Britain. He had a faith in new technologies, which if deployed correctly could produce a democratic architecture.

The Fun Palace was designed for the agit-prop theatre director, Joan Littlewood, whose brief for a theatre where the audience themselves became players, was the perfect foil for testing Price's ideas on interactive environments that put users in charge. Conceived as an ever-changing learning environment, its architecture was designed to be dismantled and reassembled and was clearly an inspiration for the Centre Pompidou in Paris. Although the project had many admirers and supporters, including **Buckminster Fuller**, it never came to fruition.

With the demise of manufacturing, Potteries Thinkbelt looked to harness the potential of the emerging information and knowledge economy, in order to revive the depressed manufacturing heartland of Britain. The project was also an implicit critique of the elitist university system, which concentrated on the arts over practical and technical education, as well as a comment on the many new university campuses being built at the time. Instead, Price proposed a travelling university on carriages that utilised the redundant railway and manufacturing sites of the area.

Price's approach perhaps most clearly embodies the role of the architect as spatial agent. Coining terms like 'anticipatory architecture' and 'beneficial change', his designs were both witty and challenging, questioning assumptions and empowering users as collaborators.

Hardingham, S. and Price, C. (2003) *Cedric Price: Opera*, Chichester: Wiley-Academy.

public works
London, UK, 1999–
www.publicworksgroup.net
Public Works is an art and architecture practice based in London which was established in 1999. Currently three of the five founding members remain: the artist Kathrin Böhm, architects Torange Khonsari and Andreas Lang, alongside artist Polly Brannan who

Park Products, Serpentine Gallery, London (2004). Ph: David Bebber

Mobile Porch, London (2000–ongoing). Ph: public works

joined in 2005. Public Works create projects that investigate how users engage with public space, devising strategies for supporting social, cultural and other initiatives in both urban and rural contexts. They employ playful methods to involve local users, residents and passers-by in their projects, often making interventions on site in order to inform and expand a given brief.

Since 2006, they have run the popular Friday sessions, inviting practitioners and theorists to speak about their work and engage in informal discussions. They have also organised a desk residency at their studio, renting out space to those working in related fields. Both the Friday sessions and the desk residency show Public Work's commitment to collaborative work and to the building and nurturing of informal networks, a concern that is followed through in their projects. Collaboration is key to their work, with a network of interested parties, experts and specialists gathered around each project.

Public Works have developed their own representational language which uses sketches, diagrams and individual websites for almost all of their projects, developed in collaboration with web designer, **Dorian Moore**. These map out the process of each project showing in detail the different actors involved, their relationships to each other and how the design evolved. This representational method allows Public Works to emphasise the importance of encounter and informal exchanges in their projects, their DIY aesthetic being able to record these important aspects quickly and clearly. This DIY ethos is also carried through in their penchant for self-publishing: they have produced fanzines (p.90) to accompany a number of projects as well as the Friday sessions. In all of their engagements Public Works take on the role of facilitators and hosts, making the conditions and spaces necessary for the types of exchanges that can create shared, social spaces.

Public works (2006) *If You Can't Find it, Give us a Ring*, Birmingham: Article Press.

Raumlabor

Berlin, Germany, 1999–
www.raumlabor-berlin.de
Raumlabor are a group of architects based in Berlin, Germany, who came together in 1999 in response to the rapid and unrestrained development of the city

following the fall of the Berlin wall. Their playful approach critiques this dominant mode of architectural production, proposing instead temporary projects that transform the urban landscape through what they call 'urban prototypes'. Pneumatic structures, submarines made out of waste materials and half-serious projects such as building a mountain from the rubble produced through uncovering a buried canal are all part of their repertoire. This approach is not only used to critique official planning processes but also to influence them, such as the 'Kolorado Plan', which was developed for a local authority in Berlin. Raumlabor proposed a long-term strategy for dealing with urban shrinkage that included small-scale interventions and involved local residents in the future of their neighbourhood.

Workshop on experimental building in Stolzenhagen, 2006. A Raumlaborberlin and Raumstation-Stolzenhagen initiative. Courtesy Raumlabor

Working in between the fields of architecture and public art, Raumlabor, whose name means 'space laboratory', create projects based around events, performance and theatre. Collaboration is a key part of their strategy with specialists including engineers, sociologists, local experts, ethnographers and citizens, being brought together around specific projects. Primarily working in public space, Raumlabor see the task of the architect as highlighting problems rather than solving them. Their projects try to open up a space of communication and negotiation in which relations can be made and conflicts played out, and they acknowledge that for them architecture is first and foremost a social phenomenon. Placing themselves within the utopian tradition of 1960's architecture, including in particular to the work of Yona Friedman, (p.151) Buckminster Fuller (p.96) and Haus-Rucker-Co, (p.155) Raumlabor preempted this contemporary turn towards an experimental and reversible architecture also practiced by Urban Catalyst (p.203) and Exyzt. (p.145)

Maier, J. and Rick, M. (eds) (2008) *Raumlabor. Acting in Public*, Berlin: Jovis Verlag.

Riwaq

Ramallah, Palestine, 1991–
www.riwaq.org

Riwaq Centre for Architectural Conservation is a Palestinian NGO based in Ramallah, founded in 1991 by Suad Amiry, a Palestinian architect and writer. The organisation deals with questions of heritage in the context of conflict and occupation working towards preserve historic buildings and neighbourhoods, as well as promoting the knowledge and use of traditional building techniques. Riwaq have since expanded their work to include community outreach and pedagogical activities, recognising that the work of conservation in the unique circumstances of Palestine where cultural heritage is being actively destroyed, cannot be left to specialists alone and must involve local residents and organisations. In this they raise an awareness of the importance of cultural heritage, whilst also working to improve the social, cultural and economic conditions of those living in areas of historic importance. Riwaq thus view conservation not as an activity that prevents change but as a practice that is fundamental to questions of development and regeneration, and in particular in establishing a sense of Palestinian identity which they argue is under continual and deliberate threat from the Israeli occupation. Their renovation projects concentrate on creating much-needed jobs, helping to transform the perception of heritage into an asset rather than a liability. The repaired buildings are often transformed into cultural and shared community spaces.

During the last three years, the group have also organised the Riwaq Biennale to promote this work and have exhibited at the 53rd Venice Biennale in 2009. Their '50 Villages' project aims at creating a network that connects the rural areas of Palestine in order to overcome the isolation of these remote areas through the promotion of cultural programmes, workshops and the renewal and provision of neighbourhood facilities. Riwaq's work creates the basis for empowerment on a larger scale, through allowing the citizens of Palestine to take control of their own environment and enabling them to take an active part in its protection.

Soueif, A. (2009) 'Reflect and Resist'. *The Guardian*, [internet] 13 June. Available HTTP: <http://www.guardian.co.uk/artanddesign/2009/jun/13/art-theatre> [accessed 10 February 2010].

Renovation project at Birzeit, Palestine for Rozana Society. Ph: Riwaq

Construction of Akron Boys and Girls Club # 2, Akron, AL (2007 Thesis Project). Courtesy Rural Studio

Rural Studio

Auburn, Alabama, USA, 1993–
www.ruralstudio.com

Rural Studio is a design/build programme attached to the architecture department of Auburn University, Alabama. Founded in 1993 by the late Samuel Mockbee, the studio has built over sixty buildings in Hale County for some of the poorest communities of rural USA. Mockbee set up Rural Studio after fourteen years in private practice as Mockbee/Coker Architects, where he developed his particular style of vernacular architecture combined with modern techniques. Although one of their first projects was a design for three 'charity houses' for low-income families, after winning prestigious awards, the practice's commissions were for increasingly wealthy clients. Funding for the charity houses was never found and this inability to create architecture for those most in need led Mockbee to propose a design/build studio at the university where he had studied. The teaching and building programme gave him an opportunity to combine his particular design approach with a pedagogical agenda that is still embedded in the work of Rural Studio.

During this first phase of its existence, Rural Studio built homes in consultation with their future users, using salvaged and donated materials; everything from carpet tiles and paper for walls to car number plates for cladding were used. This was a product of a context-specific and sustainable approach to architecture as well as a response to extremely low budgets. Financial support from Auburn University was limited and erratic and the students were expected to find funding in the form of donations and materials for their projects. The houses were built by second year students, who spent a semester working on the project, with a second set of students completing the project by the end of the academic year. Students in their fifth year built larger, more complex projects, such as a chapel and community centre, spending the whole academic year on site. Under the direction of Mockbee, Rural Studio became one of the most celebrated and successful design/build studios, inspiring other universities to set up similar programmes, such as the **BaSic Initiative**, **URBANbuild** and **Design Workshop**.

Since Mockbee's death in 2001, the programme has changed somewhat and under the direction of Andrew Freear, with the projects becoming larger and more complex. The studio is taking on more public projects as well as developing a series of prototypes for a US$20,000 house, whose design can later be given over to local builders in the hope that it will provide affordable housing and create jobs. The programme's success has meant that it now receives more regular

Consultation event at Sans Souci cinema site. Courtesy Lindsay Bremner / 26'10 South Architects

funding from Auburn University, as well as donations from charitable foundations. The impact of the Rural Studio has been profound, not least on the students who attend it. Living and working in rural Alabama, Mockbee, and later Freear and their students, immerse themselves in the community. This exposure of mostly middle-class students to extreme poverty is also considered to be part of the learning experience – Mockbee called it the 'classroom of the community'. His pedagogical approach was in fact very similar to that developed by Charles Moore at the <u>Yale Building Project</u> (p.213) during the 1960s, which manages to instil students with an understanding of the social responsibilities of the profession. It also teaches students valuable skills of working in teams, with real life situations and gives them a sense of agency.

Dean, A. O. (2002) *Rural Studio: Samuel Mockbee and an Architecture of Decency*, New York: Princeton Architectural Press.

Sans Souci Cinema

Soweto, South Africa, 2002–2009
This project takes the form of a campaign to rebuild the Sans Souci community cinema in the Soweto township district of Kliptown following its destruction

by fire in 1995. Beginning with a question rather than a design concept, architects Linsday Bremner and 26'10 South asked: 'What minimum resources does one need to turn a ruin into a cinema?' By developing the idea of the cinema's restoration through events and installations, they sought to shape an empowering memory of the Sans Souci – a spatial idea of the past that would anchor the local community's shared vision of the future.

Originally an iron cowshed, and then a dance hall, the Sans Souci became a cinema in 1948. As a public space where black people could enjoy collective urban experiences, it is significant in the context of South Africa's apartheid history. It is also associated with political resistance; some say that plans for the 1976 riots were hatched within its walls. Kliptown itself dates back to 1903; falling outside of the municipal boundaries of the city, the district developed an independent spirit associated with its multi-racial composition. It is best known as the site of the 1955 Congress of the People, held to ratify the Freedom Charter on a dusty field which has now been turned into the Walter Sisulu Square of Dedication, a major urban space framed by institutional and commercial buildings.

With almost no funding available, the architectural challenge of the Sans Souci project was to find not only a design solution but also a way to pay for it – or to shape the project's expectations and aspirations to suit strict economic constraints. In an incremental process designed to address conceptual and practical aspects of the project, the team approached the brief for the cinema's redevelopment in three related ways. Firstly, they focused on the cinema's role as a place of public spectacle. A series of performances engaged local people as actors and audience, bringing the 'ruin' to life and at the same time revitalising its role as a venue for social activity. Secondly, these events – open-air film screenings, dance workshops, festivals and displays – were linked to a business plan, winning sponsorship and building up the profile of the Sans Souci as a cultural attraction. And thirdly, capacity-building processes were embedded in the programme, so that the initiative's management team accumulated social capital in parallel with the project's reputation.

Despite early achievements the process has been uneven, success is not yet assured and the future of the project is uncertain. Reconstruction plans envisage the ruin's transformation into a multi-functional venue including a cinema and a theatre, as well as a range of performance and community facilities, according to a phased plan. The architects want visitors and residents to actively participate in remembering and recreating the history of the Sans Souci in an incremental

rebuilding programme designed to not only deliver the building but also to bring the Sans Souci back into the consciousness of the local community.

Bremner, L. (2008) 'What's the use of architecture?', *Domus*, 912(3): 15–19.

Sarai

Delhi, India, 1998–
www.sarai.net

Sarai is a programme of the Centre for the Study of Developing Societies (CSDS), an independent social science and humanities research institute based in Delhi. It was founded in 2001 by CSDS and the Raqs Media Collective as 'an alternative, non-profit space'. Through their research and practice Sarai investigate the intersection between cities, in particular South Asian cities, technology and culture, focusing on the politics of information and communication. Their output takes many forms including academic research, art practice, publications, events and the setting up of 'Media Labs'. They also provide fellowships for independent researchers in India, supporting topics that have no other source of funding. Sarai itself is supported in a number of different ways, including a space given to them by CSDS, funding from the Indian Council of Social Science Research Institute and governmental

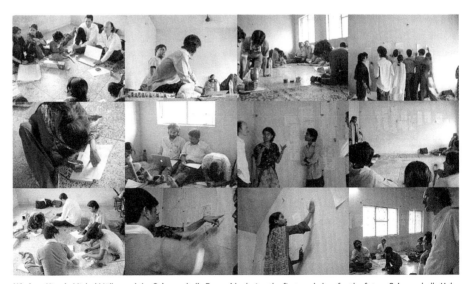

Nikolaus Hirsch, Michel Müller and the Cybermohalla Ensemble during the first workshop for the future Cybermohalla Hub in the new settlement of Ghevra (Delhi, 2007). Ph: Nikolaus Hirsch/Michel Müller

Houses built using the Segal system. Ph: Chris Moxey

funding from Holland, facilitated through their collaborations with the Waag Society.

Although dealing with new media, their work is grounded in the everyday and material realities. For example their insistence on using free software is both a political and a practical decision. In the context of India, where they have set up 'Media Labs' in deprived neighbourhoods, teaching people to use proprietary software and spending money on expensive licences is not a viable option. The 'Cybermohalla' project allows the residents of these areas, especially young people and women, to access and learn about technologies such as computers, digital photography, film-making etc. This involvement at the local level is carried out in collaboration with Ankur, (p.95) an NGO that uses learning and teaching as a tool for social change. Together they have set up a network of neighbourhood spaces where local residents carry out embedded research and take part in workshops and projects.

Sarai also publish the annual *Sarai Reader* on a specific theme whose recent issues have included 'Frontiers', 'Turbulence' and 'The Cities of Everyday Life', as well as *Deewan E Sarai*, which is the Hindi language version, and other publications related to their research. These texts are mainly aimed at academic audiences, and in keeping with Sarai's copy-left ethos, are available for free on their website.

Sarai (2001–) *Sarai Readers*, New Delhi: Impress. <http://www.sarai.net/publications/readers/> (accessed 22 May 2009).

Segal, Walter
1907–1985
www.segalselfbuild.co.uk
Walter Segal was an architect who is well-known for designing a self-build housing system based on a timber frame construction. Designed initially as a temporary and cheap housing solution for his family, Segal soon realised its durability and potential as a system that could be employed by others wanting to build their own homes. The modular system is notable for its flexibility and for its openness to user interpretation, both in the building process itself and in its future use. It empowers the user-builder to take control of their environment and can be seen as a critique of the homogenous mass housing of the time that lacked any capacity for participation or personalisation.

Segal's system was employed in Lewisham, London in the 1970s when the council made available for self-builders three sites which were too small to be developed commercially. Although the self-build method was highly suitable for the context, it still took five years of negotiation before the council finally gave permission. Designed in consultation with Jon Broome, the system makes use of materials that are readily available and simple to work with and removes the need for any wet trades. Once the positioning of the timber frame and a services and circulation core are set, the standard size panels can be positioned according to user needs. Each self-builder was provided with basic plans, sections and a specification that described the sequence of construction. Within a set grid, they were able to make adaptations to the lightweight, dry and demountable construction system, which was screwed or bolted together. Since whole families could build the houses together, with children and the elderly being welcome on site, the building process itself engendered a strong sense of community. For many, Segal's method has become an exemplary early model both in terms of construction and participation in housing design and his methods are promoted today by the Walter Segal Self-Build Trust.

Wharton, K. (1988) 'A Man on His Own [Interview]', *Architects Journal*, 187(18): 78–80.

Self-organisation

Whilst the usual frameworks of architecture and urbanism operate in ways in which local actors have little influence on their outcome, self-organised practices provide an alternate framework for the production of space. A lineage can be traced through political activism, cultural production in the form of music, art and literature, and other ways of dwelling such as squatting (p.199) or autonomous communities. All demonstrate a desire to challenge the status quo by developing fiercely independent approaches. A number of spatial practices, such as the Centri Sociali (p.117) or the Freetown of Christiania, (p.119) extend this narrative into the realm of architecture and urbanism.

In addition to informal activities, architects and artists have also begun to consider the potential of self-organisation as a tactic within their practice. Cedric Price's (p.189) experiments of the 1960s harnessed the creativity of the users of buildings and were inspired in part by the Situationists (p.178) proposals for a Unitary Urbanism, whilst atelier d'architecture autogérée's (p.105) Ecobox project developed a left-over space in Paris over five years through a deliberately slow collaborative process that involved residents, students and designers. The Isola Arts Centre in Milan also adopted a self-organised approach in its resistance to the demolition of the local neighbourhood and its own building to make way for regeneration-driven development. This tactic drew the attention of architects, artists and local residents, and this dynamic network produced a range of material that was not only oppositional in nature but also produced alternative proposals.

Veg-Out community garden in St Kilda, Melbourne, founded in 1998. Ph: Tatjana Schneider

Self-organisation in architectural terms radically challenges many of the tenets of the regulated and controlled profession. It does not simply suggest participation in something that is controlled elsewhere, but actively establishes the desire and need for a transformation in the first instance, before acting on it. This action involves the design of processes that can enable people to transform their own environments meaning that the mechanisms involved are embedded within their own locality and are not external to it. Since self-organised projects emerge from the negotiations of many different actors, they are inherently relational practices, and point towards the collective production of space.

Hughes, J. and Sadler, S. (eds) (2000) *Non-plan: Essays on Freedom, Participation and Change in Modern Architecture and Urbanism*, Oxford: Architectural Press.

Shack/Slum Dwellers International

Transnational, 1996–
www.sdinet.co.za
Shack/Slum Dwellers International (SDI) is a transnational NGO founded in 1996 and currently registered in South Africa and the Netherlands, with its member countries ranging across the continents of Africa, Asia and Latin America. It represents 'federations' of the urban poor and homeless groups who have organised themselves at a city or national level. In contrast to the prevalent post-war attitude of governments being best placed to deal with issues of poverty and development, SDI emphasises the need for the poor to be able to help themselves. They have developed a number of mechanisms or 'rituals' that facilitate this and which members have to adhere to. These focus on issues of governance and leadership with one of their key tactics being the encouragement of daily saving as a way to not only collect funds, but as a pretext for neighbourhood organisation. The daily interaction of people living in the same area under similar conditions encourages dialogue, raising opportunities to meet, discuss, and mobilise together. Although not only an organisation for women, SDI places a fundamental emphasis on their participation, contending that women's involvement is crucial to the success of initiatives based around issues of household finance and housing needs. They also highlight that women's movements have historically

tended to be non-party political whilst effecting change on a social and political level.

Organised as a network, SDI's pedagogical approach is based on horizontal exchange where members learn from each other's experiences rather than relying on the detached and often inappropriate knowledge of 'experts'. As members organise a savings group, gain land tenure regularisation, improve settlement infrastructure, or complete income generation and housing projects, they travel to other locations to meet those attempting to do the same. The growth of the SDI network increases its power and ability to influence governments and donors; the grass-roots organisation thus gains strength through numbers and is quickly becoming a large-scale social movement. It has recently become only the second NGO alongside Habitat for Humanity International (p.100) to join the Cities Alliance, an organisation consisting of donor governments and the World Bank. Herein also lies a critique of SDI, which is seen to be aligning itself more and more with neo-liberal forces, and for some becoming *the* voice for the urban poor. Nonetheless, SDI have managed to create a space for local action and mobilisation at a time when governments and political parties have failed to act.

Burra, S., D'Cruz, C. and Patel, S. (2001) 'Slum/Shack Dwellers International (SDI): Foundations to Treetops', *Environment and Urbanization*, 13: 45–59.

Simone, AbdouMaliq

AbdouMaliq Simone teaches sociology at Goldsmiths College, University of London and has taught at various universities in Africa and the US. As an urbanist, he has carried out research on African cities and more recently on Southeast Asian cities. He combines his pan-African experience working with NGOs, municipal government and community upgrading projects together with research on urban culture, policy, international relations and critical theory. Simone's research points to the inadequacy of modernist discourses in understanding the contemporary realities of non-western cities. His work focuses on the everyday experiences of people in sites and locations that are under-represented within academia, such as his 2004 book, *For the City Yet to Come*, which examined the social networks in Douala in Cameroon, Pikine, a large suburb of Dakar in Senegal, the African community in Jeddah, and Winterveld, a

Squatted house in Berlin. Ph: Chris Hamley

neighbourhood on the edge of Pretoria, South Africa. Through combining urban planning with postcolonial literature and development studies, Simone shows how African cities should be seen as examples of everyday resistance against misplaced urban and development plans, rather than being understood as failed cities as has been the prevalent view amongst planners and governments. His work reveals the potential of these cities and points to how their particular resources can be put to work for the development of urban planning policies and proposals.

Simone, A. (2004) *For the City Yet to Come: Changing African Life in Four Cities*, Durham: Duke University Press.

Squatting

Squatting is defined in the broadest sense as the occupation and transformation of land and buildings that are unused or underused. It is based on the assumption that occupation and use constitutes a right in itself above and beyond legal ownership. In this squatting is a political act, privileging direct action (p.140) to oppose the privatisation of land for speculation and individual gain. An ancient practice, one of the earliest examples of squatting was the Diggers (p.139) declaration that 'the earth is a common treasury for all', reclaiming what was common land for cultivation. A recent version

of this impulse in the UK is the movement, **The Land is Ours**, which campaigns for free and equal rights for all to the country's open spaces through policy change and land occupations.

In the global South squatting is often tied to housing rights and strategies of survival; urban organisations such as the Shack and Slum Dwellers International (p.198) or Abahlali baseMjondolo (p.89) are fighting for the land rights of those living in informal settlements whose numbers are burgeoning. The **Movimento dos Trabalhadores Rurais Sem Terra** (MST – Brazilian Landless Workers' Movement) established in 1984 is an example of a rural squatting movement, which aims at redistributing unproductive land to people who need it most to provide food and a source of income. MST has its roots in a long struggle over land in Brazil and has now become one of the largest social movements in South America. The land occupations of MST exercise a legal right enshrined in the Brazilian constitution, which allows unproductive land to be used for a 'larger social function'. The legal status of squatting thus differs across countries, from being considered a civil conflict between squatters and the legal owners, to being deemed an illegal act.

In the global North squatting is usually tied to ideological struggles and the desire to find alternative ways of living. These include the setting up of free cultural spaces and political centres, such as the large

Centri Sociali [p.117] movement of Italy or the Freetown of Christiania [p.119] in Copenhagen. Berlin has been the locus of squatting in Europe with many local initiatives such as the **K77** squat whose ten-year history has seen the refurbishment of an old uninhabitable building into a communal living and working space, through a participative and self-organised process. The US has its own phenomena of urban homesteading, where in neighbourhoods with large numbers of uninhabited abandoned homes, poorer residents take over and refurbish properties for their own use. Usually a grass-roots endeavour, urban homesteading is legal and has been used by some state governments as a solution to the lack of affordable housing. There is also a growing squatter movement in the US following the financial crisis of 2007, which has led to thousands of homes being repossessed. As the group **Take Back the Land** points out, these homes are left empty whilst evicted families are left homeless; the organisation coordinates action groups to move people back into empty homes.

In architecture, squatting has played an important role, spanning grass-roots neighbourhood initiatives such as Park Fiction, [p.181] responses by architectural professionals such as Community Technical Aid, [p.128] or writers and activists such as Colin Ward, [p.210] who uncovered another history of land rights in the UK from the Diggers to the Plotlanders, [p.187] or the many people and practices working with and for those living in informal settlements. They are all related to the squatter movement, [p.199] which whether an act of survival, a political act or both, is based in a completely different way of imagining the world than the dominant capitalist mode.

Neuwirth, R. (2004) *Shadow Cities: A Billion Squatters, A New Urban World*, New York: Routledge.

Stalker/Osservatorio Nomade
Rome, Italy, 1994–
www.osservatorionomade.net
Stalker is a collective of architects and researchers connected to the Roma Tre University who came together in the mid–1990s. In 2002, Stalker founded the research network Osservatorio Nomade (ON), which consists of architects, artists, activists and researchers working experimentally and engaging in actions to create self-organised spaces and situations.

Stalker have developed a specific methodology of urban research, using participative tools to construct a 'collective imaginary' for a place. In particular they have developed the method of collective walking to 'actuate territories', which for them is a process of bringing space into being. Stalker carry out their walks in the 'indeterminate' or void spaces of the city, which have long been disregarded or considered a problem in traditional architectural practice. Referring to their walking practice as 'transurbance', the group views it as a collective mode of expression and a tool for mapping the city and its transformations, of gathering stories, evoking memories and experiences, and immersing themselves with others in a place. They use this knowledge and experience to address urban planning and territorial issues, focusing especially on the interstices of the contemporary city-region. Starting with the edges of the Tiber river on the outskirts of Rome, Stalker have since used this method in many other cities including Milan, Paris, Berlin and Turin.

Since their early walks, Stalker/ON have developed an approach to architecture that is profoundly participa-tory. Using tactical and playful interventions, they aim at creating spatial transformations through engaging in social relations, because as they have observed, the built environment takes too long to respond to the needs and desires of those who inhabit it. Places on the periphery and communities that are marginal take centre stage in Stalker/ON's projects, working with amongst others the Roma and gypsy populations of Europe, Kurdish migrants and the homeless. Their projects show a commitment to those that society abandons and their method collectively tries to build projects with them. Through listening, making use of creative tools of mapping, walking, interventions and participation, Stalker/ON initiate processes of self-organisation that create convivial, social spaces.

Lang, P. (2001) 'Stalker on Location', in Franck, K. A. and Stevens, Q. (eds) *Loose Space*, New York: Routledge.

Supertanker
Copenhagen, Denmark, 2002–
www.supertanker.info
Supertanker is a Copenhagen based close-knit network of urban-social entrepreneurs working on the borders between action research, process design and urban

Free Trial! Designed for a conference about the future of Christiania, this concept for public meetings is organised following the format of a court case. Ph: Supertanker

development led by architect Jens Brandt, sociologist Martin Frandsen and urban geographer, Jan Lilliendahl Larsen, process designer Anders Hagedorn and artist Martin Rosenkreutz Madsen mostly based at Roskilde University. From its founding Supertanker has collaborated with diverse groups of citizens including residents, urban developers, planners, politicians, grassroots organisations and artists. The network first unfolded as a civic urban laboratory in an otherwise antagonistic political climate surrounding the redevelopment of the Copenhagen harbour in 2003. Their aim was to act as impartial mediators and in the following two years, they have experimented with different means of public dialogue and generation of ideas gradually focusing on the unnoticed and unacknowledged potentials of the urban community.

Similar to the work of muf, (p.175) Supertanker try to design situations and events that reveal the diverse claims to a space and to design processes that can include marginal voices. Through organising a series of conferences (2004, 2005 and 2006), public events and contributing to academic publications, they have developed a methodology for harnessing the creative and social potentials of urban wastelands. The focus has resulted in several techniques for political deliberation ('Free Trial!'), citizens' involvement ('Urban Process'), user driven spatial design ('Urban Workshop'), as well as social innovation ('Minority Design'). Supertanker has now established itself as an association and limited company and is funded through various social, arts and research grants.

Brandt, J. and others (2008) 'Supertanker: In Search of Urbanity', *Arq: Architectural Research Quarterly*, 12: 173–181.

Team Zoo
Japan, 1971–
www.zoz.co.jp
Team Zoo is a Japanese cooperative of small studios including architecture, urban planning, furniture makers and graphic designers. Formed in 1971 as Atelier Zō by graduates of Waseda University, Tokyo, the group was influenced by the architect and educator, Takamasa Yoshizaka, whose emphasis on regional identity and vernacular approaches they adopted. By 1978 the group had expanded, calling itself Team Zoo with each individual practice named after a different animal. The organisational structure of Team Zoo is the result of the unique Japanese context, where the rapid post-war economic growth fuelled a building boom that demanded extremely fast paced construction, something very difficult for a small office to achieve. The group therefore comes together for large-scale projects that demand such a commitment, whilst working independently in the interim. The high rents of Tokyo also saw many of the individual practices moving out to the provinces, where most of their projects were located, mainly schools, kindergartens and community buildings as well as some housing.

Many of the group's buildings are designed to be intimate in scale with large institutional buildings being broken down and clustered together. Team Zoo also insist on using local materials and craftsmen; often this has led to new workshops being set up by artisans employed by them. For example, **Atelier Iruka** in Kobe used traditional plastering methods for the exterior of their library in Wakimachi, contacting craftsmen whose skills were almost forgotten and arranging for young apprentices to be trained, thus ensuring the survival of the craft for at least another generation. They also commissioned traditional birds and dragons from a local tile factory saving it from closure. **Atelier Zo**, which is the most active of the studios, is known for its buildings expressing the zoological metaphors of the groups' names, for example Domo Cerakanto takes its shape from a mythical fish. The combination of such metaphors with vernacular traditions stand in marked contrast to much of contemporary Japanese architecture and the loose cooperative structure of the group has ensured that their slower and more individualised approach to architecture can survive in a highly competitive context.

Speidel, M. (ed) (1991) *Team Zoo: Buildings and Projects 1971–1990*, London: Thames & Hudson.

Turner, John

www.dpu-associates.net

John Turner is a British architect who has written extensively on housing and community organisation, his writings being influenced by a formative period spent working in the squatter settlements of Peru from 1957 to 1965. There, Turner studied and advised on a number of reconstruction and slum upgrading programmes which were part of a nation-wide community development initiative. During this time Peru was also a leading centre for debate on housing policy, community development and the role of self-help. Turner's own theoretical stance was formed in this context and combined aspects of the work of the Peruvian urban theorists Fernando Belaúnde, Pedro Beltrán and Carlos Delgado.

Turner's central thesis argued that housing is best provided and managed by those who are to dwell in it rather than being centrally administered by the state. In the self-building and self-management of housing and neighbourhoods, Turner asserted that the global North had much to learn from the rapidly developing cities of the global South. Through a number of empirical

studies, some of which were published in a collection for Habitat International Coalition (p.100) entitled *Building Community*, he showed clearly that neighbourhoods designed with local groups worked better since people were experts on their own situations and should be given the 'freedom to build', a phrase that became the title for an edited collection by Turner. Whether this freedom was granted by the state or wrested from it through squatting (p.199) was less important. Within this framework the state as well as private professionals such as architects and engineers, act as enablers, resulting in a shift in thinking that valorises experience and local know-how over technocratic and professionalised forms of knowledge.

In contrast to the 'aided self-help' policies of the World Bank, for which Turner is frequently credited, his vision was far more radical as he not only contended that residents should build their own houses and neighbourhoods, but that they should also have control over their finances and management. In *Freedom to Build: Dweller Control of the Housing Process*, which was first published in 1972, Turner sets out these views, which remain relevant today. Whilst there have been some attempts in Europe to involve residents in decisions regarding their built environment, such as the work of the participatory architects of the 1960s and 1970s, (p.182) the Scandinavian cohousing (p.122) movement, the Community Technical Aid Centres (p.128) of the UK and the work of architects such as Walter Segal, (p.196) the full potential of such an engagement has not yet been realised.

Turner, J. (1972) *Freedom to Build: Dweller Control of the Housing Process*, New York: Macmillan.

UN-Habitat
Transnational, 1978–
www.unhabitat.org
UN-Habitat is the United Nations (UN) agency for human habitation and settlement, first established as the United Nations Centre for Human Settlements in 1978 and becoming a full UN programme in 2002. The agency's stated aim is to provide 'shelter for all' and in this it works with both policy makers and local communities. UN-Habitat is based in Nairobi with regional offices also located in Rio de Janeiro, Brazil and Fukuoka, Japan. The agency is funded by, and reports to, the UN General Assembly and as such its reach is global, with programmes in all five continents. It runs two major worldwide campaigns – the Global Campaign on Urban Governance, and the Global Campaign for Secure Tenure. Through these campaigns and by other means, the agency focuses on a range of issues and special projects which it helps implement.

These include a joint UN-Habitat/World Bank slum upgrading initiative called the **Cities Alliance**, promoting effective housing development policies and strategies, helping develop and campaigning for housing rights, promoting sustainable cities and urban environmental planning and management, and enabling post-conflict land-management and reconstruction in countries devastated by war or natural disasters. Other projects address water, sanitation and solid waste management for towns and cities, training and capacity building for local leaders, ensuring that women's rights and gender issues are brought into urban development and management policies, helping fight crime through UN-Habitat's Safer Cities Programme, and research and monitoring of urban economic development. It also helps strengthen rural-urban linkages, and infrastructure development and public service delivery. The agency also organises the biennial World Urban Forum, the world's largest gathering based around urban issues and social justice.

UN-Habitat has some 154 technical programmes and projects in 61 countries around the world, most of them in the least developed countries. These include major projects in areas of conflict such as Afghanistan, Kosovo, Somalia, Iraq, Rwanda, and the Democratic Republic of Congo, to name a few. The agency's operational activities help governments create policies and strategies aimed at strengthening a self-reliant management capacity at both national and local levels. Its research arm has also released a number of highly influential reports.

UN-Habitat (2008) *The Challenge of Slums*, London: Earthscan.

Urban Catalyst
Berlin, Germany, 2001–2003
www.urbancatalyst.net
Urban Catalyst was a European research project based in Berlin between 2001 and 2003 that explored strategies for the temporary use of leftover sites in urban areas. Founded by Philipp Misselwitz, Philipp Oswalt and Klaus Overmeyer the project was organised as an interdisciplinary platform for research and public interventions in order to stimulate discussion amongst architects and planners about the use of void spaces in the city. The project took as its topic the various unplanned and informal uses of these spaces, which operate within informal economies and fall outside the remit of traditional urban planning. Using the city of Berlin as their site, Urban Catalyst organised a series of events, exhibitions, publications and workshops, in order to develop strategies for integrating such processes into the urban design of contemporary cities. The research explored new forms of urban development where citizens would be the initiators rather than professional developers.

Studio UC and Senatsverwaltung für Stadtentwicklung Berlin (eds) (2007) *Urban Pioneers*, Berlin: Jovis Verlag 2007.

Urban Farming
The practice of cultivating food and raising animals in an urban environment is referred to variously as urban farming or urban agriculture. Whilst small-scale and localised food production has a long history, including individual allotments which have been popular in Europe since the late C18, it is the integration of such farming practices within the economic and ecological system of towns and cities that is a newer development. This means that urban resources such as compost from food waste and wastewater from urban drainage is made use

Rotonda de Cojimar, Havana, Cuba. Ph: Jennifer Cockrall-King

The Urban Agriculture Curtain. Ph: Bohn and Viljoen

of, whilst urban problems such as the pressure on land and development also have to be negotiated.

The recent of example of **Cuba** has proven the effectiveness of urban agriculture, where it played a critical role in ensuring food security after the collapse of the Soviet Union in 1989. Cuba relied on chemical imports for fertiliser and pesticides from the Soviet Union; combined with a dramatic drop in oil availability, the country, and in particular Havana its capital city of 2.5 million people, became vulnerable to food shortages. In response, the Cuban government promoted urban agriculture at various scales, including food grown in private gardens, state-owned research gardens, and the most successful model, the popular gardens on state-owned land open to the public. Begun in 1991, the *huertos populares*, can range in size from a few square meters to three hectares and can be cultivated individually or as part of a community group. Land is provided for free as long as it is used for cultivation; the farming is organic as chemicals are expensive and difficult to get hold of. The scheme has been very successful, with an estimated 50 percent of national food production now being urban based, rising in some cities to 80 percent of all food being cultivated within the city boundary.

In Europe and the US, urban farming is becoming increasingly popular as environmental concern grows, since it reduces the carbon footprint of food production, as well as leading to greater bio-diversity and local employment. Architects, **Bohn and Viljoen** based in London, have taken the Cuban model and adapted it to suit landscaping proposals in European cities. Their 'Continuous Productive Urban Landscape' envisages an urban agriculture that takes the form of continuous green fingers running through cities to the countryside, strategically connecting allotment gardens with parks, which become more than mere ornamental landscapes. Bohn and Viljoen acknowledge that the Cuban model is dependent on its context of food shortage and a communal culture and if it were to be applied to the consumerist context of Europe, a change in attitude would also be needed. They call on ordinary people to appropriate leftover spaces such as grass verges, as do guerrilla gardeners, (p.152) but with the specific intent to cultivate food. The architects' aim is to act as agents or facilitators of a change in attitudes and habits as much as in the physical environment. As such, they have organised events such as 'The Continuous Picnic' in central London, as well designing tools and objects to facilitate such actions, for example the 'Urban Agriculture Curtain', which allows allotment style food production to be carried out in a very limited space by growing plants vertically.

In the UK city farms are also popular, where the emphasis is not on growing crops but also on raising animals, to ensure that inner city children who may never come into contact with farm animals can learn about food production. One of the earliest of these is **Mudchute Park and Farm** on the Isle of Dogs in London, established in 1977 and still operating. A piece of derelict land made from the spoil of dredging of Millwall Dock in the 1860s, it became a wilderness cherished by the local community. Plans to build a high-rise housing estate in 1974 met with local opposition and residents led by the architect Katharine Heron campaigned for a 'People's Park'. In 1977 the Mudchute Association was formed to preserve and develop the area. Farm animals and horses were introduced, trees and plants were planted by volunteers and corporate teams. Mudchute also has a clear educational mission, with local schools encouraged to use the farm.

The desire for local food production in urban areas is also reaching a global scale with the **Transition Town** movement that originated in a student project at Kinsale Further Education College in Ireland in 2006, under the supervision of Rob Hopkins, a permaculture expert. The Transition Town concept was developed to equip towns and later also villages, neighbourhoods etc. to deal with the changes that peak oil would bring. The idea was to establish a creative and holistic solution to our dependency on oil, changing energy consumption habits, food production, health, education and economy. In all these schemes local food production plays a large role in creating self-sufficient communities that are not dependent on food imports or on food that has travelled by road across the country. The Transition Town concept has already spread to many other countries, including UK, Canada, US, Australia, Chile and Italy, helped also through the emphasis on social networking, using the internet to spread the message.

Viljoen, A. (ed) (2005) *Continuous Productive Urban Landscapes: Designing Urban Agriculture for Sustainable Cities*, Oxford: Architectural Press.

Vāstu-Shilpā Consultants

Ahmedabad, India, 1956–
www.sangath.org

Vāstu-Shilpā Consultants was set up in Ahmedabad in 1956 by Balkrishna Doshi, an Indian architect, planner and educator. Doshi is considered one of the leading exponents of appropriate technology, whilst also being a key figure in the development of a modern Indian architecture, combining modernist influences with traditions from the East, specifically Doshi's interest in Hindu philosophy. The name of the practice refers to the Vāstu-Shilpā Shastras, the Hindu metaphysical design philosophy based on a system of rules related to the environment, cosmology, proportion and directional alignment. Doshi combines these influences with his experience of working with Le Corbusier, and his later collaborations with Louis Kahn, to produce an architecture that is adapted to its context, both in terms of climate and culture. As an educator he has taught at various institutions and also set up the School of Architecture and Planning in Ahmedabad, including designing its building. He is also a founding member of the Vāstu-Shilpā Foundation, a non-profit research institution that deals with issues of sustainable design, appropriate technology, vernacular architecture and urbanism.

Aranya low cost housing at Indore. Ph: Vāstu-Shilpā

Although Vāstu-Shilpā have designed private residences, offices and institutional buildings, it is perhaps their housing and urban design that is most relevant to

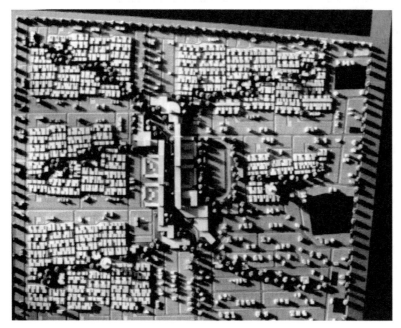

Model of Aranya low cost housing at Indore. Ph: Vāstu-Shilpā

the question of spatial agency. During the 1960s, India promoted a policy of regional industrialisation, where new factories with associated housing were to be built on the outskirts of existing towns or close to local villages. In this context, Vāstu-Shilpā developed a methodology for designing new townships which combined the demands of a growing economy with traditional skills and modes of living: prefabricated concrete elements were mixed with local materials and craft skills and a number of typologies of housing were designed that could be added to and adapted by the inhabitants. In the 1980s this model was taken further in the design of a new township, where much like the later work of Elemental, (p.143) they took advantage of the latent construction knowledge and self-building skills that low-income, squatter families acquire through need. The Aranya township incorporates a variety of income groups on an 85-hectare site, where basic infrastructure, including electricity, water and drainage are provided. Whilst in some instances whole houses were built, for poorer families there were a range of options, including purchasing a plot only; a plot with a plinth to build on; or a built 'service core' of kitchen, washroom and an additional room. Here owners could add to the given infrastructure at their own pace and

with down payments related to the average income of each family, the Aranya project tried to create a model of housing which could be afforded by those with very few resources.

It was Vāstu-Shilpā's organisational structure of a research institution affiliated to a design practice that allowed them to produce a design so well suited to the needs of squatter families. They were commissioned by the Indian government to spend a period of intensive research on such settlements gaining a thorough understanding of their physical, social and economic structures, a knowledge that was then applied to the design work.

Rybczynik, W. and Vāstu-Shilpā Foundation (1984) *How the Other Half Builds*, Montreal: McGill University.

Vélez, Simón and Villegas, Marcelo

www.marcelovillegas.com
Simón Vélez is a Colombian architect who works alongside artisan, Marcelo Villegas. Together they have pushed the limits of what can be constructed using bamboo, bringing the material to the attention of a wider international audience and at the same time challenging its perception as a building material in their

own country, where it signals poverty and marginalisation. Vélez's initial rejection of modernist architectural trends led him to research into the possibilities of constructing with bamboo, specifically the local species called *Guada*, which is an extremely strong variety. Through adapting indigenous building techniques, the pair have constructed a range of experimental buildings starting in rural Colombia and increasingly in other parts of the world.

The close working relationship between an architect and artisan has allowed Vélez and Villegas to experiment freely with construction methods and has resulted in the development of innovative techniques such as a jointing system for bamboo which uses bolts to tie the structure together rather than the traditional use of straps, which cannot accommodate for the shrinking bamboo. Other innovations include injecting mortar into certain joints, which dramatically increases structural strength, and developing foundations and roofing systems that are more appropriate to their context and materials. For example, roofs are deliberately heavy in order to provide stability in high winds, rather than the lightweight version usually favoured. Vélez and Villegas' working method combines hand-drawn sketches with full-scale mock-ups and by always

employing the same well-trained crew of workers, they build on knowledge gained over years of experimentation in the building process.

Through their innovations, Vélez and Villegas have breathed new life into an ancient building material and have transformed it into one of the best performing materials in terms of strength, stability and suitability for constructing in earthquake prone regions. Their regular seminars and workshops have been instrumental in popularising bamboo as an ecological material that can be cultivated without damage to the environment and which can provide a low-cost construction method in many developing countries, removing a dependence on imported materials and technologies. By concentrating their efforts at the level of the architectural detail the approach of Vélez and Villegas is similar to that of architect Hsieh Ying-Chun (p.106) but Vélez and Villegas' construction method does require some specialist training. In contrast, the bamboo structures built by the architect, Eko Prawoto (p.188) are friendlier to self-building but are also more modest in scale.

Velez, S. (2000) *Grow Your Own House: Simon Velez and Bamboo Architecture*, Weil am Rhein: Vitra Design Museum.

The 2008 version of the temporary Nomadic Museum in Mexico City was the largest bamboo structure ever built. Courtesy Simón Vélez

The "hand made" construction approach adapted from vernacular building techniques. Ph: Construction team/BASEhabitat

Veranda of school designed by Heringer for Dipshika in Bangladesh. Ph: Katharina Doblinger

Vernacular and Craft-based Design

There are a number of younger architects addressing issues of sustainable living and construction through combining vernacular techniques with contemporary design technologies. Most of this work is based in countries of the Global South and in deprived neighbourhoods, taking a participative approach that utilises local skills and knowhow. These architects not only design the buildings, they often raise funds and mobilise volunteers as well as organising related developmental work. For example architect Francis Kéré (p.161) has built a number of buildings in his family village in Burkina Faso by raising funds in Germany.

Sanjeev Shankar is based in New Delhi, India where his work combines traditional craft skills with an open source inclusive design process. His recent project Jugaad (2008) consisted of residents making a pavilion in their neighbourhood from nearly a thousand discarded oil cans which were worked by hand over a period of three months. The workshops provided a forum to discuss ideas on recycling and reuse and resulted in a large freestanding canopy suspended with pulleys to adjust for shade. Other projects have included collaborations with artisans from different parts of India, working with materials such as leather and bamboo and using traditional skills to produce modern designs.

The utilisation of local materials and skills has also been key to **Anna Heringer** and **Eike Roswag's** design for the Meti School in Rudrapur, Bangladesh, built in 2005. The building was designed for the Bangladeshi NGO, Dipshika, who look to reduce migration to cities by improving village life through providing better facilities and employment opportunities. The school was designed to promote creative, student-centred learning and its construction was aimed at using local knowledge and providing jobs for the villagers. The architects refined the vernacular building technique of using wet loam and straw by adding a damp proof course and brick foundations, whilst an upper storey was built using bamboo construction. Heringer and Roswag organised the construction of the school over a period of four months with only the foundation being built by a commercial company. The rest of the building was constructed by hand by local builders who were trained by specialists from Germany and with the help of architecture students from Bangladesh and Austria.

Slessor, C. (2009) 'Magic carpet: Sanjeev Shankar's New Delhi art installation', *Architectural Review*, 225(1345): 82–85.

Viennese Co-operative Garden City movement

Defeat in WWI was preceded by the economic and political collapse of Vienna with the municipal government no longer being able to provide for its citizens. With an acute shortage of housing many people turned to subsistence farming on squatted (p.199) land and lived in self-built shelters; by 1918 over 100,000 people were living in such conditions. The period of 1919–1923 saw the Social Democratic city council undertaking a series of radical reforms, including the construction of the *Wiener Gemeindebauten*, which is arguably one of the largest and most successful of co-operative housing projects built in Europe. Overhauled in the 1980s, they remain popular today and retain their co-operative community ethos, although the residents are a more heterogeneous mix than the industrial workers that the housing was originally built for. Based on Ebenezer Howard's garden cities (p.168) approach of self-sustaining satellite settlements to major cities, they consisted of 400 communal housing blocks with shared facilities such as kindergartens, libraries, medical centres, laundries, workshops, co-operative stores and sports facilities, as well as some space for subsistence gardening.

One of the initial moves was the setting up of a *Zentralstelle*, an organisation that administered and built the settlements; for a time Adolf Loos was its chief architect. However, it was not the architectural design of the built schemes that made them so successful and interesting but their organisational structure and management. There was a small participative element to the building process but mostly future residents were involved through their labour, which provided up to 80 percent of the total labour, and was used as a form of sweat equity to reduce costs. Ten to fifteen per cent of construction costs were covered in this way. All profit making ventures were excluded from the building process, including the supply and handling of material, with a public corporation set up for this purpose. Very few resources were wasted through the re-use of surplus material elsewhere and these strict rules resulting in there being no requirement to raise capital for construction. With no form of mortgage, the city kept the title to the land and leased it to the building co-operative.

This way of building and managing co-operatively gave a collective spirit to these settlements but also created frictions with their middle-income neighbours. That Vienna's socialist council was working in direct opposition to the right-wing, conservative national government also meant that the building programme was short-lived. Although the schemes resulted in good quality low income housing produced at the lowest costs they were abandoned in 1930 as the emergency conditions of housing and food shortages of WWI were alleviated and more profitable ventures were sought.

Blau, E. (1999) *The Architecture of Red Vienna, 1919–1934*, Cambridge, MA: MIT Press.

Rotenberg, R. (1995) *Landscape and Power in Vienna*, Baltimore, MD: John Hopkins University Press.

Ward, Colin
1924–2010

Colin Ward was an architect and one of the leading figures of the UK anarchist movement; he wrote extensively on the welfare system and the social history of Britain, and in particular on issues of housing and planning. From 1947 to 1960 he was the editor of the anarchist newspaper, *Freedom*, and from 1961 to 1970 the editor of the journal *Anarchy*, gathering round him a group of writers and thinkers who would go on to be influential in their own right. Ward theorised a 'pragmatist anarchism' that looked towards removing authoritarian forms of organisation and governance in favour of informal and self-organised mechanisms based on non-hierarchical structures. Unlike other anarchists, Ward recognised that a wholly anarchist society was a theoretical impossibility, as universal consent was unlikely without the use of force or coercion. Ward's pragmatist anarchism thus strove for a *freer* society rather than a 'free society'.

Ward's writings are characterised by a combination of theoretical discussion on the nature of anarchism with a practical sensibility that looked for empirical results and solutions that could transform real-life situations and everyday living conditions. One of the key themes of his work was the promotion of cooperative self-help strategies, in the form of squatting, (p.199) tenant cooperatives and self-build projects. Ward was an admirer of Walter Segal (p.196) whose self-building system he saw as exemplary of such an approach to housing, promoting participation and dweller control. Much of Ward's later

writing was historical in nature, in *Cotters and Squatters* he wrote a history of informal customs for the appropriation of land in Britain that included the Digger (p.139) movement, the Plotlanders (p.187) of southern England and the Welsh tradition of *T Unnos*, where a house is built in one night, which also has its echoes in the geçekondu of Turkey and the amateur building tactics (p.92) of the global South. Other books uncovered the history of allotments or the creative ways in which children inhabit their environments.

Ward's writings did much to dispel popular myths and stereotypes associated with anarchism, as well as demonstrating the practical applicability of such an approach to a wide range of issues pertinent to architecture.

Ward, C. (1976) *Housing: An Anarchist Approach*, London: Freedom Press.

Weisman, Leslie Kanes

Leslie Kanes Weisman is a feminist architect, educator and community activist whose work starts from the premise that the built environment is an expression of an established social order, meaning that space and the relationships it sustains reflect and reinforce existing gender, race and class relations in society. Weisman thus views access to space and its appropriation as political acts, and her research and teaching aim at subverting existing power relations in order to construct fairer cities. As a pedagogue Weisman has emphasised the role of both professionals and concerned citizens in ensuring the built environment does not exclude or discriminate. In the context of the women's movement of the 1960–70s, she co-founded the Women's School of Planning and Architecture (WSPA) in 1974, which fitted in with a wider move to form women's organisations in professions dominated by men. WSPA was organised as a summer school for women taught entirely by women, in which the content as well as the mode of teaching moved beyond traditional methods. The aim was to create an atmosphere where the hierarchies between teacher and student were broken down through simple and creative means such as allowing everyone to propose sessions with the help of a calendar to which all could add. Weisman also co-founded the Sheltering Ourselves education forum in 1987, which was an association of women involved in housing and community

Women and children in attendance at the first WSPA session in 1975. Courtesy Leslie Kanes Weisman

development. The network included architects, policy makers, grass-roots organisations, lawyers and housing cooperatives, taking the position that housing should be viewed as a human right.

For Weisman the relationships between women and the built environment are also seen as a prism for viewing the relationships between those who build our cities, and make decisions about them, and those who dwell in them. Her recent work takes these issues first raised in her book, *Discriminating by Design* published in 1992, and updates it with discussions on Universal Design, which advocates design solutions that do not exclude anyone, including those with disabilities. Universal Design has many resonances with the early work on signage and the provision of women's

services that was carried out in the UK by Women's Design Service. (p.212)

Weisman's approach to architecture has always been highly pragmatic and since 2002 has led her into a career in politics. She is serving as a member of the Zoning Board of Appeals, in Southold Town, Long Island, a body that interprets planning regulations on a case-by-case basis. That change in architecture is inextricably linked with the need to adapt and revise laws and regulations is a stance she shares with a growing number of architects, such as Teddy Cruz. (p.144) Weisman's move from an educator/activist to a politician demonstrates clearly these dependencies between architecture and politics and the need sometimes to gain a position of power in order to effect change, a position that is also demonstrated well in the example of Curitiba, (p.166) Brazil and its architect/mayor.

Weisman, L. K. (1992) *Discrimination by Design: A Feminist Critique of the Man-Made Environment*, Urbana: University of Illinois Press.

Whole Earth Catalog

Menlo Park, California, USA, 1968–1972
www.wholeearth.com

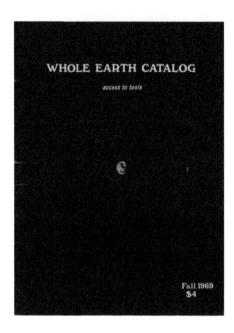

Published regularly between 1968 and 1972, the Whole Earth Catalog listed products, such as books, maps, specialist journals, camping equipment, tools and machinery, alongside methods for building, planting and specialist articles on topics ranging from organic farming, resource depletion, solar power, recycling and wind energy. It was essentially a handbook for those wanting to live self-sufficiently, full of tips and suggestions. Today, its name is synonymous with the American counter-cultural scene of the late 1960s. The Catalog was the brainchild of Stewart Brand, who was the editor; together with his collaborators, the mathematician Lois Jennings and the graphic designer James Baldwin, the Catalog was published as a series of regular editions until 1972 and intermittent editions until 1998.

The Whole Earth Catalog embraced systems theory and cybernetic evolutionism; its conceptual stance of a holistic model for society was inspired by the works of the anthropologist Gregory Bateson, the theorist Marshall McLuhan, architect Buckminster Fuller (p.96) and the mathematician Nobert Wiener. What began as an interest in communes and happenings (Brand was partly inspired by Drop City, (p.141) the artists' settlement in Colorado) evolved into a long-lasting interest in computers and alternative technology. The Whole Earth endeavour became a way of researching how a grass-roots movement could be furnished with information and energy, of how it could become a reality. The Catalog's sister organisation, the **Farallones Institute**, which was funded by the same non-profit educational institution, the Portola Institute in Menlo Park, California, concentrated on developing alternative technology solutions.

There was nothing for sale in the Catalogs, instead they were a repository of information, giving contact details of retailers, prices for items, facilitating access. Its DIY approach valorised the amateur through providing what the catalog's strap line called 'access to tools'. The ambition of the Whole Earth Catalog was huge; it was a paper based database that has been described variously as a conceptual forerunner to the Internet and as democratising access to information, likened in its operation to Google's earlier more benign ambitions. Over the years, the Catalog evolved into a number of different forms, including *Whole Earth Supplement*, *Whole Earth Review*, and *CoEvolution Quarterly*.

Sadler, S. (2008) 'An Architecture of the Whole', *Journal of Architectural Education*, 61(4): 108–129.

Women's Design Service

London, UK, 1984–
www.wds.org.uk
Women's Design Service (WDS) was set up in London in 1984 as a worker's co-operative dedicated to improving the built environment for women. Its initial members were working for the Greater London Council (GLC) as part of Support Community Building Design (a Community Technical Aid Centre (p.128)), where they identified a need for an organisation that could promote women's interests. WDS was thus founded as an overtly feminist organisation in the belief that women's voices were not being heard, and that women had to live and work in environments that were unsuitable for them.

WOMEN'S SAFETY ON HOUSING ESTATES

Published by Women's Design Service

Initially funded by the GLC, the group's remit was to provide an advisory service to community groups, write feasibility studies and assist in applying for funding. With the abolishment of the GLC in 1986, funding was harder to come by and WDS restructured itself and set out to establish a coherent body of work on women and the built environment. The organisation became a resource and information centre as well as providing **pre-feasibility** studies for community projects. At this time WDS produced some of their most important work, publications such as *It's not all Swings and Round-abouts* and *At Women's Convenience*, which dealt with specific issues such as women's safety in public places, children's playgrounds and the lack of public toilet facilities. This work has left a lasting impact on the built environment in the UK, for example the requirement by law of baby changing facilities is a direct result of the work the group carried out.

From the outset WDS has led a precarious existence relying mostly on governmental funding and grants with a supplementary income from consultancy. The group are currently involved in regeneration schemes, acting on behalf of residents and although Community Technical Aid has long since ceased, their work embodies the same ethos.

Women's Design Service (1990) *At Women's Convenience: A Handbook on the Design of Womens' Public Toilets*, London: WDS.

Eeva Berglund (2009) *Doing Things Differently: WDS at 20*, London: WDS

Yale Building Project

New Haven, Connecticut, USA, 1967–
www.architecture.yale.edu/drupal/student_work/building_project
Yale Building Project is a compulsory part of the first year architecture course at Yale University in which students design and build their own structure. Seen as an early precursor to the design-build studios that are

more popular today in the US, such as the **BaSic Initiative**, **URBANbuild** and **Design Workshop** amongst others, Yale's programme was the only one of its kind when Charles Moore set it up in 1967. Whilst the school already had a fledgling design-build culture, with past students having built houses for each other's families and ski chalets in one case, Moore gave these activities an ethical dimension. Built in some of the poorest areas of the USA, the programme exposed students to a kind of poverty that many had not encountered before. Believing that architectural education should be much more than the ability to draw, Moore's tenure as chairman at Yale broke with the Beaux-Arts tradition of students working on one-off buildings such as museums and art galleries. Instead he focused on the everyday, on how to design good quality and affordable buildings for dwelling. Although Moore himself was crucial to the process, his vision sat well with the politics of the 1960s and students' desire for a socially relevant form of architecture, and they themselves were instrumental in identifying many of the early sites and communities for the projects.

Over the years, the basic teaching model has remained largely unchanged with students working first individually and then in groups to develop designs to a given brief in consultation with residents. Later in the academic year, clients and tutors judge projects and a single design is chosen to be worked on collectively, drawn in detail and built. Students work in teams, each group being responsible for a certain aspect of the project with tutors acting as advisors. Since the inception of the programme, projects have varied from early community buildings in rural Appalachia, to more modest pavilion-type buildings in the 1980s that were the result of budget limitations, to recent projects carried out in partnership with housing organisations such as **Habitat for Humanity** and **Neighbourhood Housing Services**. The type and nature of drawings produced by students has also evolved, from the basic sketches that were made for the first building to the full set of working drawings produced today.

The pedagogical approach developed at Yale moves away from a purely academic teaching system towards a model for learning based on doing. Students take responsibility for the construction, learning to work collaboratively, making collective decisions in a process that is often chaotic and difficult. The emphasis on mutual knowledge gained alongside fellow students, users and other interested parties, teaches essential skills of negotiation and frames architecture as a collective practice in contrast to modernist notions of the individual architect.

Hayes, R. W. (2007) *The Yale Building Project: The First 40 Years*, New Haven: Yale University Press.

SELECTED BIBLIOGRAPHY

A key reference to the work of each group discussed in the book is given at the end of each entry, with more details to be found on the website. Secondary references are in the footnotes at the end of each chapter. The following is a short selection of some of the most useful writings on spatial agency and the issues around it.

An Architektur, 'An Architektur. Produktion und Gebrauch gebauter Umwelt', An Architektur, 2002.

The journal An Architektur which is produced by the Berlin based group with the same name since 2002 has become one of the most comprehensive resources for everyone interested in the critical analysis of the production of the built environment.

Brian Anson, *I'll fight you for it! : behind the struggle for Covent Garden* (London: Cape, 1981).

The book is an account of the struggle for the preservation of dwellings and other buildings in London's Covent Garden area. It continues to inspire both students and others involved in and pressing for community involvement.

John Chase, Margaret Crawford and John Kaliski, *Everyday Urbanism* (Monacelli Press, 1999).

One of the few books about western cities that shifts the attention to the everyday scene, and shows how theories such as Henri Lefebvre's are played out on the ground.

The Dictionary of Alternatives: Utopianism and Organization, ed. by Martin Parker, Valerie Fournier and Patrick Reedy (London: Zed Books Ltd, 2007).

A good selection of optimistic alternatives; some overlap with Spatial Agency.

Paulo Freire, *Pedagogy of the Oppressed*, trans. Myra Bergman Ramos (London: Sheed and Ward, 1972).

This is a foundational text of critical pedagogy in which Friere explores the relationships between student, teacher and society and highlights the role of education in challenging oppression.

Anthony Giddens, *The Constitution of Society: Outline of the Theory of Structuration* (Berkeley: University of California Press, 1984).

This book, and others written by Giddens in the 1970s and 80s, are important for formulating the concept of agency.

Robert Goodman, *After the planners* (Harmondsworth: Penguin Books, 1972).

A provocative critique of the focus on objects of architecture and planning professions, arguing that these bodies should not be ends in themselves but instead serve the people using their buildings and spaces.

Félix Guattari, *The Three Ecologies*, trans. Ian Pindar and Paul Sutton (London: Athlone Press, 2000).

Here Guattari traces his concept of 'ecosophy' that relates the mental, social and environmental worlds. It is a useful introduction to his activist poltiics that seeks to make transversal links betwen these three domains.

Henri Lefebvre, *A Critique of Everyday Life*, 3 vols (London: Verso, 1991–2008).

The trilogy was one of the main inspirations behind the student protests of 1968 in Paris and also for the Situationists. A thorough exploration of the alienating nature of capitalism and a critique of consumerist society.

Making Space. Women and the Man-Made Environ-
ment, ed. by Matrix (London: Pluto Press, 1984).

Beyond its feminist focus on and of the world, this book is an important reminder that the production of space is not neutral.

Karl Marx, *Capital. A Critique of Political Economy.* Volume I Book One: The Process of Production of Capital, 1887.

Capital has been one of the most influential, and best-selling, books ever. It is a critical analysis of capitalism, yet, despite its relevance for the understanding of capitalism's production of space, the book typically can't be found in architectural libraries. Marx is also important for his definition of praxis as "revolutionary, critical-practical activity" – a key idea of this book and one which inspired the definition of spatial agency.

Samuel Mockbee, 'The Rural Studio', in *The Everyday and Architecture*, ed. by Jeremy Till and Sarah Wigglesworth (London: Academy Editions, 1998). Reprinted in *Constructing a New Agenda: Architectural Theory 1993–2009*, ed. by A. Krista Sykes (Princeton: Princeton Architectural Press, 2010), 107–115.

A short but passionate plea for reconsidering the role of architects, and in particular their social responsibility. An inspirational text for students, educators and architects, particularly when read in conjunction with the output of the Rural Studio, which Mockbee founded.

Non-Plan: Essays on Freedom, Participation and Change in Modern Architecture and Urbanism, ed. by Jonathan Hughes and Simon Sadler (Architectural Press, 1999).

A collection of essays referring to the original article of the same name, in which Cedric Price and others set out a new agenda for planning and other built environment disciplines

John Turner, *Housing by People* (London: Marion Boyars, 1976).

This book, and the earlier *Freedom to Build* (now out of print), set out Turner's seminal contribution to the way that the built environment should primarily be shaped by its users. Learning from his experience in Latin America, Turner's manifesto has renewed relevance in the context of spatial agency.

ACKNOWLEDGEMENTS

This book arose out of a research grant from the UK's Arts and Humanities Research Council, and we are exceptionally grateful for the support given, without which we could not have completed the project. We'd like to thank An Architektur who organised the Camp for Oppositional Architecture in 2006 and provided a possibility to present our project before it had even started. Early on we put in place a steering group, who throughout have provided advice, acting as a vital sounding board, so great our thanks go to its members: Tom Bolton, Julia Dwyer, Andreas Lang and John Worthington. Others such as Liza Fior of muf, Steve McAdam & Christina Norton of fluid, Nigel Coates, Markus Miessen, Kathrin Böhm and Andreas Lang of public works, Geoff Shearcroft and Daisy Froud of AOC and Jane Rendell discussed the project with us in the first few months, and helped us develop the concept. The project has included a number of accompanying events, all of which helped shaped the argument. First was the 'Alternate Currents' symposium held in Sheffield in 2007, then came the AHRA (Architectural Humanities Research Association) annual conference in 2008 which was organised by the Agency Research Group at the School of Architecture, University of Sheffield (Cristina Cerulli, Prue Chiles, Florian Kossak, Doina Petrescu, Tatjana Schneider, Renata Tyszczuk, Jeremy Till, Stephen Walker, and Sarah Wigglesworth), and finally the 2009 RIBA Research Symposium 'Changing Practices' which we curated. We would like to thank all the participants in those events, and the people who helped organise them as well as the RIBA Research Committee and officers, especially Sebastian Macmillan, Keith Snook and Bethany Winning. We are also indebted to the students at the School of Architecture, University of Sheffield, without whom the first two events would not have been as successful as they were. They, too, conducted interviews, rattled at arguments and through their work pushed at the boundaries of what it means to be an architect. The students of the design studio, SoftPraxis, which Jeremy and Tatjana convened in 2007/2008, were happy to experiment with our ideas and the educational context of architecture.

The compilation of the entries in the book has been, in the spirit of spatial agency, a collaborative enterprise, and we are indebted to people who have helped fill important geographical gaps. These included Matthew Barac (who also very generously wrote some of the entries), Axel Beccera, Jose Manuel Catedra Castillo, Esther Charlesworth, Lu Feng, Paul Jenkins, Yara Sharif and Sam Vardy (who also wrote an entry). Adam Dainow helped to compile the huge range of photographic material.

We have been very grateful for the support that we have received throughout the project from our publishers Routledge, and in particular Francesca Ford, the commissioning editor for architecture, and Laura Williamson. The reviews that we received for our book proposal were both encouraging and directing, and we thank those who wrote them, in particular Murray Fraser who relinquished his anonymity so that we could discuss the important issues he raised. As with Tatjana and Jeremy's previous book on Flexible Housing, it has been a pleasure to work with the same graphic designer, Ben Weaver, who brilliantly adjusts his style to suit each project. The project's success is also founded on the website, which has already received numerous hits thanks in large to the design by Dorian Moore of The Useful Arts Organisation, who made a disarmingly simple but very clever site.

Of course this book and project would not have been possible without the active engagement of the people included in it – the spatial agents – and we have been bowled over by everyone's generosity in answering queries and sourcing images. The names of people who helped are listed on a separate page; we are grateful to them all.

Finally, at a personal level Nishat would like to thank Phil Langley and Doina Petrescu who are always there for support and advice. Tatjana would like thank Florian Kossak for his continuous critical support and Sander for his endurance in coming with us to almost every event as well as being dragged into teaching and reviews at such a young age. To both: "Thanks a million. Thanks without end." Jeremy is indebted as ever to the support of Sarah Wigglesworth, who has engaged in lengthy discussions on the subject, because she too is a spatial agent.

We would like to thank the following for their response to requests and the provision of images: Abahlali baseMjondolo, Nazmi Al-Jubeh at Riwaq, Samuel Alcázar, An Architektur, ArchNet and William O'Reilly at Aga Khan Trust for Culture, Steve Badanes of Jersey Devil and Joshua Polansky at University of Washington, College of Built Environments, Visual Resources Collection, Markus Bader of raumlabor, Ana Paula Baltazar and Silke Kapp of MOM, Ursula Biemann, Peter Blundell Jones, Katrin Bohn of Bohn and Viljoen, Carin Bolles at Findhorn Foundation, John Bosma (http://www.flickr.com/photos/15262666@N05/4178972681/), Jens Brandt of Supertanker, Josef Bray-Ali, Lindsay Bremner of 26'10 South Architects, David Anthony Brown, Paul Bruins, Kim Bryan at Centre for Alternative Technology, Claudia Buhmann at Kéré Architecture, Bureau d'études, Graham Burnett at www.spiralseed.co.uk, Stephanie Cannizzo and Genevieve Cottraux at University of California, Berkeley Art Museum and Pacific Film Archive, Claire Carroll and Liza Fior of muf architecture/art, Craig Chamberlain, Andrew Clayton, Nelson Clemente, Jennifer Cockrall-King, Mathew Coolidge of Center for Land Use Interpretation, Deborah Cowen of Planning Action, Luciano DeSouza, Ewout Dorman and Michelle Provoost of Crimson, Julia Dwyer of Matrix, Jessica Eisenthal at Lombard-Freid Projects, Sarah Ernst, Simon Fairlie of The Land is Ours, Ronda Flanzbaum at Dome Village, Iram Ghufran of Sarai, Graham Gifford, Dennis Gilbert, Cay Green, Justin Goh and Rozalinda at Mess Hall, Lisbet Harboe, Arif Hasan, John Hill, Nikolaus Hirsch, Susanne Hofmann and Iliana Rieger of Baupiloten, Janna Hohn at Chora, Sarah Hollingworth at OO:/, Kirsten Jacobsen at Earthship Biotecture, Wes Janz of onesmallproject and Ball State University, Daria Der Kaloustian at Canadian Centre for Architecture, Hanne Sue Kirsch at Soleri Archives, Florian Kossak, Anne Lacaton of Lacaton & Vassal Architectes, Andreas Lang of public works, Melaine Lefeuvre (www.flickr.com/photos/citesouvrieres), Max Lindegger and Robin Harpley at EcoLogical Solutions, Chip Lord of Ant Farm, Kieran Lynam, Yvonne Magener, Carol McGuigan, Anthony McInnis at the University of Vermont, Helge Mooshammer and Peter Mörtenböck of ThinkArchitecture, Chris Moxey, Víctor Oddó at Elemental, Lauren Oliver at Noero Wolff Architects, Doina Petrescu of atelier d'architecture autogérée, Sylwia Piechowska, Marjetica Potrč, Eko Prawoto, Jean-François Prost of Adaptive Actions, Lee Pruett, Beate Quaschning at Ortner & Ortner Baukunst, Tasmi Quazi of Asiye eTafuleni, Michael Rakowitz, Damon Rich and Rosten Woo of Center for Urban Pedagogy, Clark Richert, Santo Rizzuto, Rodrigo, Amir Saifee of Orangi Pilot Project Research and Training Institute, Daniela Schaffart of Bauhäusle, Jim Segers of City Mine(d), William Sherlaw, Patrick Skingley, Sarah Smith at Planners Network, Olaf Sobczak, Julian Stallabrass, Helen Stratford and Katie Lloyd Thomas of taking place, Stefan Szczelkun at University of Westminster, Department of English, Linguistics and Cultural Studies, John Todd of Ocean Arks International, Uomi, Joseph Varughese at Västu-Shilpā Foundation, Simón Vélez, Danny Wicke of Rural Studio, Tom Woolley, Tony Wrench, Jan Zimmermann.

INDEX